Cage Talk

Eastman Studies in Music

Ralph P. Locke, Senior Editor
Eastman School of Music

(ISSN 1071–9989)

Additional Titles in Music since 1900

CageTalk

Dialogues with and about John Cage

EDITED BY PETER DICKINSON

UNIVERSITY OF ROCHESTER PRESS

The publication of this volume was made possible, in part, through support from the Howard Hanson Institute for American Music at the Eastman School of Music of the University of Rochester, and the Barbara Whatmore Charitable Trust in England.

First published 2006
Reprinted in paperback and transferred to digital printing 2014

University of Rochester Press
668 Mt. Hope Avenue, Rochester, NY 14620, USA
www.urpress.com
and Boydell & Brewer Limited
PO Box 9, Woodbridge, Suffolk IP12 3DF, UK
www.boydellandbrewer.com

ISSN: 1071-9989
hardcover ISBN: 978-1-58046-237-2
paperback ISBN: 978-1-58046-509-0

Library of Congress Cataloging-in-Publication Data
CageTalk : dialogues with and about John Cage / edited by Peter Dickinson.
    p. cm. – (Eastman studies in music, ISSN 1071-9989 ; v. 38)
    Includes bibliographical references (p.) and index.
    ISBN 1-58046-237-5 (hardcover : alk. paper) 1. Cage, John—Interviews. 2. Cage, John—Criticism and interpretation. 3. Composers—United States—Interviews. I. Series.
    ML410.C24D53 2006
    780.92–dc22
    [B]
                                                                    2006011603

A catalogue record for this title is available from the British Library.

Cover image: John Cage at piano overlaid by Sonata No. 4 (*Sonatas* and *Interludes* 1948). Used by permission of Special Collections, F. W. Olin Library, Mills College. Cover design by Adam B. Bohannon.

This publication is printed on acid-free paper.

John Cage, ca. 1970. Photograph by Horace. Courtesy of the John Cage Trust.

Contents

Part IV: Extravaganzas

Illustrations

Preface to the Paperback Edition

The interviews that form the main part of this book took place over twenty-five years ago. Since then the Cage centenary has confirmed the centrality of almost everything Cage stood for. In my acknowledgments to the hardcover edition I indicated the importance of the biography by Kenneth Silverman, which was then in preparation.[1] He brought the tools of a Pulitzer Prize–winning biographer to the task, which was not always appreciated by those who had known Cage from the inside or had been part of the group of his admirers.[2] In his review of Silverman's *Begin Again*, John Adams explained:

> Cage studies is by now a small industry. The flow of new books about him, his music and his aesthetics seems unstoppable, and it is not unthinkable that he will eventually dethrone the likes of Joyce or Proust as the favored subject of college humanities departments. The problem with so much writing about Cage is the difficulty of finding critical balance. He has gone from being unfairly considered a fool and a charlatan to an equally unreasonable status as sacred cow. Criticizing Cage's aesthetic doctrines is by now a perilous venture because his defenders have become so skilled at turning any questioning around and using it as proof of the critic's poverty of awareness.[3]

This emergence of a Cage establishment is at odds with the view of Cage from a generation earlier when Charles Hamm pointed out that aligning oneself with Cage, even into the 1970s, was not "a wise career choice."[4]

---

1. Kenneth Singleton, *Begin Again: A Biography of John Cage* (New York: Knopf, 2010).
2. See Richard Kostelanetz, "Why Me? Another Biography of John Cage," *New English Review*, May 2013, http://www.newenglishreview.org/custpage.cfm/frm/138520/sec_id/138520; William Brooks, review of *Begin Again: A Biography of John Cage*, by Kenneth Singleton, *American Music* 30, no. 1 (2012): 113–15.
3. John Adams, "The Zen of Silence," *New York Times Book Review*, November 19, 2010.
4. See note 54 on page 16 in this volume. Further page references are given parenthetically in text.

There were, of course, difficulties created by Cage himself, which militated against acceptance of all he did, however logical in terms of his philosophy. Philip Kennicott, reviewing *Begin Again* in the *New Republic*, gave one example:

> When asked to give the Norton Lectures at Harvard in 1988, Cage gathered quotations from Thoreau, Wittgenstein, McLuhan, Buckminster Fuller, and various magazines and newspapers. He then used a computer to randomly select various words upon which he created his own favorite poetic form, the mesostic, an acrostic with the keyword in the middle of the poetic lines. Recordings of Cage speaking similar texts in a pitched incantation suggest that this could be hypnotic for a while, but such writing was hardly worthy of the Norton audience, and it is surprising that anyone still takes large chunks of Cage's output seriously. . . . The defensive crouch of many defenders of contemporary music makes it difficult for such a fairly obvious assessment to take root in the cultural record.[5]

I asked Arnold Whittall for his assessment of the situation since *CageTalk* appeared in 2006:[6]

> There has been little sign of any falling off of interest in Cage documentation. I would mention Kyle Gann's *No Such Thing as Silence: John Cage's 4'33"* (New Haven: Yale University Press, 2010) and Martin Iddon's *John Cage and David Tudor: Correspondence on Interpretation and Performance* (Cambridge: Cambridge University Press, 2013). There is also renewed acknowledgment of Cage's influence in establishing an "experimental" alternative to more mainstream compositional activity, which is clear from the way he is discussed in both *The Ashgate Research Companion to Experimental Music*, edited by James Saunders (Farnham, 2009) and *The Ashgate Research Companion to Minimalist and Postminimalist Music*, edited by Keith Potter, Kyle Gann, and Pwyll ap Siôn (Farnham, 2013). This latter is particularly interesting if one feels that minimalism has built on, but perhaps betrayed, aspects of Cage and other experimentalists to promote what has become an alternative "mainstream" to more conventionally modernist music. All of this is in keeping with Michael Nyman's original discussion in *Experimental Music: Cage and Beyond* (London: Studio Vista, 1974).
>
> Moving further afield, it is of no little interest that at least one writer specializing in the aesthetics of modern/contemporary music, Lydia Goehr, can use philosopher Arthur C. Danto's focus on the art of the 1960s—Warhol, Rauschenberg, Cage—to explore the continued relevance of such issues more than fifty years later (*Elective Affinities: Musical Essays on the History of Aesthetic Theory* [New York: Columbia University Press 2008]). The current pluralistic "steady-state" in post-1970s contemporary composition would therefore be a good deal less diverse were it not for the continued role that post-Cage experimentalists and minimalists

---

5. Philip Kennicott, "The Fool of Chance," *New Republic*, December 2, 2010.
6. See Arnold Whittall, *Musical Composition in the Twentieth Century* (Oxford: Oxford University Press, 1999).

play. Adams's mixture of admiration and resistance to Cage in his autobiography, *Hallelujah Junction: Composing an American Life* (New York: Picador, 2008) is probably more typical now than uncritical enthusiasm, but I imagine that British composers such as Gavin Bryars and Howard Skempton would still regard him as a liberating force whose example remains as stimulating today as it was in 1960.[7]

David Nicholls followed his *Cambridge Companion to John Cage* (2002) with his concise *John Cage* (Urbana: University of Illinois Press, 2007). His introduction is defensive: "Cage has often been characterized as, at best, a comedian and, at worst, a charlatan. Unable or unwilling to allow Cage and his work a fair hearing, or even to speak for themselves, musicians and commentators alike have frequently subverted his performances and misrepresented his ideas. . . . Yet Cage has had a profound—and essentially positive—influence on contemporary culture."[8]

Seven years after that was written, Cage and his ideas are increasingly and internationally getting "a fair hearing," but both Cornelius Cardew and John Tilbury, pioneering British supporters of Cage, turned against him for political reasons. As early as 1972, in an article for the *Listener* Cardew castigated Cage as a contributor to fashionable bourgeois culture.[9] This was premature then but is perhaps confirmed when the Aldeburgh Festival, in Benjamin Britten's home town, put on *Musicircus* for Cage's centenary in 2012; it was voted the most popular event of the festival; and consequently in 2014 *An Aldeburgh Musicircus* encompassed the entire town. Audiences may be bourgeois, but they do get the message.

With many issues about Cage remaining unresolved I asked those of my interview subjects who were still alive if they would like to comment. John Rockwell offered a partial recantation:

> I still find a lot of the late Cage something of a trial, the very music that sends my friend Mark Swed[10] into ecstasies; I envy him for that. But not too long after this 1987 interview, I heard a piece of late Cage—I can't remember which one—in a

---

7. Email to me, March 19, 2014.
8. David Nicholls, *John Cage* (Urbana: University of Illinois Press, 2007), 3.
9. Cornelius Cardew, "John Cage: Ghost or Monster?," in *Stockhausen Serves Imperialism, and Other Articles* (London: Latimer, 1974). However, in 1964 Cardew had written, "Cage's work represents unquestionably the most important development in musical composition since the war, and will exert more influence . . . than the work of any European composer." Cardew, "Cage and Cunningham," *Musical Times* 105, no. 1479 (1964): 659–60.
10. See Mark Swed, "John Cage's Genius an L.A. Story," *Los Angeles Times*, December 8, 2012. Swed stresses Cage's West Coast origins: "The composer is among the most innovative figures of the 20th century. Yet his formative years in the cultural stew of 1920s and 30s L.A. get overlooked."

mixed program. All the other music was very intentional, very busy, very composer-controlled. Cage's music was like a quiet pool of water, cool and refreshing. So maybe in the interview I undervalued him as a composer. Let's see a hundred years from now.[11]

Kurt Schwertsik, the Viennese composer and admirer of Erik Satie, confirmed his position: "I have just read our Cage interview again and was very pleased about the correctness and completeness of my recollections. It is exactly what I think about Cage—the combination of religious and Dadaist thinking in his ideas. It also shows how much this combination became part of my way of life and the great influence that Cage had on me!"[12]

Pauline Oliveros remained sympathetic to Cage's ethos:

I was pleasantly surprised by my answers concerning Cage in the interview. I certainly stand behind what I said then and for now. Cage did open the world of sound for everyone with his compositions. I still like to play *Water Walk* for my students for the understanding of how concert performance practice applies to sounds of any kind. What matters is how it is done. Cage was a consummate performer as well as composer. He also expressed his interest in sound in a context that was primed for it by the Futurists and others. Today it is unlikely that *Atlas Eclipticalis* would receive such rude treatment by the New York Philharmonic as it did in 1964. Shortly after that infamous performance I met Cage at the San Francisco Tape Music Center where we performed *Atlas Eclipticalis* tutored by David Tudor. Our performance embraced Cage and showed that our generation was ready for him. Cage would have made creative use of the internet much as he used analog tools in his early ground breaking work. Now that it is possible to detect micro as well as macro wave forms, Cage would probably wake us up to the possibility of expanding our musical sensibilities far beyond present day musical practice into the microcosmos and macrocosmos. It would be wonderful to see how he would apply performance practice to this new range.[13]

Much closer to the whole scene from his schooldays onwards was Christian Wolff, who studied with Cage. In 2006 Wolff gave me his reactions to the typescript of *CageTalk*, but he was not included, for reasons of schedule, in the original set of BBC interview subjects. Consequently I was delighted when he agreed to answer a few questions of the kind I had asked the others in 1987 but now following widespread attention to Cage and the plethora of recordings since his death.[14]

---

11. Email to me, March 10, 2014.
12. Email to me, March 8, 2014.
13. Email to me, March 4, 2014.
14. Emails to me, March 5, 14 and 17, 2014. See Amy Beal's review of *CageTalk*, in *Twentieth-Century Music* 5, no. 1 (2008): 146–49, where she kindly provided corrections, now made, and suggested an interview with Christian Wolff.

PD   What was your impression of the Cage centenary? Were you surprised by the global scale of the celebrations?

CW   I don't think I was surprised by the many Cage celebratory events in 2012, though it's nice to have the interest his work continues to stir up confirmed. And I expect some people are catching up. His name is simply part of our current arts culture.

PD   How do you see his relevance in a context where—maybe—he doesn't have to be explained as in the past?

CW   His relevance? The music would be at the center of that, rather than the ideas, which are in fact mostly second hand. What's notable is their application to the music. There are some composers—I think especially of the Wandelweiser group[15]—who sometimes use chance procedures and who are not shy of much silence and extremely sparse textures, as in Cage's late work, but I don't have any trouble distinguishing Cage's work from theirs. Generally I don't see Cage musically influencing younger composers. He matters simply because of his music, and as an example of independent integrity and the impulse of continuous exploration. As you suggest, no really good composer needs to be explained "as in the past," and Cage is certainly a good composer.

PD   In your email to me in 2005, which I footnoted in the book (p. 168), you asked if the "ordinary concertgoer"—my category—could respond to works like late Beethoven string quartets, *The Art of Fugue*, and Schoenberg or Varèse any more easily than to one of John's number pieces. So how can the technical mastery in the work of those older composers be equated with the number pieces?

CW   To relate the "technical mastery" in the older composers and in Cage's number pieces—I would include all of Cage's work—is hard. What in the twentieth–twenty-first century constitutes technical mastery? There is no standard technical basis for composing any more. More generally, in a somewhat darker mood, I'd say that the qualities we think of as the highest achievements of Western classical music are simply not available at this time. For a variety of reasons, having to do with the historical development of our world, largely under the effect of relentlessly spreading capitalist values—money, profit above all else. For a comparison from the visual arts, would you say that, for instance, Philip Guston or Jasper Johns—wonderful artists as they are, and I love both—are on a level with, especially

---

15. Wandelweiser is a group of European composer-performers, founded in 1992 by Antoine Beuger and Burkhard Schlothauer, which operates its own publishing and recording outlets.

in "technical mastery," Velasquez or Piero della Francesca? Or, back to music, can Cage, or any other more or less contemporary composer—Schoenberg and Stravinsky included—be on a level with Bach or Josquin? Well, all we composers can do is the best we can, which involves careful, inventive, and honest work. I think Cage certainly did that. And he invented—imaginatively, I think—his technical requirements and followed them stringently, with great discipline and consistency.

PD   Stockhausen said (p. 133) that Cage "doesn't hear" and couldn't be regarded as a composer in any traditional sense.

CW   Well, it's possible. Cage did say he didn't have a good ear, and his way of composing is far removed from any "traditional sense," except maybe insofar as it sets up "technical" conditions and then works strictly with them. These conditions are more stringent than, say, isorhythmic counterpoint, but maybe not that much more. Both involve a conception—vision—of what kind of sound and temporal texture will result. And what is—or is the relevance of—a "traditional sense?"

PD   John has talked about the end of art (p. 46). What does that mean now?

CW   "End of art" sounds more like Feldman.[16] This is speculative. The end of art as previously conceived, sure. But "art" is a shifting social/historical construct. I'd say what it "is" changes, but some notion like "art," as playful invention with some social presence continues, and I'd say Cage did not give up on it. After all, he kept writing music to the very end, and spent quite a lot of time making visual art as well.

PD   Earle Brown complains that John didn't understand the orchestral situation with *Atlas Eclipticalis* (p. 143). In *Cheap Imitation* the requirements of the orchestral schedule guarantee that no professional group can consider performing it. Does this impracticality matter or are there more important issues?

CW   Cage and the orchestra? Well, he was "impractical" or utopian, somewhat uncharacteristically—he was also quite pragmatic. I sympathize. The orchestra as we have it is such a problematic institution that any effort to change it even somewhat is worthwhile. You could say John understood the orchestral situation perfectly well, but wanted to get some changes into it.

---

16. Walter Zimmerman, ed., *Morton Feldman Essays* (Wasserburg, Kerpen: Beginner Press, 1985), 92.

PD   Kurt Schwertsik quotes John as saying that sounds are "beings" with their own rights. Do you agree? Is it comparable to your own notion of no sound being preferable to any other?[17]

CW   Don't know what to say. My notion "no sound being preferable to any other," stated as such, I don't hold to anymore. Let's say that any sound is possible. And sounds other than those composed, coming in from the environment—those I'm perfectly happy with. When I compose I do make choices, or, if choices are left open, consider the possible results, which will affect how the choices are set up. It's also worth remembering the heuristic effect of using chance procedures— discovering things you would otherwise not have thought of, an enlivening effect.

PD   You encountered Cage in your later teens. Did that meeting and friendship set the course for all your own work?

CW   Well, sure, and over the years he was always loyal—loyalty was important for him. He was always there with support and encouragement, which would, especially in the early years, have been very hard if not impossible to find otherwise. After a while the support and encouragement weren't so necessary, though always welcome. When I write music, including what I did especially in the later 1970s and early 1980s with politics in mind, I do think about what he would make of it. He's my reference audience, though not the only one. Also, in general, I think that he and I, of the group with Feldman and Earle Brown, had and still have the most in common musically—for instance, with regard to the element of pedagogy in the music's performance. He has remarked that his music has a pedagogical aspect. It's about learning things, as much as about the pleasures of musical sound. What things? For instance, selflessness, devotion, work, discipline, and endurance: this also includes the more or less explicit social presence of the music.

PD   Is it misleading to view Cage in terms of Western culture when everything is, as he said, an "interpenetration between East and West" (p. 231)? Should all Cage after 1952 be thought of in that way? Was

---

17. William Bland and David Patterson, "Christian Wolff," in *The New Grove Dictionary of Music and Musicians*, ed. Stanley Sadie (London: Macmillan, 2001), 28:504. Also Walter Zimmerman, "Christian Wolff," in *Desert Plants: Conversations with 23 American Musicians* (Vancouver: ARC Publications 1976), 21–46; Geoff Smith and Nicola Walker Smith, "Christian Wolff" in *American Originals: Interviews with 25 Contemporary Composers* (London: Faber and Faber, 1994), 253–59; William Duckworth, "Christian Wolff," in *Talking Music: Conversations with John Cage, Philip Glass, Laurie Anderson, and Five Generations of American Experimental Composers* (New York: Da Capo Press, 1999), 179–205.

John Rockwell right to regard these pieces as "meditative exercises" (p. 163)?

CW   By now everything is an interpenetration of East and West, or rather an increasing takeover by Western economic values and models of the whole world—China, India, the former Soviet Union, etc. Cage's values run counter to that, whether or not there are still traditional Eastern elements in them. I don't really see Cage's music, any of it, as particularly "meditation" inducing, at least not in the 1960s sense, which is where Rockwell is coming from.

PD   Interest in Cage is now increasingly strong in the art world, where Duchamp is seen as a crucial figure. Is Cage also an ancestor of concept art and other developments?

CW   Art world interest in Cage goes way back—in the 1940s he was already close to Mark Tobey and Morris Graves. Concept art doesn't seem especially Cageian to me, except insofar as he represented the possibility of doing new things in and with art.

PD   Jackson Mac Low said that Cage's writings are "wonderful works of literature and will eventually be regarded as such," (pp. 97–98). Can the outcome of random techniques to texts by Joyce and others "stand alongside practically anything in American poetry"?

CW   I don't have a strong opinion here. Mac Low has written the best thing I know on Cage's writings.[18] And the writings have been appearing in poetry or new writing anthologies.

PD   You questioned the amount of reception history I included in *CageTalk* and said: "The reviewers (newspaper and journals) are mostly tiresomely ignorant, closed-minded, and not very intelligent." Were you expecting an uncritical acceptance of Cage?

CW   I wasn't at all looking for an uncritical acceptance. On the contrary, I welcome intelligent writing about him, of which there is some. But the level of regular music reviewers, today included, is very low—art criticism is rather better and more interesting.

PD   Is it misleading that Cage is known to the wider public largely for *4'33"* and extravaganzas like *HPSCHD* and *Musicircus?* Do you regret that these conceptual gestures are detracting from fine pieces from all periods?

CW   *4'33"* makes the name Cage known, and he said that he regarded it as his favorite piece (p. 41). But I don't think its notoriety needs to interfere with the appreciation of the rest of his work, which, as far as

---

18. Jackson Mac Low, "Something about the Writings of John Cage," in *Writings about John Cage*, ed. Richard Kostelanetz (Ann Arbor: University of Michigan Press, 1993), 279–82.

I can make out, is doing pretty well, remembering the relatively small numbers of people who listen to any nonpop music.

Fifty years ago I made the case for Cage in the first long article about him in any British periodical.[19] I described Cage as the originator of the avant-garde, not restricted to traditional Western music, and suggested that questions of judgment about his later work were irrelevant. Now many musicians recognize this, but more recently the art world has embraced Cage following the deification of Marcel Duchamp and, in particular, his notorious urinal, entitled *Fountain*, submitted to the Society of Independent Artists for exhibition in New York under the name of R. Mutt in 1917. This most blatant example of Duchamp's ready-mades was rejected, but it soon became iconic: "*Fountain* brought into the open a debate about modern art in the industrial age in America and the effect of its anti-aesthetic on the New York avant-garde was long-lasting."[20] Not just in America but worldwide and continuing, as Roger Malbert confirms: "Today, John Cage's significance for artists is probably greater than at any time since the 1970s. After Duchamp he is the avant-garde hero most likely to be invoked by anyone interested in expanding the conceptual boundaries of contemporary art."[21]

As Philip Kennicott indicated, Cage's later writings, especially those emerging from his mesostic treatments, have not convinced a literary establishment that still has difficulty with Gertrude Stein (p. 98). Cage's contribution to what Jackson Mac Low referred to as language-writing reflects Cage as anarchist: in his Charles Eliot Norton Lectures he said he preferred anarchy to government. But he also admitted—surprisingly—that the results he obtained from processing his chosen texts through chance operations were then further adjusted to what he needed.[22] Cage's earlier books, especially *Silence*, had a considerable impact as John Rockwell recognized (p. 169), but it is hard to see how the later writings could be as influential as Cage's work in music and the visual arts. Words are more resistant to randomization than sounds or drawings.

Finally, when William Brooks was assessing the future of Copland's work he said: "A composer's stature is measured in part by the questions he leaves

19. Peter Dickinson, "Way Out with John Cage," *Music and Musicians*, February 1965, 32–34, 54, 56.
20. Dawn Ades, Neil Cox, David Hopkins, *Marcel Duchamp* (London: Thames & Hudson, 1999), 131.
21. Roger Mallet, "Introduction," *Every Day Is a Good Day: The Visual Art of John Cage* (London: Hayward Publishing, 2010), 9.
22. John Cage, *I—VI* (Cambridge, MA: Harvard University Press, 1990).

us wondering about."[23] Cage did that to perfection. Later Brooks returned to this idea and summed up Cage: "His was a music not of solutions but of questions, and his hope was that the right question at the right time would precipitate a change of mind that would have social as well as artistic reverberations."[24]

23. Peter Dickinson, ed., *Copland Connotations: Studies and Interviews* (Woodbridge, UK: Boydell, 2002), 183.
24. William Brooks, "Music and Society," in *The Cambridge Companion to John Cage*, ed. David Nicholls (Cambridge: Cambridge University Press, 2002), 214.

Acknowledgments

This book started with the initiative of the British Broadcasting Corporation, represented by Anthony Cheevers, producer of our one-hour Radio 3 documentary *John Cage: Inventor of Genius*, broadcast on November 20, 1989, and October 18, 1990, and repeated on August 13, 1992, immediately after Cage's death. I owe much to Cheevers' interest in Cage and am also grateful to Jacqueline Kavanagh, written archivist of the BBC, for permission to use the interviews and hereby make full acknowledgment.

My first debt is, of course, to John Cage himself for being such a stimulating and cooperative interview subject on several occasions from 1963 to 1987 and to the John Cage Trust for permission to edit and print the interviews here, as well as to use photographs. Thanks to the other interview subjects or their heirs, all of whom saw the transcripts: Merce Cunningham; Heidi Smith, daughter of Bonnie Bird, and her interviewer, Rebecca Boyle; Mimi Johnson for expediting permission to use the David Tudor interview; Ann Tardos for commenting on and allowing use of the interview with her late husband, Jackson Mac Low; Carol Oja, Minna Lederman's executor, and Anthony Cheevers who conducted that interview; Alexis Hart at the Virgil Thomson Trust; Catherine Luening for permission to use my interview with her late husband and for providing further information; Kathinka Pasveer for arranging permission with Karlheinz Stockhausen; Micah Silver of the Earle Brown Music Foundation, who also provided photographs; Kurt Schwertsik; La Monte Young and Marian Zazeela; John Rockwell; Pauline Oliveros; Paul Zukofsky; Naomi Sylvester, on behalf of her late father; Roger Smalley; Frank Kermode; Michael Downing, Michael Oliver's executor; Mel Mercier for permission to use the interview with his late father, Peader Mercier, and for giving me further detail; and Anthony Cheevers again, for his own interview with Cage about *Europeras*. It has been a pleasure to deal with everybody. I have been extremely fortunate in having the continued support of Laura Kuhn at the John Cage Trust. Apart from arranging permissions and commenting on sections en route, she read the typescript and made valuable suggestions. She led me to Kenneth Silverman, who is working on what will be a most important biography of Cage, and he kindly provided some Cage family dates. That veteran of Cage studies, Charles Hamm, also read the typescript and made constructive points. So did William Brooks, now at the University of York; and H. Wiley Hitchcock helped tighten the book's structure. The response of Christian Wolff falls in a special category in view of his close personal association with the whole story—he generously saved me from some misunderstandings, disagreed with me in ways that I have indicated, and sharpened interpretation.

Many others helped with details. Thanks to Robert Orledge for comments on the section about Satie in my Introduction; Carolyn Brown for telling me about the dance *Pelican* and other issues; David Vaughan for dance information; Stephanie Jordan for reading the Cunningham interview; Peter Ward Jones at the Bodleian Library, Oxford, for trying to trace Cage's 1958 visit there; Romeo Whou at the University of Buffalo Music Library; Elvira Wiendenhöft at Frankfurt Opera for putting me in touch with Meri Raad; David Fisher of the Bath House Cultural Center in Dallas for finding Kim Corbet, who remembered Cage's visit in such detail; Irwin Kremen, who recalled his connections as dedicatee of $4'33''$ and routed me to essential sources that Volker Schirp at Peters Edition quickly provided; and Janice Braun, Special Collections Curator at the F. W. Olin Library, Mills College, for providing a photograph that was drawn to my attention by Warner Jepson.

I have had a long series of e-mails with Ralph Locke of the University of Rochester Press and have valued his experience at all stages, as well as my contact with Suzanne E. Guiod, editorial director of the Press, and her colleagues, including my fastidious copyeditor, Cheryl Carnahan. Comments from the anonymous readers engaged by the Press helped to clarify the focus of the book. I have also had advice from Bruce Phillips at Boydell and Brewer in England and have appreciated details from Gary McDowell, as well as encouragement when he was director of the Institute of United States Studies at the University of London, where I was Head of Music. Thanks to my sister, Meriel Dickinson, for providing cuttings from the *Guardian* over many years, and to my son Francis for assistance with the title.

I am grateful to all the writers cited in the notes and bibliography for their pioneering work on Cage—especially Richard Kostelanetz, even though he seldom uses an index; David Revell and James Pritchett for their monographs; and the editors of compilations published in the 1990s, including David Bernstein, David Nicholls, David W. Patterson, Marjorie Perloff and Charles Junkerman, and Joan Retallack. I have appreciated the assistance of John Woolf at the Park Lane Group and I want to pay a special tribute to the generosity of the Barbara Whatmore Charitable Trust in England and the enthusiasm of Luke Gardiner for providing funds to support the production costs of this book. A grant from the Howard Hanson Institute for American Music (directed by James Undercofler) likewise helped the book see the light of day.

Peter Dickinson
Aldeburgh, Suffolk, 2006

Introduction

Peter Dickinson

CageTalk is based on the series of interviews, starting in 1987, I conducted for a BBC Radio 3 documentary on John Cage first broadcast in 1989. The program was aimed at a general rather than a specialist audience, and that focus is retained here. As the book developed, however, it became clear that some earlier British interviews with Cage might otherwise be lost if not included. These show him being quizzed by the art critic David Sylvester and the literary critic Frank Kermode, among others, and the later interview with Bonnie Bird contains unique material. There is also a slight difference of perspective because some of the interviews took place outside the United States, and, in any case, Cage and his colleagues must have been aware that they were reaching an international audience through the BBC—not just a local radio station. The purpose of *CageTalk* is to make this material available both as an introduction to Cage and his context and as a resource for scholars in the future.

As an interview subject, Cage was a consummate performer, a virtuoso with skills worthy of study in their own right. He knew precisely how to recycle familiar material, when to refer his interviewer to sources elsewhere, and how to sidestep awkward issues in a most ingratiating and ingenious way. But occasionally his guard slipped and he provided information from a different angle. Readers already interested in Cage will be well aware of interviews and biographical statements elsewhere. However, it seemed worthwhile to footnote some of these connections for ease of comparison, occasionally within the book—from interview to interview—and outside the book in what is becoming a vast, almost impenetrable field of Cage documentation. Cage's books lack indexes, as do some of the published collections of material. There is no attempt at comprehensive references here, but some British resources have been included since they are less accessible than U.S. sources and—from a different slant—can be revealing.

Some aspects of Cage are barely touched on in these interviews, reflecting his impact in Britain. He is a uniquely demanding subject because the ramifications of his wide-ranging interests and concerns are colossal. His utopian ideas about how society should operate increasingly entered into his conversations and writings but are only touched on here.[1] In that sense *Cage Talk* gives an incomplete picture of Cage, since his justifications lie outside music, although his impact on music of many kinds has been formidable.

His productions as a writer are included in the discussion with Jackson Mac Low, but there is nothing about Cage's work as a visual artist in later life since it had received negligible exposure in Britain at the time of these interviews. He did have an exhibition at the Fruitmarket Gallery, Edinburgh, in 1984, but his first exhibition in London was at the Anthony d'Offay Gallery in 1989. It was called *Dancers on a Plane* and consisted of paintings by Jasper Johns (at astronomical prices), videos of Merce Cunningham, and the manuscript pages of the piano part of Cage's *Concert for Piano and Orchestra* (1958). In the catalog, Sylvester wrote about Cage's Crown Point Press prints: "They are works whose interest is independent of Cage's greatness as a composer and importance as a writer; indeed it seems to me that the best of them—for instance the series of four drypoints, *Where R = Ryoanji* (1983)—are among the most beautiful prints and drawings made anywhere in the 1980s."[2] From 1951 onward, Cage used the ancient Chinese Book of Changes, the *I Ching*, as a mechanism to produce random numbers from one to sixty-four. These chance techniques, driven by Zen philosophy, operate in similar ways whether the medium is graphics, words, or music. In 1987 Cage confirmed this: "I have more and more written my texts in the same way I write my music, and make my prints, through the use of chance operations."[3]

Another aspect of Cage missing from this volume concerns the work of his final period, composed after most of the interviews here were conducted.

---

1. A rare example of Cage in discussion with biologists and sociologists is documented, but not fully edited by the participants, from a 1969 symposium held at Chichen Itza, Yucatán, Mexico. See Conrad Hal Waddington, ed., *Biology and the History of the Future: An IUBS/UNESCO Symposium with John Cage, Carl-Goeran Heden, Margaret Mead, John Papaioannou, John Platt, Ruth Sager, and Gunther Stent* (Edinburgh: University of Edinburgh Press, 1972). See also William Brooks, "Music and Society," in David Nicholls, ed., *The Cambridge Companion to John Cage* (Cambridge: Cambridge University Press, 2002), 214–26.
2. David Sylvester, "John Cage," in Judy Adams, ed., *Dancers on a Plane: Cage—Cunningham—Johns* (London: Anthony d'Offay Gallery, 1989), 51. The exhibition was in London from October 31 to December 2, 1989, and at the Tate Gallery, Liverpool, from January 23 to March 25, 1990. See Cage's interview with Sylvester and Roger Smalley, chapter 16, 185.
3. Cage, "Foreword," in *X: Writings '79–'82* (Middletown, CT: Wesleyan University Press, 1979).

On May 23, 1985, at the Institute of Contemporary Arts in London, Cage discussed what have come to be called the number pieces of his last years, where there were notated parts within time brackets but no scores. Each part was fixed, but the relation between them was not. The many recordings of these works usually feature a kind of endless sostenuto in transcendental calm. At the Institute Cage also said his greatest pleasure was "keeping my ears open wherever I happen to be." When questioned about whether he wanted to change society, he said he was struck by the social nature of music and wanted "to show the practicality of anarchy—and, I hope, desirability."

The importance of Eastern philosophies for creative artists in the twentieth century emerges from several participants in *CageTalk*. Significantly, Cage grew up with dance and the visual arts as his natural context, and he was always interested in technology. It was the musical world that had the most trouble accommodating him: if some of the comments here are anything to go by, it still does. Music is too confining a category for Cage, as he realized in 1957: "Where do we go from here? Towards theatre. That art more than music resembles nature. We have eyes as well as ears, and it is our business while we are alive to use them."[4]

In some ways this book is a personal anthology, since I first met Cage more than forty-five years ago and have followed his work and its reception ever since. I have included extracts from our intermittent correspondence. During this period Cage did not lack British supporters. For example, there were performances of *Sonatas and Interludes* and other keyboard works for more than forty years by pianist John Tilbury, often with Cornelius Cardew; Michael Nyman's pioneering book *Experimental Music: Cage and Beyond* ([1974] 1999); a compact study by Paul Griffiths (1981); a biography by David Revill (1992); the writings of Keith Potter, Gavin Bryars, and especially David Nicholls; the activities of Americans living in London, such as Richard Bernas and Stephen Montague; groups that commissioned Cage, such as Electric Phoenix and the Arditti Quartet; festivals in London, Huddersfield, and Glasgow that featured Cage prominently; and, of course, the BBC with its interviews, reviews, and performances—including its *John Cage Uncaged* weekend at the Barbican, London, January 16–18, 2004 (see Appendix II, 235). British publishers, notably Cambridge University Press, have brought out important studies. Cage had a following in France, with Daniel Charles, and in Germany, with Hans Helms, Heinz-Klaus Metzger, and Klaus Schöning—and he still does—but that is a separate subject.

Going further back, Cage's British appearances date from 1954, his third trip to Europe, when he and the pianist David Tudor did a European tour.

---

4. John Cage, *Silence: Lectures and Writings* (Middletown, CT: Wesleyan University Press, 1961), 12.

He was invited to speak at Composers' Concourse in London, for which he wrote *45' for a Speaker*.[5] He also introduced his music at Tudor's recital, presented by the Institute of Contemporary Arts at Mahatma Ghandi Hall, London, on October 29. The British reception, in the rigidly conservative postwar climate, was decidedly frosty. The program opened with *Battle Piece* (1943–47) by Stefan Wolpe and *Extensions 3* (1952) by Morton Feldman. The Britten and Mahler specialist Donald Mitchell, in the *Musical Times*, admitted that both pieces "taxed Tudor's technical gifts to the utmost," whereas "musically the works were of no interest whatsoever." The prepared piano music was "hardly less barren of artistic significance." Then came Cage's *Water Music* (1952) and *Music for Piano 4–19* (1953). Mitchell reported with some relief that Cage said his work need not be described as music and concluded that his "assembly of totally unrelated sounds extended beyond the reach of aesthetic criteria."[6] The British critic Rollo Myers, who wrote the first study of Erik Satie in English, caught Cage and Tudor at the CDMI Festival in Paris on the same trip: "The organizers committed a serious blunder in inviting John Cage and partner to give what was really a scandalous exhibition of buffoonery on two 'prepared' pianos which they subjected to every kind of brutality. . . . This kind of thing can only bring discredit on the whole experimental school, which after all has some backing among serious musicians and has the official encouragement of the French Radio."[7]

Cage's next British connection may have been when William Glock published the short article *"Experimental Music"* in 1955.[8] David Tudor played Parts 1 and 4 of *Music of Changes* (1951) at the International Music Association in London on December 17, 1956, as part of a European tour that covered six countries. The 1962 Peters Edition catalog has an entry for *Winter Music*, with Cage and Tudor apparently appearing at Oxford University in 1958, but it has not been possible to confirm this.[9] But by

---

5. Ibid., 146–92. Cage's name was not included when Composers' Concourse announced its program in the *Musical Times* 95, no. 1339 (September 1954): 474.

6. Donald Mitchell, "London Music," *Musical Times* 95, no. 1342 (December 1954): 667.

7. Rollo Myers, "Notes from Abroad," *Musical Times* 95, no. 1342 (December 1954): 671.

8. *Score and I. M. A. Magazine*, June 1955, 65–68, edited by Glock. Also in Cage, *Silence*, 13. Glock became the influential Controller of Music, BBC Radio 3 (1959–73).

9. Apparently on October 20. Peter Ward Jones, music librarian at the Bodleian, tells me this was not a University Musical Club and Union event, it was not included in the program of the recently founded Oxford University Contemporary Music Society, and it was not reported in the local press.

1964, with the triumphal visit of the Merce Cunningham Dance Company to London, things were changing. Cornelius Cardew, who had worked as Karlheinz Stockhausen's assistant and pioneered performances of Cage's music in England, wrote: "Cage's work represents unquestionably the most important development in musical composition since the war, and will exert more influence on the future evolution and changes in composition and performance than the work of any European composer."[10] It was in that year that I had a long interview with Cage in London.

The main body of interviews in *CageTalk* creates a snapshot of Cage, friends, and colleagues five years before his death in 1992. Since then, Bonnie Bird, Earle Brown, Otto Luening, Jackson Mac Low, David Tudor, Minna Lederman, and Virgil Thomson have all died. Among the interviewers, so have David Sylvester and Michael Oliver. I have not attempted to bring in further interview subjects, which would have changed the focus and enlarged an already substantial volume, although I have referred to both previous and subsequent publications in the notes. Pierre Boulez and Elliott Carter declined the BBC's invitation to take part in the original radio documentary. This reminded me that when Carter visited the University of Keele on October 17, 1977, he answered questions in front of an audience after a recital of his music. He was asked, "Mr. Carter, what do you think of John Cage?" and replied, "I don't think of John Cage!"

I have provided biographical background in the introductions to each interview, but with some subjects, such as Cage himself, these details emerge in their own discussions. Individuals and sources mentioned in the interviews are identified mostly in footnotes at their mention, if not in the introductions.

I was at the Britten-Pears Library, Aldeburgh, Suffolk, on Wednesday, August 12, 1992, when a message arrived from the BBC that John Cage had died and they wanted to repeat my radio documentary the following day with a new introduction. The symbolic juxtaposition could hardly have been more acute. Hans Keller, that great exemplar of the Austro-German tradition, wrote: "Britten and Cage: could there be greater polarity? Without Britten and his world, present and past, we wouldn't have had anything Cage could have liberated us from. . . . There is nobody who is safe from Cage's rescue act; its elemental historical force has therefore become historic."[11] I went to BBC Radio Suffolk at Ipswich to take part in a brief tribute, with

---

10. Cornelius Cardew, "Cage and Cunningham," *Musical Times* 105, no. 1479 (September 1964): 659–60.
11. Hans Keller (1919–85), "Caged," *Spectator*, June 24, 1978, 27. Keller describes Cage's *Empty Words: Writings '73–'78* as "as close as anything Cage has done to the apotheosis of stupidity."

Anthony Burton in London, interviewing me from there and Mark Swed in New York City.[12] This is what I added to the program:

> Yesterday the American composer, writer, artist and unique personality John Cage died from a stroke at St Vincent's Hospital in New York City. Even though he would have been eighty on September 5 it was always difficult to think of him as in any way old. His approach to life was continually fresh and exploratory. He opened up new possibilities in all the arts in a way that made you feel you were using only half your mind. Contact with him personally had the same effect:—one always felt better for meeting him, and his sense of humor was a tonic. He got so accustomed to being interviewed that he developed his own technique of fending off awkward questions with a joke.
>
> It was in 1987 that I went to New York to interview Cage and some of his friends and colleagues. The program was first broadcast in November 1989, and for the title we used Schoenberg's description of Cage as "an inventor of genius."[13] Now there's great sadness that Cage can't take part himself in eightieth birthday tributes all over the world as he'd planned. But his ideas have transformed our perception of art and life in the twentieth century and, whether we like it or not, nothing will ever be the same again.

My initial meetings with Cage must have been around the time of the three concerts of avant-garde music given in 1960 at the Living Theater in Greenwich Village, New York City, featuring the pianist David Tudor, who had an essential role in Cage's development. As my reviews of these concerts for the *Musical Courier*, in New York, and the *Musical Times*, in London, showed, I was not convinced by the more extreme aspects of the new music, but I was fascinated by the whole phenomenon.[14] After spending three years in New York, I returned to England in 1961 and met Cage next in London when he was with the Merce Cunningham Dance Company on its

---

12. BBC Radio 3 documentary *John Cage: Inventor of Genius*, broadcast on November 20, 1989, and October 18, 1990, with an unscheduled repeat on August 13, 1992. Producer: Anthony Cheevers.
13. The source of this frequently cited remark seems to be Peter Yates, *Twentieth Century Music: Its Evolution from the End of the Harmonic Era into the Present Era of Sound* (London: George Allen and Unwin, 1968), 243: "At our last meeting I asked [Schoenberg] about his disciples and students. In reply, he spoke only of Cage, without any prompting and indeed to my astonishment, since Cage had ceased studying with him rather abruptly and had strongly and publicly criticized the twelve-tone method. Schoenberg said of Cage: 'He is not a composer, but an inventor—of genius.'" See also Michael Hicks, "John Cage's Studies with Schoenberg," *American Music* 8 , no. 2 (1990): 125–40.
14. For details of these concerts, see interview with La Monte Young, chapter 12, 154n8.

triumphant six-month world tour. In late August 1964 he gave me an interview, and as a result I wrote the first long study about him and his work to appear in a British periodical, *Music and Musicians*.[15] I sent him a copy of the article, and he wrote back:

Stony Point, NY 10980, December 27, 1965
Dear Peter,
Thankyou for magazine & letters and your good news. I am well so don't be sorry re health. I think yr. article is very good. And congratulate you on it. I may be (next summer) in Europe & England and hope we may meet again then.
As ever,
John

In the discussion that follows, apart from related digressions, I am quoting from that article as well as from the notes I made at the time. My case for Cage recognized some obstacles from a British perspective:

He has given few recitals here, consequently his work is presented by others whose intentions are sometimes better than their competence; he has been dismissed along with the entire so-called lunatic fringe of the avant-garde, whereas he is in fact the originator who stands far above the latest generation of *bruitistes*; and his work is prematurely and unfairly judged as if it were merely a contribution to Western music—this frame of reference is too narrow, and the question of judgment may not arise at all.

I then mentioned the difficulty of obtaining his scores at a reasonable price at that time, but I was able to welcome the publication of Cage's first volume of writings, *Silence* (1961), which had not yet achieved its later influential position; the Peters Edition catalog (1962), with the first of Cage's interviews with Roger Reynolds; and sympathetic discussion of Cage by Wilfrid Mellers in his seminal book *Music in a New Found Land*.[16] Cage said

---

15. Peter Dickinson, "Way Out with John Cage," *Music and Musicians* (February 1965): 32–34, 54, 56. This was not my title. I made a case for regarding Cage's then little-known *String Quartet in Four Parts* (1950) as a masterpiece in "Case of Neglect 3: Cage String Quartet," *Music and Musicians* (January 1972): 28–29. Reprinted as "Cage String Quartet (1972)," in Richard Kostelanetz, ed., *Writings about John Cage* (Ann Arbor: University of Michigan Press, 1993), 77–81.
16. Wilfrid Mellers, "From Noise to Silence: Harry Partch, John Cage and Morton Feldman," in *Music in a New Found Land* (London: Barrie and Rockliff, 1964), 177–88. In 1964 Mellers started the influential Music Department at the University of York and was Visiting Mellon Professor at the University of Pittsburgh from 1960 to 1962.

he knew Mellers's writings but found him too dogmatic; he alerted me to the two numbers of the *Times Literary Supplement* on the avant-garde[17] and referred me to Marshall McLuhan's recently published *Understanding Media* (1964). In general, Cage said he felt that the success of the Merce Cunningham Dance Company and the interest in Robert Rauschenberg, its resident designer who had had an exhibition at the Whitechapel Gallery, showed that London was becoming more receptive to new ideas. He said he was concerned with "increasing awareness rather than the capacity to make judgments." He wanted listeners to "be aware like a tourist, curious," and stressed that "the experience itself is the thing and not the judgment."[18]

Cage realized then that his work gave people plenty to do, with countless directions open: he said music should not be separated from the other arts or science and composers should be aware of things outside music as well as inside. Change would be brought about by electronics now that we were at the end of the print culture established in the Renaissance.[19] His plans included what he called "instant electronic music," and he was interested in a system that would distort a sound so that "any other sound" would emerge—even then this technique was baffling orchestral players to the point of hostility in works such as *Atlas Eclipticalis* (1962).[20] Cage described the acceptance of the results of such a system as "transubstantiation, a religious experience." I assumed this was a reference to the Catholic doctrine of transubstantiation where, at the Eucharist, the bread and wine are converted into the body and blood of Christ. But when I asked Cage if he regarded himself as a practicing Buddhist, he simply said he considered himself a composer. In fact, he expected a spiritual discipline close to Zen

---

17. Various, "The Changing Guard," *The Times Literary Supplement*, August 6 and September 3, 1964.

18. In 1969 Cage, on a panel with biologists and social scientists (see note 1), made the same point: "In my music I want space for surprise. I want us not to be inhabitants, but tourists, meeting new experiences." Margaret Mead challenged him: "You dislike formal governments; but we have got to survive. . . . We can't have everybody [be] tourists." Waddington, *Biology and the History of the Future*, 45–46. Cage used an identical phrase near the end of his life: "What I'm proposing, to myself and other people, is what I often call the tourist attitude—that you act as though you've never been there before." Joan Retallack, ed., *MUSICAGE: Cage Muses on Words Art Music* (Hanover, NH: Wesleyan University Press and University of New England Press, 1996), 129–30.

19. For the classic statement of this position see Leonard B. Meyer, "The End of the Renaissance?" in *Music, the Arts, and Ideas: Patterns and Predictions in Twentieth-Century Culture* (Chicago: University of Chicago Press, 1967), 68–86.

20. See interview with Earle Brown, chapter 10, 142.

from both his performers and listeners; he gave many the impression of being a saintly person, but in 1987 he told William Duckworth he did not believe in God.[21] Two weeks before he died he equated God with government or the police and therefore not required by anarchists.[22]

Cage confirmed he was devoted to Erik Satie. In 1948 he had put on a Satie Festival of twenty-five concerts at Black Mountain College in North Carolina. In an article in 1958 he had said: "It's not a question of Satie's relevance. He's indispensable."[23] *Cheap Imitation*, based note-for-note on *Socrate*, Satie's so-called symphonic drama on the life and death of Socrates, would follow in 1971—and would also cause trouble with orchestras.[24] By May 1985, in the talk he gave with David Tudor at the Institute of Contemporary Arts in London, Cage said, "I still feel Satie's great importance for this century." Near the end of his life, in December 1991, Cage found between Satie and Beethoven "a break between music that involved going somewhere and a music which is not going anywhere." He regarded Satie as more radical than Ives—"a great new beginning for music . . . after Beethoven"—and concluded, "in fact, without Satie, we can't do anything."[25]

But it was back in 1963 at the Pocket Theater, New York, on September 9 and 10, that Cage had put on his overnight performance of Satie's *Vexations*—the short piano piece dating from around 1893 when the composer had been providing austere liturgical music for the Rosicrucian sect and equally strange background music for esoteric plays in Paris. Henri Sauguet lent Cage a copy of the manuscript when he was in Paris in 1949, and Cage arranged for it to be published in the review *Contrepoints*.[26] Known for his ironic captions aimed at the performer, Satie had placed at the top of the score: "Pour se jouer 840 fois de suite ce motif, il sera bon de se préparer au préalable, et dans le plus grand silence, par des immobilités sérieuses." Instead of regarding the invitation as hypothetical—"If one wants to play this motif 840 times in succession, it will be as well to prepare oneself in advance, and in the deepest silence, through serious contemplation/meditation"—Cage decided to actually perform the piece 840 times with his relay team of pianists, and it took over eighteen hours. He thought

21. William Duckworth, *Talking Music: Conversations with John Cage, Philip Glass, Laurie Anderson, and Five Generations of American Experimental Composers* (New York: Da Capo, 1995), 24–25.
22. Retallack, *MUSICAGE*, 292.
23. Cage, *Silence*, 82.
24. See interview with Cage, chapter 1, 44n56.
25. Andrew Ford, "Illegal Harmony: John Cage," in *Composer to Composer: Conversations about Contemporary Music* (London, Quartet Books, 1993), 178.
26. Vol. 6 (1949), opp. 8.

the text was in the spirit of Zen Buddhism, and this treatment of *Vexations* has become almost as notorious as Cage's so-called silent piece *4′ 33″*—but it must be regarded as Cage rather than Satie, and it is time his interpretation was challenged.[27]

According to Robert Orledge, "Satie's performance note is not a definite instruction but rather a suggestion."[28] Noelle Mann considers that the implication could even be "if one wants to play for oneself this motif," in the sense of imagining it rather than playing it at all.[29] However, Calvin Tomkins refers to "the composer's blithe notation.' "[30] *Vexations* was performed overnight by a relay team of pianists at the BBC's *John Cage Uncaged* weekend. The program note says: "The composer instructs the pianist."

Interestingly, the seventeenth piece of Satie's *Sports et Divertissements* (1914), the text of which Cage used as a mesostic in 1989, is "Le Tango," which we are told is the devil's favorite dance—he dances it to cool off and so do his wife, children, and servants. It is marked "perpetuel" and there are repeat marks, but, as far as I know, nobody seems to take this caption literally. The symbolism is far more acute than *Vexations*—the dance is perpetual, and so is evil in the world.

All the same, Cage told me he found the experience of the relay performance as on a par with such highly regarded religious works as Bach's Mass in B Minor.[31] In 1950 Cage had written a letter to *Musical America* energetically defending Satie, explaining that he was not simply taking refuge in a sense of humor. Even at this stage Cage said: "My mind runs now to Satie's *Vexations*, a short piece to be played 840 times in a row. A performance of this piece would be a measure—accurate as a mirror—of one's 'poverty of spirit,' without which, incidentally, one loses the kingdom of heaven."[32] By 1958 Cage had different ideas: "True, one could not endure a performance of *Vexations* (lasting—my estimate—twenty-four hours)."[33] Cage never felt

---

27. Cage made his own case in a 1973 interview; see Richard Kostelanetz, ed., *Conversing with Cage* (New York: Limelight Editions, 1988), 48–49.
28. Robert Orledge, "Understanding Satie's 'Vexations,'" *Music and Letters* 79, no. 3 (August 1998): 386–95.
29. E-mail, May 11, 2005.
30. Calvin Tomkins, *The Bride and the Bachelors: The Heretical Courtship in Modern Art* (New York: Viking, 1965), 104.
31. Two years later Cage used similar terms: "The *Vexations* of Satie I would be willing to equate in terms of experience with any religious work of any culture, any of the Bach Passions and so forth." David Sylvester, *Interviews with American Artists* (London: Chatto and Windus, 2001), 125.
32. Richard Kostelanetz, ed., *John Cage* (New York: Praeger, 1970), 90.
33. Cage, *Silence*, 78.

the need to be consistent, so, looking back from the late 1960s, he said: "Even those of us who were playing thought we were headed for something repetitive. . . . But this is what happened. In the middle of those eighteen hours of performance, our lives changed. We were dumbfounded, because something was happening which we had not considered and which we were a thousand miles away from being able to foresee."[34] In spite of his defense of Satie's sense of humor, Cage seems to have missed it himself in connection with *Vexations*, which he turned into a severe ritual. Robert Orledge has pointed out that the chords in *Vexations*—an important clue—link it directly to a fragment called *Bonjour Biqui* (1893), which refers to Suzanne Valadon, with whom Satie was having his only known affair.[35] The 840 times could well have been a private reference within their vexatious relationship.[36]

In 1983 Gavin Bryars listed full-scale performances of *Vexations* that, as it happens, may have begun with a British schoolboy of thirteen in 1958.[37] Cage's involvement with this mystical piece continued when he applied his *Cheap Imitation* technique—Satie's rhythms but pitches by chance—to *Extended Lullaby*, used for Cunningham's dance *Beach Birds*, to some of *Songbooks* and some of the late number pieces. In terms of extended durations, Cage said he was also impressed by the spiritual quality induced by the repetition of minimal materials in pieces by La Monte Young, which he said had changed his way of hearing.[38]

In a letter to Cage on July 18, 1989, I asked whether he knew Alan M. Gillmor's book on Satie and drew his attention to the fact that Alphonse Allais had exhibited paintings that were all black (Negroes fighting in a cave at night), all white (anemic young nuns going to their first communion in a

---

34. John Cage, *For the Birds: John Cage in Conversation with Daniel Charles* (London: Marion Boyars, 1981), 153.
35. Robert Orledge, *Satie the Composer* (Cambridge: Cambridge University Press, 1990), 144. See also Rollo Myers, *Erik Satie* (London: Dennis Dobson, 1948), for "Bonjour Biqui," opp. 32. Ned Rorem, who spent many years in France and understands French music, thought differently: "Where for me Satie's quips were plaintive, to John they were campy, and to take at face value Satie's designation . . . 'to be repeated 840 times,' and then to rent a hall plus a relay team of pianists and to do precisely that for twenty-five hours, is to take Satie literally where he was being merely whimsical." Ned Rorem, *Knowing When to Stop: A Memoir* (New York: Simon and Schuster, 1994), 232.
36. Christian Wolff, who took part in Cage's New York performance of *Vexations*, doesn't think Satie's sense of humor is much at work and, based on their experience in playing it, considers that Satie did set out to write a piece that could be repeated 840 times. E-mail, September 20, 2005.
37. Gavin Bryars, "Vexations and Its Performers," *Contact* 26 (Spring 1983): 12–20.
38. See introduction to interview with La Monte Young, chapter 12, 153.

blizzard), and all gray (drunkards dancing in a fog). He also wrote a funeral march for a deaf man on blank manuscript paper—just like the first version of *4′33″*. These items had been published in Paris in the second volume of the Allais *Oeuvres posthumes* edition in 1966, but I was curious to find out if Cage knew about them. He replied on July 22: "I do know the Gillmor book and I agree it is the best. I know about Allais' work but I didn't know about the silent funeral march before *4′33″*. I knew about an empty book that had been published here in the nineteenth century. . . . Marcel Duchamp, the evening he died, had been reading Allais and chuckling."[39]

There were other works that, like *Vexations*, Cage interpreted idiosyncratically. In the later 1930s he was particularly impressed by Bach's *Art of Fugue*, which he heard Richard Buhlig play many times in southern California and had studied in Schoenberg's classes: "I had the feeling that I needed no other music really than that to hear."[40] This is a justifiable response to the summit of Bach's fugal technique, and earlier he had felt the same way about Grieg's piano works. But Cage's lecture, *Indeterminacy*, shows that he regarded the *Art of Fugue* as for unspecified instrumentation—a common view at the time—and therefore a precursor of indeterminacy when it is actually keyboard music.[41] In terms of Baroque performance practice, little is indeterminate, in Cage's sense, about the *Art of Fugue*. Further, Cage wrongly cited arrangements of it by Webern and Schoenberg. Webern scored the Ricercare from *The Musical Offering*, and Schoenberg scored the Prelude and Fugue in E-flat Major, BVW 552.[42]

I asked Cage in 1964 whether he felt that absolutely anybody could now be regarded as a composer, and he reminded me that it was Charles Ives who had envisaged this. He must have been thinking of

> The instinctive and progressive interest of every man in art . . . until the day will come when every man while digging his own potatoes will breathe his own epics; and as he sits of an evening in his backyard . . . watching his brave children in *their*

---

39. Alan M. Gillmor, *Erik Satie* (London: Macmillan, 1988). Cage's response to my question was made known in my review of this and other books on Satie in the *Musical Quarterly* 75, no. 3 (1991): 404–9. Erik Satie (1866–1925) was born in Honfleur, and so was Alphonse Allais (1854–1905). For more on the precursors of *4′33″*, see Erik de Visscher, "Die Künstlergruppe 'Les Incohérents' und die Vorgeschichte zu *4′33″*," in Stefan Schädler and Walter Zimmerman, eds., *John Cage: Anarchic Harmony* (Mainz: Schott, 1992), 73–76.
40. Kostelanetz, *Conversing with Cage*, 37.
41. Cage, *Silence*, 35.
42. Cage related Bach to a desire for order, jazz, and the church. Ibid., 262–63.

fun of building *their* themes and *their* sonatas of *their* life, he will hear the transcendental strains of the day's symphony resounding in their many choirs.[43]

Cage said he had not felt it necessary to meet Ives, who died in 1954, but
now realized he should have done so.
He claimed it was the American spirit that avoided judgment, and he saw
this as essential to the American idea. He came back to this pronouncement
in 1966 when Richard Kostelanetz asked him if he was bothered by the fact
that anyone, regardless of skill, could be an artist: "That's a European question, you know, not an American question, this whole thing of hierarchy—
of wanting to make the most the best. And it took us ages, relatively
speaking, to get out of that European thing."[44] When I asked him about
British music, he said that, like Lou Harrison, he liked old English music—
presumably the Elizabethan composers. It was Harrison who drew Cage's
attention to "a passage by Thomas Mace written in England in 1676 to the
effect that the purpose of music was to season and sober the mind, thus making it susceptible to divine influences."[45] On the then current British scene
Cage said he had complete confidence in Cornelius Cardew[46] but no interest in Britten. He said he had been planning to hear the *War Requiem* (1962)
but didn't do so.

My 1965 article discussed the *Six Short Inventions, First Construction in Metal,
Imaginary Landscape No. 1, Sonatas and Interludes, Music of Changes,* and *Music
for Carillon No. 1,* all with music examples, to demonstrate Cage's credentials
as a composer. This was a way of trying to convince a skeptical British public

---

43. Charles Ives, "Postface" to *114 Songs* (Redding, CT: 1922; New York and Bryn
Mawr, PA: AMP/Peer/Presser, 1975). Paul Griffiths considers *4′33″* to be "not just a
window into the world of non-intended sound but also potentially, as Ives once fore-
saw in prophesying a utopian anarchy in which artists are no longer needed, it is for
each individual his own symphony." Griffiths, *Cage,* 45.
44. Kostelanetz, *John Cage,* 12.
45. Kostelanetz, *John Cage: Writer. Previously Uncollected Pieces* (New York: Limelight
Editions, 1993), 41. This may not be an exact quote from Thomas Mace's publication *Music's Monument; or, A Remembrancer of the Best in Practical Music, Both Divine and
Civil That Has Ever Been in the World.* See Austin Clarkson, "The Intent of the Musical
Moment," in David W. Bernstein and Christopher Hatch, eds., *Writings through John
Cage's Music, Poetry + Art* (Chicago: University of Chicago Press, 2001), 79.
46. This estimate of Cornelius Cardew (1936–81) within Cage's circle was confirmed
at his memorial concert in Symphony Space, New York, in May 1982 when Christian
Wolff wrote in the program book that Cardew was "to a remarkably large number of
us the most important composer in England, because of the quality of his music,
because of his organizing, because of his thinking, speaking and writing." Andrew
Porter, *Musical Events, a Chronicle 1980–83* (London: Grafton Books, 1988), 266.

that if Cage started from here with the seminal works for percussion and prepared piano, then it might be worth taking more seriously the results of his apparent abdication to chance mechanisms around 1950. When Paul Griffiths wrote his short monograph on Cage in 1981, he looked back over thirty years at the same problem: "The influence of his ideas during this period cannot be questioned, and yet the relative neglect of his earlier music has often led to a misrepresentation of his attitudes."[47] However, in 1958 Cage said about the *Sonatas and Interludes*, "Nothing about the structure was determined by the nature of the materials which were to occur in it; it was conceived, in fact, so that it could be as well expressed by the absence of these materials as by their presence."[48] So although the materials were chosen "as one chooses shells while walking on the beach," irrational elements were built in even at this stage. The attractions of both the percussion and prepared piano works derive largely from the sheer novelty of their autonomous sounds ventilated by silence.

As the permissive sixties developed, Cage's name became inextricably associated with the notion that anything goes[49]—thanks to well-publicized environmental extravaganzas such as *Variations IV*, *Musicircus*,[50] and *HPSCHD* and the fact that he was known to be using chance operations through the *I Ching* as the virtually exclusive basis for compositional decisions. Extreme gestures such as *4′33″* were misinterpreted or ridiculed.[51]

---

47. Griffiths, *Cage*, 1.
48. Cage, *Silence*, 19.
49. Dick Higgins, who was in Cage's class at the New School for Social Research in New York in 1958, said: "But the best thing that happened to us in Cage's class was the sense he gave that 'anything goes,' at least potentially." Kostelanetz, *John Cage*, 116. "He gave you permission to be yourself. Anything goes, provided—as he would always say—that you take 'nothing' as the base." Gavin Bryars in "The Music of Chance," *Guardian*, January 16, 2004, 10–11.
50. See About *Musicircus*, chapter 19, 211.
51. The copyright status of *4′33″* became an issue in England when a CD by Mike Batt included a track called "A One-Minute Silence." See Steven Poole, "A Kind of Hush: John Cage's Publishers Think a Rival Composer Has Ripped off His Famous Silent Piece, *4′33″*," *Guardian*, July 18, 2002. The resolution: "Womble Man Batt's £100,000 Keeps the Peace: Composer and Wombles creator Mike Batt, 50, today paid at least £100,000 for the sound of silence. He settled outside the High Court with representatives of the late avant-garde composer John Cage, whose music publishers had threatened legal action claiming Batt stole the concept of a minute of silence from a piece Cage wrote in 1952. Batt said: 'We are making a donation without any admission there has been any plagiarism.'" *Evening Standard*, September 9, 2002. However, I am assured by Cage's publisher, who did not benefit directly, that the report is misleading and the figure inaccurate.

My correspondence with Cage had covered the all-black and all-white paintings exhibited by Alphonse Allais, but the British novelist and biographer Sir Harold Acton had a curious experience. He was visiting a mental hospital in Oahu, and an old Italian man with dignity and charm came up to him and presented him with some pieces of paper. Acton had lived in Florence for many years and was surprised to find that the old man, speaking to him in Italian, knew this. The man gave him several sheets of paper; asked him not to look at them until the moon was full, and told him they represented "the only truth." When Acton examined them, he found they were blank. This left him musing on the whole encounter: "So often is the virgin sheet of paper more real than what one has to say, and so often one regrets having marred it."[52]

The influential educationist Maria Montessori employed a teaching technique called the Silence Game:

> To quicken a child's attention in special relation to sounds there is a most important exercise which . . . consists not in producing but in eliminating as far as possible, all sounds from the environment. My "lesson of silence" has been very widely applied . . . for the sake of its practical effect on the discipline of the children.
> The children are taught "not to move"; to inhibit all those motor impulses which may arise from any cause whatsoever, and in order to induce in them real "immobility," it is necessary to initiate them in the *control* of all their movements. . . . Then it is that slight sounds, unnoticed before, are heard; the ticking of the clock, the chirp of a sparrow in the garden, the flight of a butterfly. The world becomes full of imperceptible sounds which invade that deep silence.[53]

It may be instructive to ask what has changed since I first put the case for Cage in 1965 and now, over forty years later. Following his pioneering work in the article on Cage in the 1980 *New Grove Dictionary of Music and Musicians*, Charles Hamm asked the same question fifteen years later and concluded that Cage had anticipated virtually everything in postmodern art, theory, and criticism.[54] But there was a defining moment in the meantime—Cage's death

---

52. Sir Harold Acton (1904–94), *Memoirs of an Aesthete* (London: Methuen, 1948), 252–53.

53. Taken from Maria Montessori (1870–1952), *Dr Montessori's Own Handbook* (English, 1914) and quoted in Bernarr Rainbow, *Music in Educational Thought and Practice: A Survey from 800 BC* (Aberystwyth, Wales: Boethius, 1989), 283.

54. Charles Hamm, "John Cage," in Stanley Sadie, ed., *The New Grove Dictionary of Music and Musicians* (London: Macmillan, 1980), 3: 597–603. See also Charles Hamm, "Epilogue: John Cage Revisited," in *Putting Popular Music in Its Place* (Cambridge: Cambridge University Press, 1995), 381–85. Hamm also pointed out

in 1992. In obituaries he was celebrated as the grand old man of the universal avant-garde; tribute was paid to his work as composer, writer, artist, and philosopher, as well as to the breadth of his influence on music, dance, and the visual arts.[55] Away from the American centers and less inclined to accept Cage in terms of his own celebrity, critics in London were more cautious. Andrew Porter led the opposition: "He said a lot of silly things and wrote a lot of silly music. But everyone was fond of him." However, Porter did quote Lutoslawski, who said that a radio broadcast of Cage's *Concert for Piano and Orchestra* (wrongly cited as *Concerto*) "changed my life decisively. . . . I suddenly realized that I could compose music differently."[56] Michael White visited Cage in New York in 1983 and was surprised to hear him say he was not interested in other living composers such as Boulez, Messiaen, or Britten. When White pointed out that Britten had died seven years earlier Cage quipped, "Well, some living composers are more dead than alive . . . and some dead ones just live on!" In his obituary White prophesied that it would be Cage's ideas that would live on rather than his music, which would not survive on CD—soon to be proved wrong. But he signaled the way Cage's works "threw down a massive challenge to the way audiences evaluate sound and respond to the artifice of performance."[57] For the *Daily Telegraph*, Cage was "the most iconoclastic and influential representative of that radical, saltishly independent strain in American music. . . . Whereas for many of his eager young disciples Cage represented liberation and the freedom to do

that aligning oneself with Cage in the 1950s, 60s, and 70s, when he was "still a highly controversial figure," was "not a wise career choice." See his Introduction to David W. Patterson, ed., *John Cage: Music, Philosophy, and Intention 1933–1950* (New York: Routledge, 2002), 3. I discovered this myself when I applied for a post in music at the University of St. Andrews, Scotland, in 1962. Immediately after the interview I was told that somebody who knew John Cage and liked Stockhausen was overqualified.

55. Allan Kozinn, "John Cage, 79, a Minimalist Enchanted with Sound, Dies," *New York Times*, August 13, 1992.

56. Andrew Porter, "Chance Master," *Observer*, August 18, 1992. I interviewed Lutoslawski in London on June 24, 1973, and he said it was *Jeux Vénitiens* (1960) that was inspired by Cage as a result of hearing the *Concert for Piano and Orchestra* broadcast on Westdeutscher Rundfunk. He then said he realized he could compose in a different way. From the concrete to the whole design: simple to sophisticated. He realized he could start from chaos. Lutoslawski told Cage about this, and Cage then asked him for a contribution to his collection called *Notations* (New York: Something Else, 1969). He sent Cage the whole manuscript and seemed surprised when he sold it. However, Cage intended the collection to benefit the Foundation for Contemporary Performance Arts.

57. Michael White, "An Artist Who Dared to Be Indifferent," *Independent on Sunday*, August 18, 1992.

exactly what they liked, for others he quickly became the object of ridicule and the most aggressive hostility."[58]

The Times described Cage as "American composer, philosopher and writer" who "forty years ago was a giant among rebels, shaking up the American musical establishment that was dominated and awed by elderly European émigrés. . . . Few composers have caused as many ripples as Cage—with his theory of art as a random event depending on chance—in the philosophies of other avant-garde art-forms: of dance, particularly, and of visual art, rock music and theater."[59]

Paul Driver saw Cage as "in some sense a musical surrealist . . . but all too close to the spirit of Andy Warhol and his American conceptual chic. Like Warhol, Cage easily gives the impression of devising indigenous art by filling a vacuum with a vacuum."[60] But, like Paul Griffiths and me, he recognized the substance of earlier works such as the *Constructions in Metal* and *Sonatas and Interludes*, as well as the later notated pieces such as the *Freeman Etudes*.[61]

Andrew Clements described Cage as

in many ways . . . the most influential figure in post-war music, one whose ideas ramified across the avant-garde arts. His own works may not endure . . . but his significant position among the convolutions of music in the second half of the 20th century is secure. . . . Cage's intentions . . . subversive in the best sense of the word . . . provided a necessary corrective to over-insistent dogmas of the post-war years and can take much of the credit for the polyglot musical world in which composers today can work.[62]

Hugo Cole, who had been sympathetic toward Cage for some years, hailed him as "one of the most original and influential composers of the twentieth century" who "liked to bemuse the public; but he was a true musician with a sharp intellect, as well as a great original, with the fertility of invention which marks the true genius."[63]

Extracts from these British obituary tributes have been quoted in ascending order of commendation, and it was finally Cole who brought up the

---

58. Unsigned, "Obituary. John Cage," *Daily Telegraph*, August 14, 1992.
59. Unsigned, "Obituary. John Cage," *The Times*, August 14, 1992.
60. Cage has been compared to Andy Warhol (1928–87), who began his career as a successful commercial artist, made an impact in the early 1960s with his repetitive images as American pop art, then made deliberately boring films while continuing to manage his image as a celebrity.
61. Paul Driver, "Obituaries: John Cage," *Independent*, August 14, 1992.
62. Andrew Clements, "John Cage," *Financial Times*, August 14, 1992.
63. Hugo Cole, "Breaking the Sound Barrier," *Guardian*, August 14, 1992.

notion of genius. Peter Yates, who first met Cage in 1939 and had followed his development for the next thirty years, remembered that for him "the name Beethoven symbolizes all that is lumped together in misuse of the word genius." He went on to claim that "the musical growth of John Cage has been as exact, exacting, and creatively logical as that of Beethoven or Schoenberg."[64]

Anyone who spent time with Cage can confirm that his personality endeared him to people who might otherwise have been reluctant to take him seriously. David Revill, Cage's British biographer, found this too. He felt that Cage's "potentially greatest legacy will stay largely unnoticed: the value and power of seriousness, integrity and discipline. And the greatest loss will be soonest forgotten—the fact, against which cultural polemics pall, that Cage was a good human being." He then quoted Cage: "I have no regrets: I've enjoyed the whole thing, every bit of it."[65]

British critics like Driver and White were not alone in thinking that Cage's music would not endure. Donal Henehan, reviewing *For the Birds*, Cage's interviews with Daniel Charles, in the *New York Times* in 1981, went out on a limb: "If I were asked to name the Cage works that might still have an audience in 2001, I would list only four."[66] And these, astonishingly, were not music but Cage's first four books. Henehan concluded that "John Cage is, no matter on what scale you weigh him, a remarkable man who has raised contrariness to the status of art."

As a fellow composer sympathetic to Buddhism, Jonathan Harvey wrote, in an obituary tribute: "When attending to music we use our cultural experience to decode significance. When attending to Cage we perceive chance and non-intentionality and therefore our cultural experience is phantasmagoric at best, useless at worst." Harvey imagined Cage as "a complete Buddhist, a shining example" but found he never enjoyed the sound of Cage after *Music of Changes*.[67] He also questioned "the worrying dualism in Cage's practice where he opposes chance to control, carefully eliminating the latter." Harvey quoted Alan Watts in justification: "For Zen there is no duality, no conflict between the natural element of chance and the human element of control."[68]

---

64. Yates, *Twentieth Century Music*, 309.
65. David Revill, "Obituaries: John Cage," *Independent*, August 14, 1992. See also David Revill, *The Roaring Silence—John Cage: A Life* (London: Bloomsbury, 1992).
66. Donal Henehan, "The Random Cage," *New York Times*, August 23, 1981.
67. Jonathan Harvey, "John Cage: Four Envois," *Perspectives of New Music* 31, no. 2 (Summer 1993): 133–34.
68. Alan W. Watts, *The Way of Zen* (Harmondsworth, Middlesex: Penguin Books, 1962), 193.

Reviewing the BBC's *John Cage Uncaged* weekend, Paul Driver moved into attack mode: "It worries me that John Cage's music is not being quickly forgotten. I had assumed that, like many a composer feted in his lifetime, he would slip into prompt obscurity on his death."[69] Driver, one of the few remaining modernist critics in Britain, particularly objected to the random choices that lay behind *Atlas Eclipticalis* and *Apartment House 1776* and finally sided with Stockhausen, quoting what he told me in 1987: "It is just a shock in the history of European traditions that someone like him can be called a composer."[70] At the other extreme, Sean Doran, then director of English National Opera, said: "I do believe the future, let's say 25–50 years from now, will place Cage as the most important composer of the twentieth century. . . . Cage's sound-worlds are fashioned foremost to be beautiful—a prism that helps us refocus the world already within and around us."[71] More balanced was Michael Berkeley, who admired the works for prepared piano and for percussion and added, "Cage is that rare thing, a maverick who has taught us to re-evaluate the way in which we perceive music through creations that, though frequently conceived with childlike simplicity, both scintillate and enchant the ear."[72]

During the 1990s things began to change. Cage was increasingly taken up by musicologists—a multidisciplinary industry becoming comparable to literary studies of James Joyce.[73] As with Joyce, Cage's stature was rising as a result of the opportunities his work provided for labyrinthine critical elucidation. Christopher Shultis claimed, "John Cage was not only a great composer: he was also a great writer."[74] Against many of the prophecies, Cage was taken up by a younger generation of performers who relished the opportunities his pieces gave them to enter into the creative process—and to prove it one has only to scan the CD catalog. In the British Classical Record catalog alone, in 2005 the figures for the number of different recordings speak for themselves: *In a Landscape*, for harp or piano (12);[75] *Sonatas and Interludes*,

---

69. Paul Driver, "The Follies of Cage," *Sunday Times*, January 25, 2004, culture section, 29–30.

70. See interview with Stockhausen, chapter 9, 134.

71. Sean Doran in "The Music of Chance," *Guardian*, January 16, 2004, 11.

72. Michael Berkeley in ibid.

73. See Danae Stefanou, "Mapping a Museum without Walls: John Cage and Musicology," *Journal of the Royal Musical Association* 128, no. 2 (2003): 319–28.

74. "Cage and Europe," in David Nicholls, ed., *The Cambridge Companion to John Cage* (Cambridge: Cambridge University Press, 2002), 20.

75. The mesmeric quality of this unusual piece explains its attraction. It was written in the rhythmic structure of a dance by Louise Lippold, wife of sculptor Richard Lippold, and premiered on August 20, 1948, at Black Mountain College. In 2005 Merce Cunningham told David Vaughan that he didn't remember much about the

the complete cycle for prepared piano (11); *Bacchanale,* the first piece for prepared piano (8); *The Wonderful Widow of Eighteen Springs,* song for voice and closed piano (7); *Second* and *Third Construction in Metal* for percussion ensemble (6 each); and *Concerto for Prepared Piano and Orchestra* (3). Of the late number pieces, there were recordings of *Five* (8) and *Four* (4).[76]

The figures show the distribution of these works among performers of various nationalities and prove that Cage is not remembered for his ideas rather than his music. There are remarkable individual achievements such as the Complete Piano Music by the German pianist Steffen Schleiermacher[77] and the Complete John Cage Edition on Mode Records, which already runs to over thirty volumes. The percussion works have become classics in the medium, but there are surprises where Cage enters the mainstream. For example, Paul Hillier's group, Theater of Voices, has performed Cage with the dedication it previously brought to Arvo Pärt and early music, showing that Cage can escape from the avant-garde he did so much to establish.[78]

The first section of the book is "Cage and Friends." My 1987 interview with Cage, who was in typical genial form, sets up the parameters of the discussions that follow, where I deliberately came back to some of the same issues. As usual, Cage took refuge in Zen that, through him, was transmitted to Cunningham in the medium of dance. The dancer, choreographer, and teacher Bonnie Bird recalls the context of this extraordinary professional and personal partnership, which originated in 1938 when she took Cage on as her accompanist at the Cornish School in Seattle, where Cunningham was one of her students. Bird's interview with Rebecca Boyle took place at the Laban Centre in London, where there were regular interruptions, but she kept to the point throughout. By 1944 Cage and Cunningham, both in New York, were giving recitals together, and in 1950 what has become known as the New York School came together—Cage with Morton Feldman, David Tudor, Christian Wolff, and, two years later, Earle Brown. Tudor and Cunningham were in London with the Merce Cunningham Dance Company when I interviewed them. Both were relaxed and communicative, but Tudor offers unique insights, especially about the background of *4′ 33″*. Tudor has not often been interviewed and is disarmingly modest about his significant

dance except that it was "very beautiful, with small gestures, but she moved around a lot." E-mail from David Vaughan, September 6, 2005.

76. James Jolly, ed., *Redmuse Classical Catalogue 2005* (London: Gramophone, 2005), published in association with *The Gramophone.*

77. Dabringhaus und Grimm, MDG 613 series (1997 onward).

78. John Cage, "Litany for the Whale," Theater of Voices/Paul Hillier, Harmonia Mundi HMU90 7187 (2000).

role. I met the writer Jackson Mac Low in his loft, surrounded by great shelves of books. He came to know Cage well from 1953 onward, but Minna Lederman had published Cage's contributions to the journal she edited, *Modern Music*, well before this time.[79]

Those interviews deal with insiders in Cage's circle, but to see the picture whole we need to come to terms with different views and some opposition. The section of the book called "Colleagues and Criticism" is opened by Virgil Thomson who, at the time of the interview, was ninety years old and very deaf. He and Cage had their differences, but his early support for Cage in newspaper reviews was crucial, and he ends up being loyal. Matters reach an extreme with Stockhausen who, in spite of lobbying for Cage at Darmstadt in the 1950s, is no longer able to regard him as a composer. Earle Brown, too, was troubled by the insistent impracticality of Cage's dealings with professional orchestras as opposed to his fruitful relationship with dedicated performers such as David Tudor. The Austrian composer Kurt Schwertsik relishes the delights of Cage and the liberation he offered young composers but also recognizes the demands he made and continues to make of his audiences. La Monte Young, too, respects Cage, absorbed his ethos at a crucial stage in his own development, but finds Cage's work has lost the original element of surprise. John Rockwell, like Young, admires Cage's dedicated career, accepts his influence—especially through his writings—but has doubts about his musical significance beyond the earlier works. Pauline Oliveros, a fellow composer also on the fringes of the Western tradition, understands Cage; and Paul Zukofsky, a performer-collaborator less central than David Tudor, nevertheless has qualified insights to offer.

The section called "Earlier Interviews" reproduces some BBC interviews made before mine. As far back as 1966, the art critic David Sylvester, along with composer Roger Smalley, conducted a sympathetic exploration of Cage's position that ends with his Zen contradictions. In 1970, with the astute literary critic Frank Kermode, Cage was just as consistent and concluded with the kind of anarchistic social gospel he increasingly propounded. By 1980, with Michael Oliver, Cage's idiosyncratic mixture of subversion and charm was expertly polished.

The next section deals with what I have called "Extravaganzas." *Musicircus* (1967) reached England in performances with my students five years after its U.S. premiere and got a mixed reception from the London critics, although some were ready to give it the benefit of the doubt. *Roaratorio* (1979), which began as a radio play, was stunning to watch, with the Merce Cunningham Dance Company in The Royal Albert Hall at the BBC Promenade Concert in 1987, but the BBC received complaints from those who merely

---

79. See introduction to interview with Minna Lederman, chapter 6, 102.

heard it on the radio. Finally, *Europeras,* in some ways an extension of Cage's 1960s ideas but taking the circus principle into opera, were in progress when Cage talked to Anthony Cheevers in 1988. At that point Cage had completed only the first two of these pieces and was engaged in what turned out to be his final works—the series of number pieces, which occupy a unique position as his last testament.

Figure 1. John Cage preparing a piano, before 1950. Photograph by Ross Welser. Courtesy of the John Cage Trust.

Figure 2. John Cage and David Tudor in Japan, 1962. Photographer unknown. Courtesy of the John Cage Trust.

Figure 3. Unidentified female dancer in *Europeras 1 & 2*, Frankfurt, 1987. Photograph by Maria Eggert. Courtesy of the John Cage Trust.

Figure 4. John Cage and Merce Cunningham, ca. 1983. Photograph by Didier Allard. Courtesy of the John Cage Trust.

Figure 5. John Cage with Karlheinz Stockhausen at a reception after a performance of his *Sternklang,* Englischen Garten, Munich, 1982. From the Archives of the Stockhausen Foundation for Music, Kürten, Germany.

Figure 6. Merce Cunningham and unidentified female dancer from the Merce Cunningham Dance Company, in *Roaratorio*, 1983. Photograph by Delahaye. Courtesy of the John Cage Trust.

Figure 7. David Tudor, onlooker, and John Cage, 1962. Photograph by Earle Brown. Courtesy of the Earle Brown Music Foundation.

Figure 8. John Cage, Earle Brown (both standing), Matthew Raimondi, Kenji Kobayashi (violins), Walter Trampler (viola), and David Soyer (cello), 1962. Photograph in Earle Brown studio. Courtesy of the Earle Brown Music Foundation.

Figure 9. The New York School: Christian Wolff, Earle Brown, John Cage, David Tudor, and Morton Feldman, 1962. Photograph in Earle Brown studio. Courtesy of the Earle Brown Music Foundation.

Part I
Cage and Friends

Chapter One

John Cage

Interview with Peter Dickinson, BBC studios, New York City, June 29, 1987

By permission of the John Cage Trust

Introduction

John Milton Cage was born in Los Angeles on September 5, 1912, and died in New York City on August 12, 1992. He often mentioned his impressively named paternal grandfather, Gustavus Adolphus Williamson Cage, who took a first degree at CU-Boulder and did postgraduate work at the University of Denver. After that, Cage's grandfather became a dogmatic and rather intolerant minister in the Methodist Episcopalian Church, and he was apparently suspicious of music. Cage's father, an engineer and inventor who worked in various fields with limited success, was also named John Milton Cage (1886–1964), and his wife, Lucretia Harvey (1885–1968), was the pianist at the local church. Later, she took part in the activities of women's clubs and reported on them for the *Los Angeles Times.* Cage took up the story of his family background and his first musical influences and training through his aunts. Significantly, he came across the work of Gertrude Stein when he was at Pomona College—and subsequently became a dropout.

But Cage returned to academic institutions later. In 1948 and 1952 he taught at Black Mountain College, North Carolina; in 1956 and 1959 he gave classes at the New School for Social Research in New York City; and he was a Fellow at the Center for Advanced Studies at Wesleyan University, Middletown, Connecticut, in 1960 and again in 1970. He was composer in residence at the University of Cincinnati, was artist in residence at the University of California at Davis, was elected University of California Regents Lecturer at San Diego, and became Charles Eliot Norton Professor of Poetry at Harvard in 1988–89. From the 1960s onward he increasingly received international commissions and awards, and his work in the visual arts was widely exhibited. This recognition moved to a climax with plans toward his eightieth birthday, which he did not live to see.

Interview

PD   I'm interested in the background of musicians from their earliest times. Somehow it all fits. Your father was an inventor?

JC   Right.

PD   But on your mother's side there were professional musicians?[1]

JC   My mother's sisters were. My Aunt Phoebe was a singer, pianist, and piano teacher. Aunt Marge had a contralto voice. She sang in a Protestant church. I used to go and sit in the front row. Her voice was so beautiful it would bring tears to my eyes. That's why I never liked my Uncle Walter because, when he married Marge, he said, "There's to be no more singing." And I never forgave him. He wanted her to take care of the house, to raise the family, and so forth. You know my story about Aunt Marge and the washing machine?

PD   No.

JC   I was visiting my Aunt Marge, she was doing her laundry, she turned to me and said, "I love this machine much more than I do your Uncle Walter!"[2] But when he died he went straight to heaven—in her estimation.

PD   Did she go back to her singing?

JC   No, she was too old then.

PD   What a sad story.

JC   It is very sad, but she went on laughing. I think I could call her laugh coloratura. It was absolutely beautiful: it came descending from above like a laughter-fall.

PD   That's a Joyceism! You've inherited that kind of "sunny disposition," you called it once.[3]

JC   Yes.

---

1. Cage described his background in "A Composer's Confession" (1948), in Richard Kostelanetz, ed., *John Cage: Writer. Previously Uncollected Pieces* (New York: Limelight Editions, 1993), 27.

2. John Cage, *Silence: Lectures and Writings* (Middletown, CT: Wesleyan University Press, 1961), 85.

3. John Cage, *A Year from Monday: New Lectures and Writings* (Middletown, CT: Wesleyan University Press, 1967), x.

PD What about Fanny Charles Dillon, who does get her own entry in the *New Grove Dictionary of Music* as a pianist and teacher?[4]
JC She was also a composer of music in relation to birdsongs.
PD She provides a link with nature, doesn't she?
JC Yes. She was before Messiaen.[5]
PD She wrote birdcalls down and put them into salon pieces. Do you remember hearing those?
JC Yes. I was in high school and in a group of students. Instead of having private lessons it was a class studying piano with her. There must have been between ten and twenty students. She was very serious. I admired her.
PD It was through her that you got interested in Grieg?
JC No, it was through my Aunt Phoebe.[6] She had absolute confidence in sight-reading. I would go to the Los Angeles Public Library and get stacks of music and bring them home and sight-read. We had at that time, on the piano, *Music the Whole World Loves to Play*, and it was there that I came to know of Grieg. So when I'd go to the library I'd get out as much Grieg as I could.[7]
PD I don't think it's entirely fanciful to see a connection between those very adventurous *Lyric Pieces*, the focus of pieces by Satie, and your own works like the *Toy Piano Suite* and *In a Landscape*?[8]
JC No, it's true.
PD Among the large figures clearly in your background is Gertrude Stein.[9] You must have come into contact with her work at college when you wrote those essays?

4. Fanny Charles Dillon (1881–1947), composer and pianist, born in Denver, studied with Leopold Godowsky in Berlin, and made her debut in Los Angeles in 1908.
5. Olivier Messiaen (1908–92) notated birdsong and incorporated it as a primary source in many of his works. In his early work Cage used measured lengths of time, whether of sound or silence, and Messiaen employed extended rhythmic patterns derived from the talas of Indian music.
6. For more about Aunt Phoebe James see Kostelanetz, *John Cage: Writer*, 27–28.
7. Cage, *Silence*, 115.
8. *In a Landscape* and *Suite for Toy Piano* were both written in 1948, the year Cage presented a festival of the music of Erik Satie (1866–1925) at Black Mountain College.
9. One of Cage's earliest surviving works is *Three Songs* (1933) to fragments from Gertrude Stein (1874–1946). *Living Room Music* (1940) is for four percussionists playing unspecified household objects and includes a spoken text from Stein. The manuscript of *Three Songs* is headed Piano Pieces 1, 2, 3, but this is crossed out and under it Songs 1, 2, 3 is written. However, on November 4, 1990, I played the piano version at a reception given by the late Marjorie and Jerry Shapiro at their house, 441 East 84th Street, New York. John Cage was there, and he told me he thought the *Three Songs* were "more mysterious when not being sung" and said the text came from

JC   Actually, it was when I left college—you know I'm a college dropout—
and went to Europe, and it was there through a friend Don Sample
who was a little older than I and was the one who introduced me to
transition magazine.[10] It was through him that I came to know Joyce
and Stein, Cummings, Eliot, and Pound.[11]

PD   But you say yourself that you wrote an essay in the style of Gertrude
Stein at college?[12]

Stein's *Useful Knowledge* (1928). When Meriel Dickinson and I were planning to perform these songs, I asked Cage if I could adapt the last one for low voice so that some
of the vocal line was an octave lower and the roulades were only in the piano. I sent
him a written-out realization. On August 30, 1990, he replied: "Down an octave is fine
but then very emphatically. I think the doubling of the voice with the piano is so to
speak part of it." Cage considered this version to be the European premiere of the
songs, given at the Muziekcentrum de Ysbreker, Amsterdam, on September 29, 1990.
10. *transition: an international quarterly for creative experiment*. It was founded in Paris
in 1927 and edited by Eugene Jolas and Elliot Paul. Don Sample was a close friend
in Paris, and he and Cage were together in Los Angeles. See Thomas S. Hines, "Then
Not Yet Cage," in Marjorie Perloff and Charles Junkerman, eds., *John Cage: Composed
in America* (Chicago: University of Chicago Press, 1994), 81–85, and chapter 20,
Introducing Roaratorio, 217.
11. Cage's involvement with James Joyce (1882–1941) included settings of *The
Wonderful Widow of Eighteen Springs* (1942) and *Nowth upon Nacht* (1984) and climaxed
with *Roaratorio* (1979) and the series of *Writings through Finnegans Wake*. He set E. E.
Cummings (1894–1962) in *Five Songs* (1938) and *Experiences No. 2* (1948). When I sent
him copies of programs that included his *Five Songs*, he told me: "I've never heard the
Five Songs. Glad you enjoy them." Letter of May 2, 1971. When I sent him a copy of the
LP *American Anthology*, Unicorn RHS 253 (1978), made by mezzo Meriel Dickinson and
me, he said: "Yes, I received the disc and thank you very much. I don't keep a machine
for playing records but I keep the records and send them ultimately to Northwestern
University, the Music Library [Evanston, Illinois]." Letter of January 29, 1979. For more
on Cage's attitude toward recordings see the interviews with the four-LP set *Music before
Revolution*, Ensemble Musica Negativa, EMI (1972) 1 C 165-28 954 Y, with Cage's *Credo
in US, Imaginary Landscape No. 1, Concert for Piano and Orchestra, Solo for Voice 1 & 2, Rozart
Mix*, and works by Brown, Feldman, Wolff, and Ichiyanagi. Hans Helms asked Cage
about the use of a recording, and he replied: "I don't think it has any use, because people think they can use records as music. What they finally have to understand is that they
have to use them as records. And music instructs us, I would say, that the uses of things,
if they are meaningful, are creative. Therefore the only lively thing that will happen with
a record is if somehow you would use it to make something which it isn't. You could, for
instance, make another piece of music with a record and other sounds of the environment or other musical instruments—that I would find interesting." Cage responded to
Ezra Pound (1885–1972) in "Writing through the Cantos," in *X: Writings '79–'82*
(Middletown, CT: Wesleyan University Press, 1983), 109.
12. For more detail about Cage's introduction to Stein see David Revill, *The Roaring
Silence—John Cage: A Life* (London: Bloomsbury, 1992), 33–34.

JC   That is true. So I knew about Stein before that. I wonder how that happened. I don't have the least idea.

PD   What amused me was that the first essay you wrote in her style got an A and the second one failed!

JC   Right. That was good Zen teaching! [*laughs*]

PD   That time when you were in France and around Europe you were writing poems and painting. What happened to these?

JC   I sent the poems as letters to my mother and father. Finally, my father said, "Don't send us any of your writing: we want to know what's happening." [*laughs*] He wanted real information.

PD   What about the paintings? In view of your later career in graphics, how interesting they would be if we could see them.

JC   I don't know where they are. I gave one of the more interesting ones to Richard Buhlig.[13] I think it might not be too difficult to find out where it is.

PD   What about the music of this period, such as the works before the *Three Songs*?

JC   Well, those are gone. I threw them away, unfortunately. I wrote them by means of some mathematical formulas—they can't have been very complicated. I mean to say the formulas couldn't have been very complicated, but the music was sufficiently complicated to seem to me not to be music—with my then point of view.

PD   Do you remember when you destroyed them?

JC   I tended to move around a good deal, and I remember that when I would pack up to go someplace I had a tendency to eliminate anything that I didn't need to carry because I wanted to reduce the luggage. But I think it could have been the move from Majorca, where I wrote them, back to California.[14]

PD   So it wasn't much later when you were more widely known?

JC   It was in Majorca that I had a piano and I wrote those pieces, and it was there that I decided that they weren't musical. So I must have left them there.

PD   Did the influence of Satie start in that period?

JC   I have no confidence in my memory, and my lack of confidence is redoubled by your having shown me that I knew about Stein in college! I have no idea when Satie begins. He could well have begun quite early with that collection of simple modern pieces called *Das Neue*

---

13. Richard Buhlig (1880–1952), American pianist, born in Chicago, who studied with Theodor Leschetizky in Vienna. Taught Cage and Henry Cowell.

14. See also "An Autobiographical Statement" (1989), in Kostelanetz, *John Cage: Writer*, 238, where he confirms that he left these scores behind in Majorca.

Klavierbuch. I'm sure there was some Satie in that. One of the *Enfantines?*[15]

PD   At this time you met Henry Cowell and you read his book *New Musical Resources.*[16] What did you learn from it?

JC   For one thing, he carried on the notion of gruppettos, so that instead of having just thirds and fourths of notes you could have fifths and sevenths and ninths.[17] He suggested giving different shapes for those notes. That set my mind working in terms of fractions, which reaches its most complex point in my *Music of Changes,* where I found a way of equating the space on the page to time so that I could have two-sevenths of a note without the other five-sevenths. I could measure them, and I could go from sevenths to thirds and so on. And you could do that perfectly practically with magnetic tape. It was subsequent to that that I did it with the *Williams Mix.* I did it first on paper with the *Music of Changes.*

---

15. The three volumes of *Das Neue Klavierbuch* (Mainz: B. Schott's Söhne's, 1927–29) were brought to Cage's attention by John Kirkpatrick in Paris. He told William Duckworth, "I began writing music in response to all that music." Duckworth, *Talking Music: Conversations with John Cage, Philip Glass, Laurie Anderson, and Five Generations of American Experimental Composers* (New York: Da Capo, 1995), 7. However, the volumes contain nothing by Satie or Schoenberg. In Joan Retallack, ed., *MUSICAGE: Cage Muses on Words Art Music* (Hanover, NH: Wesleyan University Press and University of New England Press, 1996), 84, Cage still thought there were pieces by Satie and Schoenberg in these volumes. The three sets of Satie's easy piano pieces, *Enfantines,* were published in 1914.

16. Henry Cowell (1897–1965) anticipated Cage's piano preparations and also wrote music influenced by both Eastern and Western traditions. His *New Musical Resources* was first published in 1930, but see Cowell and David Nicholls, ed., *New Musical Resources* (Cambridge: Cambridge University Press, 1996). On April 4, 1987, his widow Sidney Cowell wrote to me: "[T]he concept of the prepared piano, which in effect creates an instrument of definitely predetermined timbres, was entirely John's—a combination, it always seemed to me, of a Schoenbergian tone-row, of timbres instead of pitches, and the piano-string gamelan sounds John probably first heard from Henry. The difference is in the consistency of preparation for an entire composition. John has spent years of his life explaining that he owes the initial idea to Henry, and I have spent years of my life explaining that John picked up an idea from Henry that he carried much further, methodically. Finally we agreed that this was a waste of time because it was never going to get definitive in anybody's mind, and we just agreed to let people think how they like." Quoted in part in my review of William Lichtenwanger, *The Music of Henry Cowell: A Descriptive Catalog* (New York: Institute for Studies in American Music, 1986) in *Music and Letters* 69, no. 2 (April 1988): 292–93.

17. Cage means dividing a measure or a space in notation into five or seven equal parts rather than the conventional three or four, as outlined in Cowell's chapter on rhythm.

PD It's intriguing to find an early influence bearing fruit much later.

JC That must surely have come from the early experience of Henry Cowell's book on rhythm, which I copied out by hand since it wasn't published then. I think the activity of copying something by hand is a natural resource, which we no longer have.

PD You've got to love something if you take the trouble. . .

JC And if you copy it out by hand it steals its way into you.

PD Looking back at when you went to Schoenberg's classes, did he seem very strange to you?[18]

JC Well, I worshipped him. It sounds foolish to say that I thought he was extraordinary, but I mean that in every sense. I thought of him as superior to other people.

PD But he stood for so many different things that, as an American, you could hardly have understood.

JC I know, but for someone to come from another country and to know the English language better than we did—which he did—was just fantastic. I mean, it just added to his musicality. His treatment of language, his insistence on the fine points of language. He would ask us a question and we would give one answer after another, all of which displeased him. Then, when he finally accepted an answer or gave us the true answer, we would tend to say, "Oh, but we said that earlier" with another word. And then he would show us that the other word was not the same.

PD Did you think of him as a kind of Zen master who had authority and power?

JC I've never until this moment connected him with Zen [*laughs*]. He was something quite different from a Zen teacher. He was a law giver, but he was a law taker-backer too. [*laughs*] He would encourage you to take freedom, and then you would do that and he would say "Why do you break the rules?" Then you'd follow the rules and he'd say "Why don't you take a little freedom?" and so on. So nothing ever satisfied him.

PD It's not as mad as it seems. This quality is part of the Zen approach, isn't it?

---

18. Arnold Schoenberg (1874–1951) moved to the United States in 1933. In 1935–36 he taught at the University of Southern California and took a professorship at the University of California in Los Angeles the following year. Cage attended classes with Schoenberg in 1935 and 1936 and regularly spoke of this in interviews. He often said he worshipped Schoenberg, but his letters at the time tell a different story. See Michael Hicks, "John Cage's Studies with Schoenberg," *American Music* 8, no. 2 (Summer 1990): 125–40; Calvin Tomkins, *The Bride and the Bachelors: The Heretical Courtship in Modern Art* (New York: Viking, 1965), 85; and "John Cage Interviewed by Jeff Goldberg," *Transatlantic Review* 55–56 (1976): 103–110.

JC   Yes, but there was very little of the shock or the humor in Schoenberg.
      There was more law giving and putting you in a very uncomfortable
      position. I still have trouble connecting him with Zen. [*laughs*]
PD   Which can also put you in an uncomfortable position—give you a slap
      on the nose.
JC   I agree, but I just don't connect it with him.
PD   In desperation, you went to percussion instruments where you would-
      n't have to cope with the harmony that Schoenberg thought you ought
      to deal with. And you got away from the dilemmas of pitch.
JC   Actually, it wasn't desperation; it was a suggestion from Oskar
      Fischinger, who was an abstract filmmaker, and when we were working
      together the idea was that I would write percussion music to go with
      one of his films.[19] He was at the time using Brahms's *Hungarian
      Dances*—it would have been a step forward for both of us [*laughs*] to
      bring his films and my music together. At any rate he said, while we
      were working together—and it was very slow, tedious work, frame by
      frame by frame—I had a stick with a chicken feather on one end, and
      I would have to still these paper images that were circles or squares or
      triangles. I'd have to get them perfectly still before he could take a
      frame. In the course of that he said, "Everything in the world has its own
      spirit, and that spirit is released by setting it in vibration." It was that
      statement of his that sent me absolutely exploring the world from the
      point of view of sound. I took a group of camp counselors through a
      trip in the woods. The problem was to find sounds in the woods that
      you could take back to the camp and use for the performance of music.
PD   Before we leave Schoenberg and the percussion instruments too, I love
      that story about your asking him to go and hear your percussion
      orchestra.
JC   [*laughs*] I wanted Schoenberg to come. Right? We could perform at
      the drop of a hat and we had several pieces in rehearsal, and I called
      him and asked him to come, and he said he was busy and couldn't
      come. I said we could change the date, and then he said "but I'm
      always busy, I will never be able to come"—and he simply wouldn't
      come. . . . Isn't that how it went?
PD   He said he couldn't come any other night of the week either?
JC   I could have told the story better if I'd put in some *Ach so!* [*laughs*] I
      know how it began. I said I'd written some music—*Ach so*—and would
      you come and hear it. He said, "I'm not free."

---

19. Oskar Fischinger (1900–67), pioneer of avant-garde cinema, born in
Gelnhausen, Germany; left Berlin for Hollywood in 1936.

PD   It's at this period that you came into contact with dancers and painters. Did you find they were more open to new ideas than musicians?

JC   Oh yes, definitely. When I would show a musician some of my work, he would say, "That's not the way to write music." Then I would say, "How should one write?" Then he gave me perfectly good advice—he said, "Write the way Mozart did!" [*laughs*] What I was doing was not satisfactory from a musical point of view, but it was perfectly useful from the point of view of a dancer and it was perfectly interesting from the point of view of an artist.

PD   I love the way you use this word *useful*. Does it refer to music largely based on dancers' counts?

JC   I use it frequently in different ways. I would use it even in connection with changing one's mind—useful to change one's mind.

PD   But the music of this period is based on counts for dancers, measurable quantities. The square-root forms last until the 1950s.[20]

JC   When I came to work with modern dancers they were revolting against following the music as the ballet had done, and they wanted the music to follow the dance. When I saw that there was this kind of political situation rampant, what I wanted to provide was a space of time that was empty of both music and dance, which could have both arts go into it independent of one another. So that there wouldn't be a hierarchical situation. And that's what the rhythmic structure was.

PD   But the rhythmic structure also gave rise to pieces like the *Sonatas and Interludes* that don't require a dance.

JC   But the initial idea was one that saw that structure as a common denominator.

PD   So the dancers' counts kept you going as a composer until about 1950?

JC   Except I didn't take them as counts, I took them as part phrases.

PD   Another aspect that came in around 1939 with *Imaginary Landscape No. 1* is the use of audio equipment to generate sound rather than just reproduce it. There was that radio show with Kenneth Patchen.[21] Was that where the whole business of electronics started?

---

20. So called because the numerical proportions of the whole piece are the same as its individual units. *Sonatas and Interludes* No. IV is a simple case. Its proportions are 3+3+2+2=10. The piece consists of ten ten-measure units—three (repeated in the movement's binary form) plus two (repeated). Inside each ten-measure unit the phrasing is 3+3+2+2. This piece has created a notational problem. The third note should surely be A, not B. However, the performers in these recordings select A—Ajemian, Butterley, Schleiermacher, Karis, MacGregor; but these misread it as B—Tilbury, Vandré. This three-note figure B-C-A is anticipated in Scene IX of *Four Walls* (1944).
21. Kenneth Patchen (1911–72), American poet with whom Cage produced his radio play *The City Wears a Slouch Hat* for CBS in 1942.

JC In my mind, yes, and in my practice. What began it all was the fact that at the Cornish School in Seattle there was a radio studio, and it was very near the theater, so that it was possible to use the equipment in the radio studio and pipe it into the theater and use those sounds with the performances.

PD You must have met Bonnie Bird[22] before you met Merce Cunningham?

JC She was his teacher, and he was in her class at the Cornish School.

PD What was she like as a dancer?

JC She had come from Martha Graham and was a marvelous teacher, very attentive to detail and discipline. She was an inspiration to her students. And now she's an inspiration globally. She has in mind to bring dancers from different cultures together—not to dance together but to be aware of each other's positions, so to speak, in society.

PD Who were the important painters you met in New York around 1942? Was this when you met Marcel Duchamp for the first time?[23]

JC Yes. Before that, the people in the field of the arts who had been important for me were, first of all, Galka Scheyer in Los Angeles, who brought the Blue Four from the Bauhaus,[24] and then at Mills College I met Moholy-Nagy who was also from the Bauhaus, and other teachers.[25] But in Seattle itself I met Morris Graves and Mark Tobey. So when I got to New York I met many people, including Marcel Duchamp, but I met Mondrian, who was the one I liked the most at that time.[26] And

22. Bonnie Bird (1914–95), dancer, teacher, and choreographer who appointed Cage as her accompanist at the Cornish School in Seattle in 1938. See interview with her, chapter 3, 69.

23. Marcel Duchamp (1887–1968), French-born influential avant-garde artist involved with cubism, futurism, and dadaism. Invented ready-mades in 1913 and in 1962 claimed, "I threw the bottle rack and the urinal in their faces and now they admire them for their aesthetic beauty." In Ian Chilvers, *Concise Dictionary of Art and Artists* (Oxford: Oxford University Press, 1996), 156.

24. The Blue Four, for whom Scheyer acted as patron and agent, were Wassily Kandinsky (1866–1944), Alexei von Jawlinski (1864–1941), Paul Klee (1879–1940), and Lyonel Feininger (1871–1956).

25. Laszlo Moholy-Nagy (1895–1946), Hungarian-born modernist involved with collage, photomontage, and constructivism in art. He taught at the Bauhaus in Weimar, immigrated to the United States in 1937, and founded his own School/Institute of Design in Chicago in 1939. According to Franz van Rossum, Cage and his friend Don Sample visited the Bauhaus. See Christopher Shultis, "Cage and Europe," in David Nicholls, ed., *The Cambridge Companion to John Cage* (Cambridge: Cambridge University Press, 2002), 22.

26. Piet Mondrian (1872–1944), Dutch abstract painter. See Cage, *Silence*, 127, for Cage likening his music to Mondrian. See 78n18 for Graves and Tobey.

I visited him in his studio. He had an apartment here in New York with an arch, which he carefully masked so that there was no curve. [*laughs*]

PD It seems that the Duchamp idea of ready-mades has continued with you in a piece like *Inlets*, where you have those marvelous conch shells.

JC Yes—and the plants in the piece before, which is called *Child of Tree*, which is a quote from *Finnegans Wake*,[27] or *Branches*, playing on cactus.

PD You said about *The Perilous Night*, "I had poured a great deal of emotion into the piece and obviously I wasn't communicating this at all." At this time you extended your horizons with the Indian and Japanese traditions. Is it right to think of this period as a crisis?

JC Oh yes, it was a crisis both in my musical life and in my—so to speak— private life. It was at that time that the divorce with Xenia took place and I considered being psychoanalyzed.[28] It was at that time that I determined also to find another reason for making music than that of communication. We had all been taught—perhaps people are still being taught—to have something to say and say it. [*laughs*]

PD Whereas you said, "I have nothing to say and I am saying it and that is poetry."[29]

JC Right! But I was still having feelings and expressing them as well as I could and finding that people didn't understand. So I gave that up. I literally gave it up. I think I stopped writing, waiting for a better reason or one that I could use.

PD As we said the other day, it's the *Concerto for Prepared Piano* that is a particular landmark. [*Cage agrees*] I'd like to focus on what happened because the consequences seem to be enormous. [*Cage agrees*] What happened to you—tell me if I'm wrong—was that you came into contact with the whole ethos of Zen and its values, which are quite different from those of Western culture. Did you realize that you were taking onboard something that would change the rest of your life and your creative work?

JC I think I did and I felt, as you've put it, in need of great change—so much so that I went, as I've suggested, to a psychiatrist. He was a Jungian, I think recommended by Joseph Campbell, my friend who

---

27. Joyce's *Finnegans Wake* was published in complete form in 1939, earlier as *Work in Progress* in the magazine *transition*. Cage became obsessed with *Finnegans Wake* and created several reduced versions using his mesostic technique—see his explanation, 220–22. The title *Child of Tree* comes from *Finnegans Wake* (New York: Compass, Books, 1959), 556, the same passage used for *The Wonderful Widow of Eighteen Springs*.

28. Xenia Andreyevna Kashevaroff (1913–95), one of six daughters of Andrew Petrovich Kashevaroff (1863–1940), archpriest of the Russian Orthodox Church in Alaska.

29. Cage, *Silence*, 109.

wrote *The Hero with a Thousand Faces* and so forth.[30] Anyway, this psychiatrist said, "I can fix you so that you will write more music than you do now." And I was alarmed because I was already writing too much music, it seemed to me.

PD   In Joyce we have epiphanies; in Zen, satori is a moment of enlightenment. Was this a point with you where things became different?

JC   At what point?

PD   The Zen masters strive to achieve enlightenment, and I love those stories. Your own stories are modeled on those anecdotes, aren't they? [*Cage agrees*] Did you have a moment yourself when you could say "from that time . . . ?"

JC   [*laughs*] Oh, I don't know what to say because I'm so struck by that monk's remark where he says, "Now that I'm enlightened, I'm just as miserable as ever!"[31] [*laughs*] Don't you think that's truer?

PD   It is, but you've never given that impression to people. You have a wonderful serenity . . .

JC   No, but . . . I think I have just as much trouble as everyone else!

PD   I was going to say that your serenity enables people to accept what you're doing . . .

JC   You think I don't have any problems?

PD   No, but had it come from anybody else they wouldn't. And I try to find the sources for that in some aspect of Zen. I've been reading Suzuki, your teacher, and finding useful things.[32]

JC   I had an interesting experience here in New York the other day. I went to a show, and a young man sitting on the steps leading up to the gallery stopped me and said, "I want to thank you for having replied to my letter." It seems he wrote me a letter years and years ago, and then he told me the circumstances. He had come under the influence of Zen too, but instead of taking a smiling or affirmative attitude he took the attitude that if that was how things were it was unnecessary to do

---

30. Soon after they arrived in New York in 1942, Cage and his wife stayed with Joseph Campbell (1904–87), author, editor, and lecturer; authority on myths. He was married to the dancer Jean Erdman, who worked with Cunningham.

31. Cage, *Silence*, 193.

32. Daisetz Teitaru Suzuki (1870–1966), preeminent Buddhist scholar and philosopher whose books played a major part in bringing Buddhism to the West. He was a visiting professor at Columbia University, New York, when Cage met him and attended his lectures, probably 1951–52. Later on, Cage visited him twice in Japan. See *Silence*, 40, 46, 262; "An Autobiographical Statement (1989)," in Kostelanetz, *John Cage: Writer*, 241; also David W. Patterson, "Cage and Asia: History and Sources," in David Nicholls, ed., *The Cambridge Companion to John Cage* (Cambridge: Cambridge University Press, 2002), 41–62.

anything. And so he stopped. It was at that point when he stopped his work that he wrote to me, and I wrote back almost in a hurry—he said my letter came very quickly—and I told him that there were two forms of the ox-herding pictures. The first form ends in an empty circle in which you do indeed do nothing. But the second version, which I prefer, has a picture after the empty circle, which is that of a fat man with a smile on his face coming back to the village bearing gifts.[33]

PD   That's very nice.

JC   Don't you think?

PD   When *Roaratorio* was done in London and shown on TV,[34] a Japanese writer said: "John Cage is not trying to make Zen-inspired music but to live Zen. The sounds are the vehicle for direct realization." Were you trying to live Zen?

JC   It's difficult to say anything. I would rather listen to you tell me more things! [*laughs*] There was a lovely concert in Dallas, Texas, where I had written some improvisations for the B. L. Lacerta group.[35] They ask

---

33. Cage explained to Calvin Tomkins in 1965 that "the Zen text teaches through illustrations rather than words. . . . The fat man returned without ulterior motive . . . the idea being that after the attainment of nothingness one returns again into activity." Kostelanetz, *Conversing with Cage*, 55. "In these pictures the path of self-discipline that leads to enlightened knowledge is compared to the gradual taming of an ox. The ox becomes completely docile, and ultimately disappears entirely." James Pritchett, *The Music of John Cage* (Cambridge: Cambridge University Press, 1993), 60.
34. *Roaratorio* was given at the BBC Promenade Concerts, The Royal Albert Hall, London, on July 19, 1987, with the Merce Cunningham Dance Company. See chapter 20.
35. This is now an artistic umbrella organization at the Bath House in Dallas, helping young artists and producing multimedia events. Kim Corbet was the low brass specialist of B. L. Lacerta and recalls: "Bob Price and I picked Cage up at the airport and drove to Bob's house, where he would stay. Bob was driving an antique Datsun that was, let's face it, a lump of junk. I was always amazed it ever made it anywhere. Its noises were too numerous to describe. Everything inside rattled and squeaked, while the engine produced an inspiring array of percussive sounds. At one point, there was such a loud 'chunk' under the hood, I looked at Bob and he let out a nervous chuckle. When we thankfully reached Bob's place, I wondered what our guest thought of his limo. As he exited the car, Cage broke the tension by saying, 'Your car is a symphony.' After that, we called it the Cage Mobile. I was in the northwest corner of Horchow Auditorium the evening of that performance. My principal contribution to the Cage piece, as I recall, was an eight-orbit circumnavigation of the audience at breakneck speed while playing the highest note of my accordion. Cage also came on stage and sat in a chair next to the cellist and, mostly, engaged in Tibetan throat singing while we played his simple score, including cells of three or four notes and instructions like 'play your lowest note as long as possible' and 'play only what others are not.' I remember the night as electric, a capacity crowd, turning away almost as many as sat in a rather sweaty theater. We were so happy John Cage had brought out

composers to come to Dallas to tell them how to improvise, and then they give concerts. Anyway. Is it Bob Price, the marvelous clarinetist, with a beautiful wife whose last name is Tree? They have a lovely daughter named Rachel. Rachel, her mother, and I were sitting in the front row at the concert, and the musicians, at my suggestion, were spaced around the audience. Bob Price was back in one corner. Well, Rachel—just a little tot, still not really walking but crawling—got out of her mother's lap. The stage had just a few steps leading up to it, not large but gradual steps, so that very shortly she was on the stage. There was a group of percussion instruments on the stage. Anyway, Rachel began crawling around and she was, of course, the star of the show, and at one point she approached some wires and her mother was worried that she would get a shock, so she went up on the stage and brought her back. The point of my telling you all this is that afterward a Japanese man—again—connected this whole thing [*laughs*]—all the music and everything that happened—with Zen. Isn't that marvelous?

PD   Yes. I wasn't being frivolous; I'm trying to understand.

JC   Well, I know. And I'm trying to keep it misunderstood! [*laughs*]

PD   I've been reading Suzuki who says that the Zen masters used to set the minds of their disciples and scholars free from being oppressed by any fixed opinions or presumptions or so-called logical interpretation.

JC   Right.

PD   Now, that's what you're doing to us.

JC   Well, I hope so.

PD   That's what Western civilization finds hard to swallow.

JC   I know. The Japanese mind processes vowels on one side, consonants on the other, whereas the Western mind processes both vowels and consonants on one side of the mind and nothing on the other side [*laughs*] in terms of language. So a great deal of experience is meaningless to the Western mind, whereas all experience is meaningful to the Japanese mind. Now the thing that saves us from disaster in this whole mind situation is that out of twenty-three Japanese minds, five or six work the way the Western minds do [*laughs*], and out of twenty-three Western minds, five or six work the way the Japanese do. [*laughs*]

---

that kind of support in Dallas, an otherwise hapless desert outpost. I remember anticipating our collaboration with this great man, thinking he must have been negatively affected by a life of challenging the mainstream. I expected him to be somewhat gristly and cynical. Instead, he was the sweetest man imaginable. At our first rehearsal, he came out of the kitchen with a huge steaming bowl of macrobiotic vegetables. He served it to us over a special kind of rice he traveled with. If we were his disciples, he was certainly our messiah." E-mail communication, February 13, 2005.

PD   Are you looking so far forward that the world's cultures have really become one and that our ways of thinking have actually become merged so that we can take on a global attitude toward events?

JC   My tendency is to think that our experience, particularly nowadays, is extremely complex, so I don't think we can come to one idea.

PD   Once you've crossed the Rubicon of accepting the Zen disengagement, then all your activities—using chance or observing imperfections on the manuscript paper—are routes to the same thing—getting yourself out of the music.

JC   No, that's true. I've come to the conclusion that the common denominator of my activity, whether it be with music or now writing or graphic work, is non-intention.

PD   When you had intention, as in the *Sonatas and Interludes*, when you chose the sounds "as one chooses shells while walking along a beach," you got through to people.[36] They're classics, with many different recordings, and you received awards. By the time of *Music of Changes* you're taking yourself out. Do you ever regret this?

JC   No.

PD   Because whatever it is about you that fascinates people, it is you and not somebody else. It's your personality . . .

JC   No, but we have so many personalities we don't need one more! [*laughs*] . . . There's a piece of mine, which I'm sure is very popular, the one called *Dream*. And there was an organist who asked me to write a piece, and then when I agreed he said, "The piece of yours that I like most is *Dream*, and I would like the new piece to be like *Dream*." He'd already sent me half of the commission, and I sent it back to him and said, "I don't want to write *Dream* over again." He then sent the money back to me and said, "Do whatever you wish." Since he had given me complete freedom, I, of course, wanted to do what he wanted me to do. [*laughs*] So I wrote a rather poor piece called *Souvenir*. Then more recently I wrote—by means of chance operations and so forth—*Aslsp*, which can be played on the piano or the organ. I think it's much more beautiful than *Souvenir* or *Dream*.[37]

PD   So you started your commission like Stravinsky being asked to write a new *Firebird*; you refused but came to something quite near it in the end?

JC   Yes.

---

36. Cage, "Composition as Process" (1958), in *Silence*, 19. Also: "The *Sonatas and Interludes* were composed by playing the piano, listening to the differences, making a choice"; 34.

37. *Dream* (1948), for a dance by Cunningham; *Souvenir* (1983); *Aslsp* (1985).

PD   I'd like to try to see whether you feel the Zen involvement needs understanding by those who want to account—in a very Western, logical way—for what you've done since about 1950.

JC   I'm not sure. I'm thinking, for instance, of a very close friend with whom I feel utter sympathy—Morton Feldman.[38] I would say Morty has no closeness to Zen. His closeness is to Western psychology, don't you think?

PD   Yes, I do. But he wouldn't go all the way with you in taking his own tastes and desires, as you call it, out of his music.

JC   No, he wouldn't at all. But he feels very close to my work. He also has, so to speak, as deep an understanding and experience of my work as anyone. And yet he has no experience of Zen.

PD   The golden opportunity to get yourself out of your music was the discovery of the *I Ching?*

JC   I was first introduced to the *I Ching* by Lou Harrison[39] before I went to Seattle, and it made no impression on me, but I remembered it. And later, Christian Wolff[40] brought me a copy that his father had just published—of the Bollingen edition, a translation from the German of Wilhelm by Cary Baynes.[41] At that point, when I saw it—I'm speaking now of the chart with the hexagrams—I suddenly understood how to write the *Music of Changes.*

PD   When Feldman called out, "You've hit it?"

JC   Yes.

PD   A kind of eureka?

JC   [*laughs*] We were at a point with his work, my work, and Christian Wolff's work with the charmed help of David Tudor[42]—a very intoxicating point—where things were happening quickly and richly.

---

38. Morton Feldman (1926–87), celebrated for a high proportion of slow, quiet, and, later, extended works. In 1971 Feldman said: "The more interested I got in Cage's music, the more detached I became from his ideas. I think this happened to Cage too. As his music developed over the years he talked less and less about Zen." "Give My Regards to Eighth Street," in Thomas DeLio, ed., *The Music of Morton Feldman* (New York: Excelsior, 1996), 201.

39. Lou Harrison (1917–2003), American composer whose works draw on Eastern and Western traditions. He wrote *Double Music* (1941) in collaboration with Cage. See interview with Harrison in Duckworth, *Talking Music*, 104.

40. Christian Wolff (1934–), born in France and moved to the United States in 1941. A professor of classics and music, many of his works involve performer participation and, later, politics.

41. Richard Wilhelm, trans., and Cary F. Baynes, ed., Foreword by Carl G. Jung, *The I Ching or Book of Changes* (Princeton, NJ: Bollingen Edition, Princeton University Press, 1950).

42. David Tudor (1926–96), American pianist and composer prominently associated with Cage, as well as with the piano works of Boulez, Stockhausen, Brown, Wolff, and others. His interview, chapter 4, 81.

PD   It must have been wonderful to come across a performer like David Tudor?

JC   Yes. Another great moment that I enjoyed was the close association with Merce, Robert Rauschenberg,[43] and Jasper Johns.[44] The four of us were often together.

PD   Would you account for *4′33″*, which everybody knows and talks about in terms of Rauschenberg's completely white and completely black canvases or of the Buddhas who, when asked to make a statement, said absolutely nothing?

JC   All of that. Actually, I wrote a text, which has never been published, called "A Composer's Confessions,"[45] and in it I described the silent piece before I wrote it. But I didn't give myself the right to write it until I saw the white paintings of Bob's.

PD   You've said quite often that *4′33″* is the piece of yours that you like best.

JC   Yes.

PD   Why?

JC   Well, I listen to it all the time! [*extended laughs*] I wish you'd ask me such questions all the time. [*more laughs*]

PD   You listen to it all the time by your selection [*Cage: Yes*], but in a concert hall it's given to a paying audience.

JC   The pieces that are given [*laughs*], that aren't that, are a terrible interruption! [*extended laughs*][46]

---

43. Robert Rauschenberg (1925–), American experimental artist, studied at Black Mountain College, worked as designer with the Merce Cunningham Dance Company from 1954 to 1964. See Cage, "On Robert Rauschenberg, Artist and His Work," in *Silence*, 98–104. Note Cage's prefatory remark: "To Whom it May Concern: the white paintings came first; my silent piece came later." And: "I remember the show of the black paintings in North Carolina. Quickly! They have become masterpieces." See also Cage's letter to me, Introduction, 11–12.

44. Jasper Johns (1930–), highly successful American experimental artist identified with pop art and minimalism, friend of Rauschenberg with whom he helped promote events involving Cage and Cunningham. Johns became artistic adviser to the Merce Cunningham Dance Company in 1967 and designed posters, costumes, and decor until 1978. See "Jasper Johns: Stories and Ideas," in Cage, *A Year from Monday*, 73–84.

45. Now published—see Kostelanetz, *John Cage: Writer*, 27–44. This is Cage's 1948 Vassar Lecture in which he says he hopes to compose "a piece of uninterrupted silence and sell it to Muzak Co. It will be 3 or 4½ minutes long—those being the standard lengths of canned music—and its title will be *Silent Prayer*. It will open with a single idea, which I will attempt to make as seductive as the color and shape and fragrance of a flower. The ending will approach imperceptibly." See also David Tudor's recollections, chapter 4, 86.

46. Cage came back to this subject countless times. See "John Cage and Roger Reynolds: A Conversation," *Musical Quarterly* 65 (October 1979): 577. See also Duckworth, *Talking Music*, 7, where Cage does not select *4′33″* as his favorite piece.

PD   So all sound is an interruption of the silence?

JC   I consider it my responsibility not to interrupt that, you see.

PD   But you've also said there's no such thing as silence?

JC   True. But there are, in fact, things to be heard when you listen to noth-
      ing—to no music.

PD   This is now fascinatingly logical in the Zen manner but illogical in the
      European manner. Was it something of this sort—your insistence on
      getting yourself out of your music—that caused difficulties with Boulez
      when you were quite close at one point?

JC   I suppose so. We had a very interesting correspondence; I think ulti-
      mately it will be published.[47]

PD   Some of it was very technical?

JC   Oh yes. Some of his letters to me were just absolutely marvelous in
      terms of information. His handwriting was so very small; mine was
      scrawly and large. He wrote on pale blue, transparent airmail paper—
      on both sides—so the writing on one side affects the reading of the
      writing on the other side. It was very difficult. We used to get micro-
      scopes—because it was in French besides. [*laughs*] We were struggling
      to understand it.

PD   That was a junction where the European position of Boulez and your
      own American position were breaking company.

JC   Another thing then was that I was working—just before that corre-
      spondence and perhaps during the beginning of it—with the magic
      square, before the chance operations, and Vishnegradsky in Paris was
      doing the same thing.[48]

In 1991 *The Gramophone* sent me a review copy of John Cage's *4' 33"*, with the British
organist and pianist Wayne Marshall, on Floating Earth FCD004. The CD was fully
packed, complete with booklet notes, but *4' 33"* was the only work on it. I offered to
review it with the normal heading, then a blank space, with my name at the end. The
editor declined.

47. Now published—Jean-Jacques Nattiez, ed., Robert Samuels, trans., *The Boulez-Cage
Correspondence* (Cambridge: Cambridge University Press, 1993). Cage's use of chance
operations caused his split with Boulez. In an article published in *Nouvelle Review
Francaise* 59 (November 1, 1957) Boulez wrote, without naming Cage: "The most elementary form of the transmutation of chance is located in the addition of a philosophy dyed with orientalism and masking a fundamental weakness in the technique of
composition; this would be a recourse against the asphyxia of invention, recourse to a
more subtle poison that destroys every embryo of artisanship . . . the individual, not
feeling responsible for his work, simply throws himself into a puerile magic out of
unavowed weakness . . . chance by inadvertence." Boulez, "Alea," reprinted in *Notes of
an Apprenticeship*, trans. Herbert Weinstock (New York: Alfred A. Knopf, 1968), 35.
48. Ivan Alexandrovich Vishnegradsky (1893–1979), Russian-born microtonal composer and theorist.

PD   What I tend to think of as the Zen moment, when you get yourself out of almost everything, caused Virgil Thomson, one of your best allies, to feel that things had gone wrong.[49] Did that worry you?

JC   Oh yes. I think he could follow the chance operations. What he had difficulty with—and so did Henry Cowell—was the lack of success in *Imaginary Landscape No. 4*. They couldn't understand why the piece was so quiet.[50] They wanted it to be what Lou Harrison used to call a rabble-rouser . . . and later I wrote a radio piece that is perhaps.[51]

PD   It's completely consistent that you could use radio as one of several ingredients within a totality where you, as composer, don't mind what goes in. But in the Town Hall Retrospective Concert there were protests, which can be heard on the recording, during *Williams Mix*.[52] They were getting bored. What did you feel about that?

JC   Well, I was used to it. All the concerts since the late thirties had this sign of controversy. If, in fact, people were not refusing—if I didn't notice that—I thought I was doing something wrong! [*laughs*] I began to think of myself as properly controversial.[53]

PD   So you're really like the naughty child who wants to know how far he can go before he gets smacked?

JC   Perhaps. I even sometimes would privately think of myself as being bad—in the terms that you've just used. But I wouldn't publicly want to be thought of as bad. [*laughs*]

PD   This is like the initiate who goes to the Buddhist master and gets his face slapped?

JC   Yes.

PD   You wanted to know where and when your nose was going to be pulled?

---

49. See interview with Virgil Thomson, chapter 7, 111.

50. *Imaginary Landscape No. 4* (1951) for twelve radios, twenty-four players, and conductor is a landmark in indeterminacy since it depends on whatever happens to be on the air at the time of performance. The premiere was on May 2, 1951, in the McMillan Theater, Columbia University, New York, at the end of a long concert when very little was being broadcast.

51. *Radio Music* (1956) for from one to eight performers, each at one radio. Each tuning "to be expressed by maximum amplitude."

52. A boxed set of three LPs of the 25-Year Retrospective Concert of the Music of John Cage at Town Hall, New York, on May 15, 1958, was produced and marketed by George Avakian. Now on CD: Wergo WEA 0247-2.

53. About a year after this interview Cage said: "If there isn't opposition, I have the feeling that I'm not going in a radical enough direction. Not that I want to offend or shock people, but it's very good, it's like a thermometer." In Geoff Smith and Nicola Walker Smith, *American Originals: Interviews with 25 Contemporary Composers* (London: Faber and Faber, 1994), 73.

JC   No, it's more serious.

PD   That's serious.

JC   Yes, but it's not me really. It's what ideas, what kinds of actions are at the edge of acceptability.

PD   I remember Egon Wellesz telling me exactly when the audience reacted at the premiere of Schoenberg's Second String Quartet—the precise bar number on the first page.[54] Do you feel the same need to know the moment of crisis?

JC   No. I would want it to be bar one! [*laughs*]

PD   But it won't be bar one; it's not until the mind is overloaded.

JC   You're quite right because people are always saying that up to a certain point it would have been acceptable but beyond that, not. [*laughs*]

PD   You can do it because of your philosophical position, but you've had to deal with people who were not as gifted or as tolerant. Therefore when the New York Philharmonic played *Atlas Eclipticalis* under Bernstein in 1964 and starting wrecking the microphones, you were very annoyed and said they were like a group of gangsters.[55]

JC   I would still say that. [*laughs*]

PD   You've had other situations like this—*Cheap Imitation* with the Dutch orchestra, for example.[56] Are you attacking the administrative structure of such institutions?

---

54. Egon Wellesz (1885–1974), Austrian-born composer and associate of Schoenberg who settled in England in 1939 but remembered this 1910 performance in Vienna sixty years later.

55. Cole Gagne and Tracy Caras, *Soundpieces: Interviews with American Composers* (Metuchen, NJ: Scarecrow, 1982), 75. *Atlas Eclipticalis* (1961–62) consists of instrumental parts (86) to be played in whole or in part, any duration, in any ensemble, chamber or orchestral; with or without *Winter Music*; an electronic version is made possible by the use of contact microphones with associated amplifiers and loudspeakers operated by an assistant to the conductor. See also interview with Earle Brown, chapter 10, 142.

56. Cage provided a minimum rehearsal schedule: "Not less than two weeks before a projected performance each musician shall be given his part. During the first week he will learn the melody, at least those phrases of it in which he participates. He is to learn, among other matters, to play double sharps and double flats without writing in simpler 'equivalent' notes. During the second week there will be orchestra rehearsals on each day, each rehearsal lasting 1.5 hours. If, at anytime, it appears that any member of the orchestra does not know his part, he is to be dismissed. If as a result one of the essential 24 parts is missing, the projected performance is to be cancelled." Kostelanetz, *John Cage: Writer*, 94–95. For Cage's account of what happened at the 1972 performances, see Cage, *For the Birds: John Cage in Conversation with Daniel Charles* (London: Marion Boyars, 1981), 183–84. Cage returned to this subject in an interview with Stephen Montague: "I finally had a very good performance of an orchestral work, *30 Pieces for Five Orchestras*, done on the 1981 Metz Festival in France.

JC   I think we have to get to the musicians themselves, not the institution but to the individuals who have committed themselves to it. We have to find a way to arouse them as—what can I say?—conscientious, professional musicians.

PD   You want them to care?

JC   To pay attention and to do the best they can. On our way here we were talking about that quality of musicianship in chamber music and its frequent absence in orchestral music. I want, either from the point of view of chamber music or of orchestral music, to bring the attitude of chamber music to the orchestra.

PD   But why do you have to fix a schedule of rehearsals for *Cheap Imitation* that is so demanding that professional orchestras could never budget for it?

JC   They can't do it. But the school orchestras can. The high school in Cologne has played *Cheap Imitation* beautifully; they were able to spend a month on it, and they were grateful for the experience.[57] And now we'll be able to see in September how the *Quartets*[58] get along: probably not as well because they won't have that much rehearsal. I'm doing another thing at the moment that is a composition called *Music for . . .*[59] It began as music for six, but it's now up to something like fourteen instruments. In other words, I'm approaching the orchestra instrument by instrument and each part is that of a soloist, so I will eventually have a work of chamber music the size of a full orchestra.

And it was because I had written into the contract that there were to be ten rehearsals devoted entirely to this work. That is to say, thirty hours of rehearsal. About three-quarters of the way through rehearsals, the musicians obviously became interested in what they were doing. . . . Each time they had the chance they would leave the group and go out and listen, then go back. The performance was excellent! Do not write for an orchestra unless you have in the contract, some way that will hurt them, plenty of rehearsals." "Significant Silences of a Musical Anarchist," *Classical Music*, May 22, 1982, 11. Also Kostelenatz, *Conversing with Cage*, 132. *Cheap Imitation*, based on Satie's *Socrate*, was the fully notated score for Cunningham's dance *Second Hand* (1970), with costumes by Jasper Johns.

57. Ensemble der Musikhochschule Köln/Markus Stenz, February 14–15, 1987, during NACHTCAGETAG, Vierundzwanzig Stunden für und mit John Cage, a non-stop overnight festival for Cage's seventy-fifth birthday put on by Westdeutscher Rundfunk.

58. *Quartets I–VIII* (1976) for 24, 41, or 91 players. In 1989 Cage said, "In *Quartets* no more than four musicians play at a time, which four constantly changing. Each musician is a soloist." Kostelanetz, *John Cage: Writer*, 246.

59. *Music for . . .* (1984–87), variable chamber ensemble.

PD   *Atlas* is indeterminate, whereas in *Cheap Imitation* you specify exactly what you want. In the sixties you were saying that art's day is done and quoted Jasper Johns as imagining a world without art, which would not be a bad place. Do you retreat from that now?

JC   I think it means almost more now. It's not necessary; I really believe it. For instance, my experience of silence—ambient noise—as music satisfying musical needs is my daily experience. And much earlier, in the early forties through the work of Mark Tobey,[60] I was able to look at the environment—at the pavement I was walking on—as equivalent to a work of art. I could go from a gallery to Madison Avenue and there was no change. And yet I was still interested in buying art on the installment plan! [*laughs*]. It was actually more practical than digging up the pavement. [*laughs*]

PD   This is literally a kind of beauty in the eye of the beholder.

JC   Right.

PD   The beholder has to be ready to supply what you've sometimes called discipline. [*Cage agrees*] When you've been accused of boring people so they protest and walk out, you've said they're mean and need more discipline?

JC   Yes.

PD   You've also reduced the category of music by saying in *Empty Words*, "For many years I've noticed that music, as an activity separated from the rest of life, doesn't enter my mind. Strictly musical questions are no longer serious questions."[61]

JC   I mean by that they're not questions over which one could fight—I am trying to avoid the word *fight*. One wouldn't have to struggle to support dissonance, for instance. That's been won; we can have any dissonances we like. In fact, you can't think of anything purely musical that you couldn't support.

PD   In *A Year from Monday* you said, "Our proper work now if we love mankind and the world we live in is revolution."[62]

JC   It was through that experience I had of going to Hawaii, which I tell about in the first installment of the *Diary: How to Improve the World*.[63] I had been invited by the university, which was to the south of Oahu, but I lived with Jasper Johns and Lois Long on the north side of the island, and we went through a tunnel to get home each evening—and in the

---

60. Mark Tobey (1890–1976), American mostly abstract painter, influenced by Eastern thought, who was at the Cornish School in Seattle with Cage.

61. John Cage, "The Future of Music" (1974), in *Empty Words: Writings '73–'78* (Middletown, CT: Wesleyan University Press, 1979), 177.

62. Cage, "Foreword," in *A Year from Monday*, ix.

63. Cage, "Diary: How to Improve the World (You Will Only Make Matters Worse) 1965," in ibid., 4.

morning too. I noticed that at the top there was a crenellation of the mountain that was tunneled, and I asked people what that crenellation was. They said the people at the north used to fight the people at the south, and they used those crenellations to protect themselves when they were shooting poisoned arrows at the other people. And now that the place is tunneled, the very idea that the people at the north of the island used to fight with the people from the south is just silliness. Buckminster Fuller's view of the world is that it's one island.[64] So I equated Oahu with the world, and all of his and McLuhan's ideas fit to make a world where we won't fight with one another, where the history of having fought will be as foolish as it was on the island of Oahu.[65]

PD   It's marvelous to read Fuller saying we're all astronauts and trying to get us to think of ourselves as citizens of the world. It's a dream, but we've got to have dreams.

JC   I think it's a good idea—and to bring a closer relation between the day and the night.

PD   However did you come to admire Mao Tse Tung? It seems unlikely.[66]

JC   I know. I'm trying to think how it was. There was a book by two Australians who went to China and studied him and wrote about his work very sympathetically. I think it may have been Norman Brown who first suggested that I read their book and that I read some of Mao.[67] It made a great deal of sense to me. I love his remark that we must firmly believe that all human beings are good. Walking through a city, you can easily get the notion that most people are not worthwhile. So many people you see are derelicts, have been destroyed by the society. But for Mao to say we must believe that everyone is a nobleman is inspiring.[68]

---

64. Buckminster Fuller (1895–1983), design scientist concerned with managing world resources to eradicate poverty; inventor of the geodesic dome.

65. Marshall McLuhan (1911–80), Canadian media analyst whose *Understanding Media* (1964) was a best-seller.

66. See Jung Chang and Jon Halliday, *Mao: The Unknown Story* (London: Cape, 2005), which reveals Mao Tse Tung (1893–1976) as the greatest mass murderer in history. But before this full story became known, artists and intellectuals in the 1960s and 70s were affected by his ideas. In 1973 Cage said, "I don't know how they're getting along now but it's perfectly clear to everyone that one quarter of the world, through Mao Tse Tung, has actually improved." Interview with Alan Gillmor, *Contact* 14 (Autumn 1976): 24.

67. Norman O. Brown (1913–2002), classicist, philosopher, and critic whose idiosyncratic ideas fused Marx, Freud, and Joyce. See "John Cage: A Lecture by Norman O. Brown at Wesleyan University, February 22–7, 1988," in Richard Fleming and William Duckworth, eds., *John Cage at Seventy-Five* (Lewisburg: Bucknell University Press, 1989), 97–118.

68. See the interview with Cage in the four-LP set *Music before Revolution* (see note 11).

PD   It's difficult because he also said that the thoughts and feelings of writers and artists should be fused with those of the masses.

JC   We have to more-or-less ignore what he had to say about the arts! [*laughs*]

PD   Yes, I thought so. [*laughs*] To come back to the noise aspect. Back in 1937 you said, "I believe the use of noise to make music will continue and increase."[69] In 1968 you said, "The reason I am less and less interested in music is . . . that I find environmental sounds and noises more useful aesthetically than the sounds produced by the world's musical cultures."[70] I can see how you are able to think that, and I can too because I understand what you mean, but how . . .

JC   It's the presence in those sounds of non-intention and the awful presence of intention in music that makes the non-intentional, ambient sound more useful. By more useful I mean less irritating.

PD   Do you mean more attuned to somebody's spiritual development?

JC   All of that—more possible to live affirmatively if you find the sound of the environment beautiful. Irish musicians had a contest of heroes and the question was, "What is the most beautiful sound?" The one who won the contest said the most beautiful sound is the sound of what happens.

PD   What, then, of the great monuments of classical music—Bach, Beethoven, or Stravinsky?

JC   They are beautiful, and we don't have to give them up if we can use them. The question is whether we can use them. There is some Beethoven that I actually cannot any longer use. It's that one that sounds like movie music, constantly changing its emotional suggestions—one of the big piano sonatas with one of those special names.

PD   The *Hammerklavier?*

JC   Yes, that's it. I think it's perfectly awful. [*laughs*]

PD   I'll never forget that recording of *Variations IV*, which contains the credo from Beethoven's Mass in D.[71] It's in there with everything else, but it survives. You can't kill Beethoven.

JC   No, we don't mean to. But it becomes more palatable in certain circumstances. One thing that's very important for any music is to be played well: that holds for Beethoven. I remember feeling—as I have

---

69. Cage, "The Future of Music: Credo," in *Silence*, 3, where the lecture is dated 1937. Leta Miller points out that the Seattle Artists League meeting at which Cage spoke was actually held in 1940. "Cultural Intersections: John Cage in Seattle (1938–40)," in David W. Patterson, ed., *John Cage: Music, Philosophy and Intention, 1933–50* (New York: Routledge, 2002), 54–56.

70. Cage, "Foreword," *A Year from Monday*, ix.

71. John Cage, *Variations IV*, from a live performance at the Feigen-Palmer Gallery, Los Angeles. John Cage with David Tudor on Everest Records 3132 (1968). The Beethoven *Credo* emerges at 5'30" into side 2.

in much of my life—anti-Beethoven and then being surprised at the beauty of the Bagatelles when they were beautifully played by Grete Sultan.[72] I couldn't separate the Bagatelles then from the most modern music I have experienced. They seemed to me absolutely superb.

PD In a sense, you're working as a kind of supra-composer because you can take into your works existing music of all kinds.

JC Through the circus principle.

PD That's what you're going to do in your new opera for Frankfurt?

JC Well, not all music, but opera music. It's called *Europera*, and it makes use of literature in the public domain, from Gluck to Puccini. I think the interesting thing about *Europeras*—there are two of them[73]—is that all the theatrical elements are in collage, but no one of them is underlining or supportive of another, so the costumes don't illustrate the arias sung nor are they in any way related to anything else that is happening, so you have in the collage disassociated costumes, arias, instrumental parts, flats, lights. Is there something I've missed?

PD Recordings?

JC There will be just a few but as though in the percussion section.

PD This could be very funny?

JC I think it'll be both mirthful and wondrous.

PD Which is true about *Musicircus*, *Theatre Piece*, and other pieces that bring many separate components together.[74]

---

72. Johanna Margarete Sultan (1906–2005), known as Grete, was born in Berlin. She met Richard Buhlig before World War II, and he aided her escape to the United States in 1941. He later introduced her to Cage who wrote his *Etudes Australes* (1975) for her (Anne Midgette, "Grete Sultan, 99, a Pianist and Mentor to Cage, Is Dead," *New York Times*, July 3, 2005). The European premiere was claimed for Richard Bernas at the Institute of Contemporary Arts, London, although he played only numbers 10–14 (Dale Harris, "Spheres of Influence," *Guardian*, June 14, 1976). Sultan played 16 of the 34 etudes at The Queen Elizabeth Hall, London, on June 13, 1978. Like her recording, this performance was at a similar dynamic level throughout. Dominic Gill ("John Cage," *Financial Times*, June 14, 1978) found that Bernas "gave a more satisfying reading, more pungent, more delicate and varied." But Max Harrison ("Zukofsky, Queen Elizabeth Hall," *The Times* June 14, 1978) found the etudes "superficially all the same" but "completely unpredictable" and varied in their linear shapes. If they held one's attention, this was "partly to the credit of Grete Sultan, whose unflagging performance was one of unmistakable authority."

73. Finally there were more, but Puccini, still in copyright, was not included: *Europeras 1 & 2* (1987), *Europeras 3 & 4* (1990), and *Europera 5* (1991). For more detail see *Europeras* and After, chapter 21, 227.

74. *Theatre Piece* (1960); *Musicircus* (1967), mixed media—see About *Musicircus*, chapter 19, 211.

JC   I'm more and more aware in this work—and first I suffered from it—
       that I'm in a complicated institutional situation and it's hard to break
       through. I think I must find a way to make this viable—it's very simple,
       and I think people will finally agree with me as the date gets closer and
       closer. The show must go on! [*laughs*] Their prejudices will melt:
       they'll have to.

PD   It's always going to be hard to convince people that their experiences
       looking at the sunset or a rock formation are the equivalent of a
       Turner sunset or a Henry Moore. You want to blur that distinction
       because you say we don't need the artist distilling from our natural
       experience through his own personality. You don't want that personal-
       ity to operate.

JC   Right. I want the experience to be such that it would be available after
       the opera is over.

PD   Don't you have to be a composer, writer, or artist yourself to have that
       experience?

JC   I don't think so.

PD   You want everybody to be [*Cage: yes*] like Ives thinking of people hear-
       ing their own symphonies?[75]

JC   Right. There's a marvelous girl, Mehri Raad, who's the assistant to the
       technical director in Frankfurt for the opera. She has become so
       involved in *Europeras 1 & 2* and is so enthusiastic and very technically
       so. We were together after having had lunch and the traffic was com-
       ing by, and I think I made a step and she pulled me back, and I said
       something about the ease with which one could die. She said, "Well, it
       really doesn't matter because if you do die I'll carry on for you!
       [*laughs*] The next important step in life is to finish *Europeras I & II.*"
       Isn't that marvelous?[76]

PD   Ives didn't carry through his ideas about everybody making their own
       symphonies. Do you feel you've done it for him?

JC   These ideas on his part, my part, and, say, Thoreau's too are in the air,
       and we are having access to them because the connections have been
       established that permit us to entertain the ideas. And we are all living
       at a time when those ideas are able to be had. There's a beautiful other
       expression of it. I heard a concert in Frankfurt of the music of Giacinto

---

75. Cage wrote about Charles Ives (1874–1954): "Now that we have a music that does-
n't depend on European musical history, Ives seems like the beginning of it." Cage, *A
Year from Monday*, 38. The Ives source is quoted in my Introduction, 12–13.

76. The commitment of Frankfurt to Cage climaxed with the massive festival
Anarchic Harmony, with twenty-five concerts from August 28 to November 6, 1992.

Scelsi,[77] and he said he made music in order to make holes in the sky so that the light could come through. Isn't that beautiful? And it's very close to Ives.

PD You have had many connections with technology—there are computers in your apartment but no piano.

JC There's a toy piano, unless I've loaned it to somebody. It's in a box.

PD I played the *Suite for Toy Piano* shortly after I went to start the Music Department at Keele University,[78] and somebody came up to me afterward and said, "If you want to be taken seriously here you won't have to do things like that." [*laughter*] I thought you'd like that! I've been reading quite a lot of the Zen anecdotes.

JC They're marvelous, aren't they?

PD It's enormously helpful in explaining to people what your work is about.

JC One thing is the practicality of Zen.

PD The practicality and the impracticality—always both?

JC Yes, and it always works so beautifully. Did you come across the story with "Why are you burning the statues of the Buddha—that's sacrilegious?" Answer: "But the metal ones won't burn!"

PD Thank you very much, John. I do appreciate having this interview.

JC It's such a pleasure to talk with you. How old were you when you decided to live in England?

PD I was born in England.

JC You were? But I thought you were an American.

PD No, I came to study here. After a degree at Cambridge I had to get all that out of my system, so I came to New York.

JC I thought you were an American who had a beautiful voice! [*laughter*]

PD I went to Juilliard and then spent two more years in the United States around 1960. You'd just come back from Italy and had your Volkswagen.

JC Isn't that funny—I've spent my life thinking of you as an American.

PD You've honored me because I've a great sympathy with things American, as I hope you can tell.

---

77. Giacinto Scelsi (1905–88), Italian composer whose works involved improvisation, collaboration, and a fusion of East and West. Much later Cage admired the way Scelsi would "make a whole piece that would be one sound." Retallack, *MUSICAGE*, 109.
78. University of Keele, Staffordshire, England, where Peter Dickinson started the Music Department in 1974 with its Centre for American Music.

Chapter Two

Merce Cunningham

Interview with Peter Dickinson, Ibis Hotel, London, July 26, 1987

Introduction

At the start of a new millennium John O'Mahony was able to say: "Merce Cunningham is, without doubt, the world's greatest living choreographer. His name stands alongside Martha Graham and George Balanchine in the pantheon of mercurial figures that transformed twentieth-century dance, though his work arguably reaches further and deeper, celebrating sheer movement for its own stark, austere sake."[1]

Cunningham was born in Centralia, Washington, on April 16, 1919, the second son of Clifford D. and Marion Cunningham. His father was a lawyer of Irish descent, and his mother was a teacher. In his teens he took classes in ballroom and tap dancing, and after graduating from high school in 1936 he went to George Washington University, D.C., before attending the Cornish School in Seattle the following year. As Bonnie Bird explains in her interview (chapter 3), he joined her class in 1937, met Cage in 1938, and in 1939 went to the Bennington Summer School for Dance held at Mills College, where he met Martha Graham. This was a crucial encounter, since she was immediately impressed, and as a result Cunningham left the Cornish School and joined her company in New York. He made his debut with a lead in her *Every Soul Is a Circus* on Broadway.

Cunningham eventually became impatient with the narrative aspects of Graham's approach to dance and left her company, encouraged by Cage after he arrived in New York in 1942. David Vaughan, archivist at the

---

1. John O'Mahony, "The Dancing Master," *Guardian, Saturday Review*, October 7, 2000, 6–7.

Cunningham Dance Foundation, has said, "Movement itself is the principal subject matter of his dances: neither narrative nor musical form determines their structure."[2] Landmarks in the fifty-year Cunningham-Cage collaboration were *Credo in US* (1942), with choreography by Cunningham and Jean Erdman and music by Cage, given at Bennington College, Vermont, on August 1, 1942; and their first full New York program on April 5, 1944, with *Triple-Paced, Root of an Unfocus, Tossed as It Is Untroubled, The Unavailable Memory of, Totem Ancestor,* and *Spontaneous Earth.*[3] In 1948 Cunningham joined the faculty of the School of American Ballet, but he and Cage gave recitals of solo dance and piano music at colleges and other venues in the United States through the 1940s and 50s. In 1949 they both went to Paris.

Cage's influence on Cunningham soon became apparent when he started to use chance operations to determine his choreography. Further, the two made a historic declaration of independence between music and dance so that—controversially—the dancers rehearse in silence and do not hear any music until the actual performance. Carolyn Brown described the problems:

Cage's notions of anarchy and coexistence as practiced by Cunningham work in strange ways. Merce works secretively: the dancers in his company discover the set in the final rehearsal. . . . I will not pretend that this is not extremely difficult for the dancers. Loudness, especially unexpected loudness, can make one irritable, nauseous, even faint. Brilliant lights which come on suddenly can momentarily blind and disorient the dancer and that too affects the balance, and makes quick-moving exits hazardous; darkness cripples one's sense of space and therefore the fullness of the movement itself. . . . The dancers . . . must responsibly do their work, continually at the mercy of those whose flights of fancy with gloom and glare, noise and obstacle can inhibit their ability to dance well. Of course, it's just possible that these

---

2. David Vaughan, "A Lifetime of Dance," *Filmmaker Interview,* 2000, http://www.merce.org. See also Vaughan, "Merce Cunningham: Origins and Influences (1983)," in Richard Kostelanetz, ed., *Writings about John Cage* (Ann Arbor: University of Michigan Press, 1993), 327–33.

3. In an interview with Laura Kuhn, Cunningham indicated fourteen pivotal works in the Cage-Cunningham collaboration, which she kindly communicated to me by e-mail on August 24, 2005: "Root of an Unfocus (1944); Sixteen Dances for Soloist and Company of Three (1951); Suite for Five in Space and Time (1956); Antic Meet (1958); Variations V (1965); Second Hand (1970); Un Jour ou Deux (1973); Inlets (1977); Trails (1982); Roaratorio (1983); Points in Space (1986); Inventions (1989); Beach Birds (1991); Ocean (1994) (not technically, as realized, a Cage/Cunningham work, but the conception was clear Cage/Cunningham, hence Merce wanted to talk about it)." See "Merce Cunningham in Conversation with Laura Kuhn," in *Art Performs Life: Cunningham/Monk/Jones* (Minneapolis: Walker Art Center, 1998), 22–43.

conflicts and tensions, and the dancers' constant attempts to deal with them contribute to making the experience of Merce's theater so extraordinary.[4]

In 1980, when Cage and Cunningham were at the Laban Centre for Movement and Dance in London, Cage gave a lecture called "Music for Dance" and repeated his story about watching swimmers in a pool through the window of a café where a jukebox was playing. He observed that the music was a perfectly appropriate accompaniment to their movements.[5]

The year 1952 was a crucial one for Cage. It ushered in his so-called silent piece *4'33"*, music for tape such as *Williams Mix*, theatrical pieces like *Water Music*, and the use of indeterminate techniques such as observing imperfections in manuscript paper. Further, Cage and Cunningham were at Black Mountain College[6] where they instigated the first happening, and it was there that the Merce Cunningham Dance Company was launched, with Cage as musical director, in 1953. The dancers were Carolyn Brown, Remy Charlip, Anita Dencks, Viola Farber, Jo Anne Melsher, Marianne Preger, and Paul Taylor, with Robert Rauschenberg as resident designer and pianist David Tudor.

Those who observed these early years have said that Cage was the powerhouse behind the venture, which did not become successful overnight. It was not until 1964 that the six-month world tour brought deserved acclaim. This was supported by the sale of donated works of art from eighty painters and sculptors, including some very famous names. The company was a sensation in London, where it was seen by such luminaries as Margot Fonteyn, Frederick Ashton, and Rudolf Nureyev. The show began with a week at Sadlers Wells and continued with three more weeks at the Phoenix Theater, where the program

---

4. "Carolyn Brown," in *Merce Cunningham: Edited and with Photographs and an Introduction by James Klosty* (New York: Limelight Editions, 1986), 28. Brown studied with Cunningham in New York and danced with his company from 1953 to 1972. See also Stephanie Jordan, "Freedom from the Music: Cunningham, Cage and Collaborations," *Contact* 20 (Autumn 1979): 16–19. Jordan comments on the Certificate of Appreciation presented to Cunningham by the mayor of New York City in 1977 and questions the claim that he "freed contemporary dance from the tyranny of music." She concludes: "The development of new ways of combining the two art forms is certainly a shared effort rather than the property of Cunningham alone. In the light of the role that Cage and other composers have played in Cunningham's achievements, the somewhat emotive suggestion that Cunningham 'freed contemporary dance from the tyranny of music' is perhaps misleading. Certainly it leaves much unsaid."
5. Stephanie Jordan, "Cage and Cunningham at the Laban Centre," *Dancing Times* (October 1980): 38–39. See also *Die Reihe* 5 (English, 1971), 115.
6. Black Mountain College, Asheville, North Carolina (1933–53), revolutionized the concept of American education. The distinguished faculty included leading figures in various fields such as Walter Gropius, Willem de Kooning, Robert Motherwell, Buckminster Fuller, and Charles Olson.

from August 19–22 consisted of *Aeon* (1961) to Cage's *Atlas Eclipticalis* and *Winter Music, Changeling* (1957) to *Suite* by Christian Wolff, *Paired* (1964) to Cage's *Duet for a Cymbal,* and *Antic Meet* (1958) to Cage's *Solo for Piano with WBAI.* Costumes and decor were by Rauschenberg, and Cage and Tudor provided the music, which was becoming increasingly involved with what sounded like randomly produced electronic noises—in sharp contrast to the sophisticated and well-rehearsed dances onstage.

Peter Brook, in the program book, said Cunningham's work was "of the highest quality and of great importance . . . in the tradition of Martha Graham in many ways, but in one most of all. The very things that are criticized, laughed at and ignored will only a few months later be imitated everywhere." Alexander Bland wrote in the *Observer,* "At a blow, ballet has been brought right up in line with the front-rank experiments in the other arts."[7] Although the company still had problems, news of its triumphal reception fed back to the United States, and the rest is history. Cunningham received many national and international awards, including the French Commandeur de l'ordre des arts et des lettres (1982) and the Légion d'honneur (1989).

In an illustrated booklet, published a year before the company's world tour, Cage outlined his colleague's philosophy in terms that fit his own views about the autonomy of sounds:

> Merce Cunningham . . . has, since 1944, developed his own school of dancing and choreography, the continuity of which no longer relies on linear elements, be they narrative or psychological, nor does it rely on a movement towards and away from climax. As in abstract painting, it is assumed that an element (a movement, a sound, a change of light) is in and of itself expressive: what it communicates is in large part determined by the observer himself. It is assumed that the dance supports itself and does not need support from the music.[8]

Cunningham's partnership with Cage, who was divorced in 1945, has been little discussed on a personal level, and both men were careful to maintain their privacy.[9] What is significant is the stroke of fortune that brought them together at the Cornish School and eventually gave them most of a lifetime together. Cage needed dancers and support from the other arts at a time when the musical world would not take him seriously; Cunningham

---

7. Quoted in O'Mahony, "The Dancing Master."

8. John Cage, "A Movement, a Sound, a Change of Light," in *Merce Cunningham & Dance Company* (New York: The Foundation for Contemporary Performance Arts, 1963 [from 2005, known as The Foundation for Contemporary Arts]), 1.

9. However, see Thomas S. Hines, "Then Not Yet 'Cage': The Los Angeles Years, 1912–1938," in Marjorie Perloff and Charles Junkerman, eds., *John Cage: Composed in America* (Chicago: University of Chicago Press, 1994), 65–99. These revelations are based on five hours of interviews with Cage at his New York apartment three months

needed a promoter. Cage turned to Zen and chance at a time of great personal crisis but he also had Cunningham, and together they transformed both dance and music.

Interview

By permission of Merce Cunningham

PD I'd like to go back to the prewar days in Seattle when you first met John.
MC I was a student at the Cornish School studying theater and dance. I was there two years, and John came the second year to accompany the dance class.[10] During that year he also organized a small percussion group, and he asked me to play in it—which astonished me. But since the work was not necessarily technical but involved the rhythmic sense, which I had, he thought I could work in it. That was wonderful. We rehearsed and played pieces—things he wrote and got other composers to do at the time. I remember that toward the end of that school year Bonnie Bird, who was the teacher, left to come back to New York for a two-week period or something. John gave us a kind of composition course, which was quite fascinating to me. I can't remember it in detail except that it was about the relationship of dance and music—not strictly the way we work now, of course, but totally different from the things Bonnie Bird had been giving us to do during the year. John set up a very strict relationship between the music and the dance, which wasn't note-by-note, but there was a relationship. Previous to that, the compositional work hadn't had that kind of a structural sense. Even though it wasn't very clear to me—I must say—it was fascinating!
PD You were working together from that moment?
MC I was a student, of course, only making exercises in that situation. Then I left for New York to be in the company of Martha Graham. There was a point after I'd been in New York two years, maybe three, when I worked with a dancer named Jean Erdman, and we were planning to give a

---

before his death in 1992. Richard Kostelanetz, who knew Cage well and had seen him a week before the interviews, reacted with shocked incredulity—*John Cage (ex)plain(ed)* (New York: Schirmer, 1996), 167–69. Jonathan D. Katz, who has heard the tapes of Hines's interviews with Cage and considers them genuine, takes matters further: "John Cage's Queer Silence; or, How to Avoid Making Matters Worse," in David W. Bernstein and Christopher Hatch, eds., *Writings through John Cage's Music, Poetry, + Art* (Chicago: University of Chicago Press, 2001), 41–61. John O'Mahony (see n. 1) includes personal recollections from dancers in the company. See also Jacqueline Bograd Weld, *Peggy: The Wayward Guggenheim* (New York: E. P. Dutton, 1986), 279–81.
10. John and Xenia Cage arrived in Seattle for the fall semester 1938.

program that would consist of solos for each of us and several pieces we made together—duets and so on. One of them was a piece I thought John should do the music for. It was called *Credo in US*,[11] and I remember writing him and asking him if he would do it. I think he wrote and said he would, and then we didn't hear from him for what we thought was a long time. I remember Jean Erdman getting very nervous, but I said I was sure he would do it since he had said he would. He eventually sent the score, and the first time we did it was at Bennington College in the summer—John wasn't there, and we had to get the musicians together. I don't remember the performance very well, only because I was occupied with the dance and simply trying to get it on. But the following year John came to New York and we did the program again, and this time he was there to do the music. I have a very clear impression of the sound, which was wonderful. That's the first thing together: then, I think, the following year we gave a program together. He wrote the music for the dances, as well as music of his that was played on prepared piano.

PD   He seems to have been working at this time with dancers' counts.

MC   He always was interested in what I would call structure, exact structure in time. In the solos I made for that first program, he suggested the use of what he called rhythmic structure. Most of those solos were done with some form of rhythmic structure, which I would make for the dance and he would take to write the music to. So what he wrote was not necessarily following the dance, even though the structure was very clear, and there were short structural points rather than, as now, very long ones or none at all.

PD   Can you remember that intriguing moment when you decided you'd make a dance that would be completely unrelated to the music?

MC   I think it was in that first program because once the structure was set, he would go away and write the music and I would make the dance separately. Of course, we brought it together to rehearse at that time—different from now when it often comes together at the moment of performance. But the principle was the same—the two arts acting in time but in different ways, given this underlying structure.

PD   A kind of declaration of independence between music and dance?

MC   Yes, as John has said so often, a coexistence where one is not more prominent necessarily than the other or one does not support the other. They just coexist. And the result is something that was not

---

11. *Credo in US* (1942), a "suite of satirical character composed within the phraseology of the dance by Merce Cunningham and Jean Erdman for which it was written." Richard Dunn, ed., *John Cage* (New York: Henmar, 1962), 35.

predicted when you were working on it. [*laughs*] It doesn't mean it doesn't involve rehearsal. It does—a lot.

PD   Having made that decision about the independence of music and dance, did you ever look back and regret it?

MC   No. It was not an intellectual thing, really, but a feeling that this was an extraordinary experience. Rather than narrowing, it was widening. It seemed to me to open multiple possibilities rather than pinning it down to "I need this to help me do this." [*laughs*] Or "You have to do this," or whatever. Here was a way to have an experience I wouldn't have otherwise. That feeling has always been there.

PD   Do you think John owes his philosophical position on some of this to Zen?

MC   It has a great deal to do with it. He was very much involved and attended the lectures of Suzuki at Columbia, reading, discussing, talking, and thinking about it. But John has always worked in ways that were not conventional. His mind was not in the line most composers have followed—Schoenberg said he had no feeling for harmony.[12] John has always allowed for the idea of noise as one of the sound elements in music, which has nothing to do with harmony. He has evolved another way of working with what sound does, then has found ways to use that. From the beginning he spoke about dance and music as time arts, occupying lengths of time. I remember once in New York, in the first years I was there, there was a seminar about music and dance. John and Anthony Tudor[13] were on it. The moderator asked for comments, and John said that the first thing was that music and dance take place in the same time together. [*laughs*] The moderator started to go on, but Anthony Tudor said, "Now, wait a minute, let's go back and talk about that!" [*laughs*] It was a fascinating evening!

PD   That's exactly what John has said about *Roaratorio*[14]—the connection between the different elements is simply that they take place at the same time. But what about chance operations in dance?

MC   I have used chance operations ever since the early fifties when the idea came along and I began to understand something about it, working at it in various ways. Each piece has some element of chance operations, maybe simple or complex. What I always have to go on is the fact that I am dealing with human beings. There is the question of their running into each other—to put it on the simplest level—which could involve serious accidents or injuries. From that point of view, I involved myself with the practical aspects of dancing. At the same time, I used the

---

12. See also interview with Michael Oliver, chapter 18, 202.

13. Anthony Tudor (1908–87), British ballet dancer, choreographer, and teacher who made his U.S. debut with Ballet Theater, later called American Ballet Theater.

14. See Introducing *Roaratorio*, chapter 20, 225.

chance operations to make the continuity of the dance. It has nothing to do with the dancers performing. There is no improvisation or anything like that. The dances have been strictly choreographed, but the process of choreography is by using chance.

PD Do you actually use the *I Ching*?

MC I have used it in several dances. I could use it in all of them: sometimes because of practical necessities, such as the amount of time I have to make something, [*laughs*] I have to employ simpler ways like using coins. It's the element of chance bringing up something my own experience might not produce. Even though I have made the movements that will be utilized in the dance, I use chance operations to devise the continuity so that what comes after what can be a new experience.

PD Wasn't it when Christian Wolff's father published the *I Ching* that it became a great discovery for John?

MC I don't remember the exact moment. It must have been Christian Wolff who brought the book, and I remember very strongly the impression he [Cage] had of reading the preface where Jung asks the *I Ching* what it thought of being published in a different language. The answer was so extraordinary . . . I remember John being absolutely amazed.[15] My own experience about it was that the book is so vast and the kind of thing it allows for is so open that if you asked it a question, the answers were always pertinent. Then I began to see that the numbers themselves—not what they represented in terms of hexagrams—could be used for my purpose. It was around that time that I began thinking much about space and dancing. I'd been taught that in dance there was the proscenium stage and there was a center of interest at the center of the stage, the most important part of the space. Even before the *I Ching*, that didn't make sense to me. I didn't have any other answer, I admit. Then I happened to read this quotation of Einstein's where he said there are no fixed points in space. I thought that was perfect for the stage, and there's

15. The Swiss psychoanalyst Carl G. Jung (1875–1961) wrote in his foreword to the *I Ching*, trans. Carl G. Wilhelm, ed. Cary F. Baynes (Princeton: Bollingen Edition/Princeton University Press, 1950), xxxviii: "I submitted two questions to the method of chance represented by the coin oracle, the second question being put after I had written my analysis of the answer to the first. The first question was directed, as it were, to the *I Ching*: what had it to say about my intention to write a foreword? . . . The *I Ching* replied by comparing itself to a cauldron, a ritual vessel in need of renovation, a vessel that was finding only doubtful favor with the public." The *I Ching* is a Chinese sourcebook for Confucian and Taoist philosophy around three thousand years old. Jung experimented with it around 1920, and Cage used it to generate random numbers. See also Joan Retallack, ed., *MUSICAGE: Cage Muses on Words Art Music* (Hanover, NH: Wesleyan University Press and University of New England Press, 1996), 210.

no point that's any more important than any other. In that sense it's Buddhist or Zen. Any point could be important. Wherever anybody was, was in that sense a center. So I began to explore that by taking pieces of plain white paper and marking the imperfections, then drawing lines from one to the other; then taking another sheet of paper and drawing more lines because the imperfections are always different. Then I would superimpose them so that each sheet [represented a single] dancer's space track. Where those [tracks] happened to coincide they could do something together. That eradicated anything about the center of the stage: it didn't exist anymore. I thought that was wonderful! [*laughs*] Then I also found it was possible to make dances where the audience was all the way around you. One of the very first ones, called *Suite by Chance*, was done that way, and we presented it at Black Mountain College that summer we were there with the audience all the way around us.[16]

PD　Did you find that you and John dominated the scene there?

MC　Oh no, not at all. . . . First of all, from a practical and personal point of view, it was wonderful for me. I was there several summers, actually. The first summer John and I were there with Buckminster Fuller, Elaine and Bill de Kooning, and Albers, of course.[17] What was so amazing was that, in spite of inadequate facilities for dancing, it was still made possible for me to work. The dining hall was the only big space they had, and they'd simply clear it every day. [*laughs*] It was a community where the pupils and the teachers had a sense of interacting. You all ate at the same dining room and sat at different tables each day with different people, always having a crossing of ideas, listening to something totally out of the realm of dancing. As far as I was concerned it was marvelous [*laughs*] to get out of it for a while. You could not only hear about something different, but it could make you change your ideas.

PD　You took part in the happening at Black Mountain College in 1952. What was it like?

MC　I don't know in detail what the others did. There were about five or six of us—Bob Rauschenberg, John, David Tudor, myself, I think M. C. Richards and maybe another person.[18] I'm sure John has described this, but we each simply did what we did. That is, I danced around through the public, which sat in the center with aisles between. It was a kind of agreed-upon length of time during which these things would take

---

16. *Suite by Chance*, Urbana, Illinois, March 24, 1953, with music by Christian Wolff.
17. Willem de Kooning (1904–97), Dutch-born abstract expressionist painter, moved to the United States in 1926. Joseph Albers (1888–1976), German-born American designer.
18. Mary Caroline Richards (1916–99), potter, painter, and poet; head of the faculty at Black Mountain College (1949–51).

place. There was no connection other than what anybody looking at this could make. All these things were separate, and everybody was sitting facing a different way so that they would see or hear something in a different way. It wasn't all fixed so that everybody was to look at it one way. At the end of it they brought out coffee or something! [*laughs*][19]

PD Did it feel like something that would have reverberations right through the 1960s?

MC No. And it didn't have a name. It was just something we did. Later they called them happenings. It was an idea about theater that John had— that anything could be theater. It can, depending on how you act or think about it. It doesn't have to have a reference, a meaning, or a connection. It can simply take place.

PD John's ideas open up the skies, don't they?

MC Yes, a large mind open to so many kinds of things. His reactions to things have often been so amazing to me. He looks at it from some other point of view and his wit, humor . . .

PD Do you find you never know what he's going to say next?

MC Often! [*laughs*] Yes, he stays very bright. [*laughs*]

PD After Black Mountain another community was Stony Point.[20]

MC I didn't live there but John did. He built a house and was there for a number of years. I would visit, of course, but there was no facility there where I could work as a dancer, and my work was of necessity in New York.

PD At the 1958 Retrospective Concert at Town Hall in New York, you didn't dance but conducted the *Concert for Piano and Orchestra.*

MC It was the second time in my life I was a conductor. I conducted the school orchestra when I was about ten. [*laughs*] Very briefly, but I did. This was a far more marvelous experience as a conductor. [*laughs*] Because of what the conductor had to do physically, John thought a regular conductor couldn't do it at the time. Now others have done it; it's not that complicated. It was quite difficult in the beginning. Instead of a regular beat, this was a use of the arms. One had to do one thing and the other another in terms of time. One arm indicated something to the musicians, like the hands of a clock. In a half minute by the watch

19. See Richard Kostelanetz, ed., *Conversing with Cage* (New York: Limelight Editions, 1988), 82–83, 210–11. And Cunningham, "A Collaborative Process between Music and Dance," in Peter Gena, Jonathan Brent, and Don Gillespie, eds., *A John Cage Reader: In Celebration of His 70th Birthday* (New York: C. F. Peters, 1982), 110–11. There Cunningham describes the original happening as *Theater Piece* with John Cage (speaker), David Tudor (music), Merce Cunningham (dance), Charles Olson and M. C. Richards (poetry), and Robert Rauschenberg (paintings).

20. The Gate Hill Coop, Stony Point, Rockland County, was a cooperative community in the country just up the Hudson River from New York City.

I would show fifteen seconds by the arm, which meant the sounds were slower for the players. Or if in fifteen seconds by the watch I showed a minute, that meant they played faster—one of the ways the tempo could change. It was physically very hard in the beginning until one got used to it. To do something with your arms and take three minutes was very long for the arms to go down and up the other side.

PD   Do you recall the atmosphere of the Town Hall Retrospective?

MC   Yes. It went through the early music up to the *Concert for Piano and Orchestra* as the most recent. It was a very large public, marvelous and attentive. Arline Carmen came out to sing two of John's songs, which she did just beautifully—this beautiful woman came out in a blue dress, and behind her came John, smiling, to sit at the piano and play *She Is Asleep* and also *The Wonderful Widow.* I remember that very clearly—it was marvelous. But there were so many other things—percussion. But as the program went on and the later pieces came, the audience began to get restless. When it came to the orchestra piece at the end, the audience was really quite boisterous—obstreperous, whatever! [*laughs*] I was so concentrating on this [conducting the piece] that I didn't dare pay any attention to it, but it apparently got quite wild. One man later said this was worse than when the *Sacre* was first done! [*laughs*][21]

PD   Even before the *Concert for Piano and Orchestra,* you can hear the audience's disapproval during *Williams Mix.*

MC   Yes. That's from the fifties, and you can hear this audience changing as the program went on. [*laughs*]

PD   John seems to like this kind of disapproval as part of his relationship with an audience. It's not been the same for you. You haven't had this kind of hostility, but the music has. Is it necessary for John?

MC   Perhaps it is, or perhaps he's so used to it he'd feel there's something wrong if there isn't hostility. [*laughs*] I have a feeling that changes in sound disturb a public more than changes in sight. I'm not sure if I'm right, but I've noticed that when we first danced some pieces, the public apparently disliked both the music and the dance. Even now they may

---

21. Stravinsky's *The Rite of Spring* was premiered at the Champs-Elysées, Paris, on May 29, 1913. Ironically, the recording of the *Concert for Piano and Orchestra* at the 1958 New York Town Hall Retrospective Concert reveals a horn player quoting from *The Rite* at 3′20″—the four-note figure anticipated in the first violin four bars after figure 12 but given to the horns at figure 27. This is more likely indiscipline rather than coincidence. In December 1991 Cage showed that he knew about this: "The people who first played it—also wanting to show it was foolish—put in excerpts from Stravinsky's *Rite of Spring.* That would be what I call having too good a time. I now write in such a way that they won't put in quotations from anything." In Andrew Ford, *Composer to Composer: Conversations about Contemporary Music* (London: Quartet Books, 1993), 181.

not like the music but can see the dance. I've noticed that change over years, not yesterday or today by any means. [*laughs*] With John, he has been much concerned all his life with going on from where he is to something else, looking for a new idea constantly, not in any sense a repetition. So he has used the *I Ching* or many other things as ways to jump to the next possibility as he sees it. He's constantly looking for something he doesn't know about rather than reinforcing something he does, which could automatically put him in a position with the public—they may have gotten this far but don't know where they are when he goes on.

PD   As a choreographer, have you ever rejected any music, even though you don't come across it until the last rehearsal?

MC   No, we haven't in that sense rejected it. I remember distinctly a couple of times when the person making the music has been troublesome, difficult for us. More often than not, I have found the experience enlivening, something I found useful. Not disturbing to me. I remember one event in Westbeth, our studio in New York. Friends from Wesleyan University phoned to say there was this classical Japanese shakuhachi player who had been in residence and was on his way back to Japan and asked whether we'd be interested in having him play for one of our events. I said it sounded marvelous: I love the sound of the shakuhachi. We have a little tiny stage at the studio, and he sat in his beautiful robes very formally. I think he meditated beforehand, and we said we'd do whatever was necessary for the musician. We started to dance, and he began to play. He didn't play constantly. He would play a piece; he would stop, and we would keep on dancing. He played about six times during the course of the hour and a half. It was just marvelous. I'm sure the nature of that sound produced a different kind of effect on the dancers. We got quite quiet. [*laughs*]

PD   Does that vary the tempo? Watching you in *Roaratorio* I was checking to see whether the strong rhythm of the Irish traditional musicians was affecting the dancers.

MC   No, except that in *Roaratorio* I made up a number of jigs and reels—not authentic, but what I call jigs and reels—where the dancers dance separately but together at the same time. These do have a folk tempo, so the coincidences that happen—not the same each time—show a connection. The rhythm when the drummers are playing, for example. Peadar Mercier told me after this performance, "I tried to keep with your rhythm but you tricked me!"[22] [*laughs*]

PD   If the rhythm is just slightly faster does the dancer change pace?

MC   Some of them would and some would not. If they're doing something together they're so tied to each other that they would just keep going.

---

22. See chapter 20, 223.

It might affect them a little bit. But I've noticed individually some of them, who are quite strong about things, may very briefly go with it. Those who don't can sustain it and have decided that's what they want to do. It doesn't change the step. It's just a question of a slight change in the tempo.

PD I'd like to ask you about the different personalities of what's now called the New York School of composers.

MC I had a loft on 17th Street where I lived for many years. They needed a place to work when they were making *Williams Mix* and putting all those pieces of tape together. They came and used a long table, and Earle and Christian came and occasionally Morty—he didn't do very much [*laughs*], but he liked to be around—and John.[23] They were putting this together, and I remember that it was a question of putting sound in space rather than sound in time. You could put so many sounds in a given inch of tape—it was tape music then. They figured out they could get six hundred sounds into an inch of tape. John also said nobody's measurements were the same. Then he got different rulers and found out they weren't the same either! [*laughs*] So he decided that measurements, like everything else, were flexible. [*laughs*] Morty would come around, lurk, and make marvelous remarks. Funny is not the right word for his humor, which was so extraordinary. It's more than that.

Christian is an absolutely marvelous person, so strong. He wanted to know something about dancing, and John suggested he come watch a class with the idea that he might accompany some classes. I couldn't imagine Christian wanting to do that, but I said it was fine. He was very young then. He came and he looked at a class and, with that serious face he has, he said, "But they're just exercises!" [*laughs*] I said, "You're exactly right." [*laughs*] It's not very interesting to accompany for that. [*laughs*] It was the pianist Grete Sultan who knew the Wolffs in Berlin many years ago. She had to come to the States and then somehow, when the Wolffs were in New York, they met again. Christian came to study piano with Grete, who lived below me in this loft. He was about seventeen and went to a Quaker school in New York. He wanted to

23. Other members of the New York School—Morton Feldman (1926–87), Earle Brown (1926–2002), and Christian Wolff (1934–). Cage brought his colleagues to European attention when he discussed their work in his lectures at Darmstadt in 1958 and praised its indeterminacy. He condemned both neoclassicists and serialists and said, "In this social darkness, therefore, the work of Earle Brown, Morton Feldman, and Christian Wolff continues to present a brilliant light, for the reason that at the several points of notation, performance, and audition, action is provocative." Cage, *Silence: Lectures and Writings* (Middletown, CT: Wesleyan University Press, 1961), 52.

study composition, so Grete said she thought he should meet John Cage: [*laughs*] that's how that began.

PD And Earle Brown?

MC Earle I knew with Carolyn, his wife, who was in my company for so many years. He has taught a lot in various places and has always been—to me—very definite about what he thinks something should be in terms of music or perhaps anything else. My connection is that he wrote a piece for a dance in the fifties, and I think I used one or two others that were written as music with nothing to do with the dance.[24] He was very definite about how he wanted his music to sound: there was not any leeway. [*laughs*]

PD Not at all like John?

MC No.

PD Would you say that John influenced the art world?

MC Oh yes. By his ideas—either because people don't like them or they do. I think that by his presence and his continued concern with visual things as well as writing, he has affected artists. I remember times with Jasper Johns and Bob Rauschenberg in the early fifties when we would be together talking. I would mostly listen because the ideas were so interesting to me. It had nothing to do with dancing but simply brought something else to my experience—the way they looked at things and talked about them. Jasper, I think more than Bob, was interested in John's ideas about sound. When they talked about painting, these were ideas I felt close to, but not in the way I would deal with them and quite out of my previous experience, which had been in modern dance, particularly with Martha Graham and my brief time with ballet at the School of American Ballet. This was an eye-opener for me: wonderful years. Particularly with Rauschenberg, where we were quite sure we could work together. I remember asking him to make something for a dance. He lived in a loft down in Lower Manhattan then. I said, "Bob, I just want something in the middle of the stage the dancers can go 'round." That was all; I didn't say anything else. I went away, and two or three days later he phoned up and said he had this thing and would I come and look at it. I went down to his loft, and there he had this thing hanging down from the rafters. It was perfectly beautiful, made of comic strips, plastic, bits of wood he'd gotten from the street, and colored papers. It was just stunning. I looked at it and said, "Oh dear. Bob, it's wonderful, but I can't use it." He said, "Why?" I said, "Because we're performing on stages where there's no place to hang anything. I have to be practical and have something that will sit on the stage so we can move it." And he said, "OK, I'll make another one." [*laughs*] Three days later I came back, and there was a totally different piece. [*laughs*]

---

24. *Springweather and People* (1955), *Galaxy* (1956), and *Hands Birds* (1960).

PD Do you have a favorite piece of John's?

MC No, I like so many of them when I hear them—the *Sonatas and Interludes*, the *Book of Music*, and the *Three Dances* for prepared piano, for which I made a dance. *Credo in US* I like very much. I'm looking forward very much to hearing the orchestra version of *Cheap Imitation*, which will be played in Metz in November. He's heard it—the schoolchildren [in Cologne] played it marvelously. It's from Satie's *Socrate*, and I made a dance to it years ago.[25]

PD That's the piece where John requires a rehearsal schedule that would put most orchestras out of business because they couldn't afford it!

MC [*laughs*] Exactly—and he complains bitterly! I must say that when I hear his music played well it's a marvelous experience. I heard the Bowery Ensemble in New York a couple of years ago at Cooper Union—it was very beautiful.[26]

PD I asked John why he had to do this to orchestras when he knew they would never have the budget to do a piece like *Cheap Imitation*.

MC And what did he say? [*laughs*]

PD He wanted a particular sort of dedication that's not characteristic of these administrative organizations.

MC No, that's for sure.

PD Then we went on to the fact that he's asking for a sort of spiritual quality very hard to get in modern life.

MC Yes. I think that's one of the reasons I work the way I do. I don't mean it's better or worse than anybody else. But I've felt for many years that to have a dance company and to get the dancers to do the things the way I thought they should be done required that they have a class—in that sense, a dedication. If I were employing movements or ideas about movements that were not common through the ballet or other kinds of modern dance, then their training wouldn't work for what I was doing.

So I had to find a way to teach. One of the reasons for teaching was not simply physically to train the dancers but to give them the experience of working in a kind of dance that wasn't familiar. I still think that way, although it's terribly hard to keep up!

---

25. Cage's *Cheap Imitation*, based on Satie's *Socrate*, was used for Cunningham's ballet *Second Hand*, premiered with Cunningham and Carolyn Brown in the leading roles at the Brooklyn Academy of Music, January 8, 1970. See Cunningham, "A Collaborative Process between Music and Dance," 107–120. Also Kostelanetz, *Conversing with Cage*, 79–80. See interview with Cage, chapter 1, 44n56, for the rehearsal schedule Cage imposed for concert performances.

26. April 1982, ten hours of Cage, including the piano solo from *Concert for Piano and Orchestra* and the *Etudes Boreales*.

Chapter Three

Bonnie Bird

Interview with Rebecca Boyle, Laban Centre, London, December 7, 1993

Introduction

In this interview Bonnie Bird provides details of her background at the Cornish School of the Arts in Seattle, followed by her connection with Martha Graham and her dance company, and then, in fall 1937, her return to the Cornish School where her students included Merce Cunningham and her accompanist was John Cage.[1] She was born in Portland, Oregon, in 1914, and in 1938 she married the psychologist Ralph Gundlach.[2] They were both members of the Seattle Artists League, an organization with left-wing associations, which would cause trouble for them in the McCarthy era.

Bird left the Cornish School in 1940, discouraged by the decline in student numbers, but after World War II she went on to develop contemporary dance in universities and community arts centers. She was a founding member and president of the American Dance Guild, as well as of the Congress on Research in Dance. In 1974 she was invited by Marion North, principal of the Laban Centre in London, to become director of the Dance Theatre Department, where she set up the first British academic programs in dance with degrees ranging from BA to PhD. In 1982 Bird founded Transitions Dance Company, the leading British professional training company for young dancers, and was artistic director until her death in 1995.

---

1. For details about Cage's context at this time see Leta E. Miller, "Cultural Intersections: John Cage in Seattle (1938–40)," in David W. Patterson, ed., *John Cage: Music, Philosophy and Intention, 1933–50* (New York: Routledge, 2002), 47–82.
2. Ralph Harrelson Gundlach (1902–78), whose career was blighted in 1949 when he was dismissed from the University of Washington for alleged communist sympathies. The university issued a formal apology in 1994.

Leta E. Miller sums up Bird's importance in the Seattle period: "Among those artists who influenced Cage's work, none played a greater role than Bonnie Bird. Her impact on his compositional development extended far beyond her initial invitation for him to come to Seattle . . . she served as the catalyst for his most important innovations in this period."[3]

Rebecca Boyle took a first-class degree in music at Goldsmiths College, University of London; then, as a Fulbright Scholar at Yale University, she gained a master's degree in musicology. She spent her early career at IMG Artists, an international arts management company, working in New York, London, and Paris, before setting up a performing arts education venture, Artis, of which she is chief executive.

Interview

By permission of Heidi Smith

RB   When did you first meet John Cage and Merce Cunningham?

BB   I have to separate the two! [*laughs*] I first met Merce because he was a student of mine. I left the Martha Graham Company in 1937 at the request of Martha Graham to go to Seattle, Washington, to the Cornish School, where I had actually grown up. From the age of seven I studied dance many afternoons a week. By the time I was thirteen or fourteen I was going every day after school, and it was there that I studied with Martha Graham. It was a full-time college of the arts, headed by Miss Cornish, with about a thousand children a week studying after school in all the different departments. There was a four-year training in dance, drama, visual arts, and music.[4]

Modern dance was just developing in the United States. Graham asked me to become a member of her company and go to New York to train as an actress and a dancer at the Neighborhood Playhouse where she and Louis Horst[5] were teaching. So I apprenticed in her company while I went to school for two years and then went directly into her company and worked with her for four or five years—and was chosen to be

---

3. Miller, "Cultural Intersections," 57.
4. The Cornish School—now the Cornish College of the Arts—was founded in 1914 by Nellie Centennial Cornish (1868–1956). Her background was as a pianist, but she became involved in education in all the arts. Affectionately known as "Miss Aunt Nellie," she was the school's director until 1939 and presided over a broad and innovative curriculum quite unusual at the time.
5. Louis Horst (1884–1964), music director for various dance companies and from 1926–48 with the company of Martha Graham (1894–1991).

her assistant. So I did a lot of teaching for her, both in the studio and in universities and various places.

Miss Cornish asked her to release me from the company to go to Seattle to head the dance department I had grown up in. I was delighted to do it because I had reached a stage in my relationship with Graham where I was so identified with her—and she was an extraordinary person—that I was almost bewildered as to where she left off and I began. [*laughs*] As in a family, you have to try your own wings to find out how much you have really learned.

So I arrived in Seattle to take over the dance department I had left when I was seventeen to go to New York. One of the students in the class was a very tall, skinny young man who was about nineteen at the time, and I was probably twenty-three or four. He was an acting major and his name was Mercier Cunningham. All the actors had to take dance class, and I taught a class in the morning for the dance and acting majors. And within about three months he was so absolutely absorbed that he shifted his major to dance and worked with me that whole year.

My accompanist at the time was a young man named Ralph Gilbert, who wanted very much to go and work with Martha Graham, so I was looking for a new person. An accompanist always sounds like a second-class citizen, but it wasn't at all—he was a composer/improviser with great facility.[6] I was in San Francisco and had been asked to teach at Mills College for the summer, and I knew the composer Lou Harrison who was then also a dancer. I asked Lou if he would like to come [to the Cornish School] and be music director and accompanist for the dance department, but he said he couldn't because he was dancing in a company and had committed himself during the year to a certain number of performances, as well as to what he did all the time—writing the music. He said, "I know somebody who I think would be very interested. He is looking for a job, and I'll call him."

So he did, and it was John Cage, who was living that summer in Carmel just south of San Francisco. John and I met—actually in front of the San Francisco Art Museum. We liked each other very much immediately, and he said he would come. He was married at that time to Xenia Kashevaroff, daughter of the head of the Russian Orthodox Church in Sitka, Alaska. She had a face like a Modigliani painting and was very small and slight, a very interesting person—an artist. So they both came to Seattle.

RB   Had you heard any of John Cage's music before you met him?

---

6. Gilbert had studied at the Cornish School and was much admired by Graham. Miller, "Cultural Intersections," 50.

BB   I knew a little bit about it but he hadn't done very much then, having just completed being a student with Schoenberg in Los Angeles. I absolutely trusted Lou's judgment about this. [*laughs*] I knew Cage was an experimentalist, but so was I so that was fine. He turned out not to be the world's greatest accompanist, but in a funny way he made a terrific contribution to the class even so—sometimes through his marvelous humor, sometimes through the fact that he would get involved in the class. I finally had him take over sections of the class. He had new ideas about how you could teach rhythm or how to read a score. He'd lay it on the floor in chalk, and he'd make relationships between space and time and the distance of a step. He would make the students walk the size of a beat on the floor and then split it up and so on. So he was getting them physically to visualize the music but putting it into their movement.

These were very short experimental things, more like one off, but they were always very intriguing, and John and I had a lovely time working together. He was also composer for the dance department, and I had a couple of students who were completing their fourth year. One of them was an absolutely beautiful black girl named Syvilla Fort, who had been dancing since she was a child. Her mother was the housekeeper for Miss Cornish, who lived in this big building with all the studios. When Syvilla and I were discussing her graduation concert, I said she could have two or three pieces written for her by different composers available from the music department—and John was one of them. She had to prepare the rough outline of the dance so they had something to see, and then she worked with the composers. John came to me after seeing the dance and said, "I have to have a gamelan orchestra." I laughed at him and said, "John, you're absolutely crazy—we can't even afford fifty cents!" We had no budget whatsoever. He said, "But she's done an absolutely beautiful work called *Bacchanale,* which has many textures that would be so right with the gamelan."[7] So I said, "It's not possible, we can't even buy a gong." There were a few old instruments around that we could borrow. John played for class on a beat-up grand piano—the dance studios tended to get the leftovers from the music students. It wasn't in the greatest condition; I had a little box behind the piano where I kept all the nuts and bolts and things that fell off!

At the same time, he was writing music for me for a couple of works I was doing. One was a piece called *Les Mariés de la Tour Eiffel,* a script written by Jean Cocteau and originally danced by John Borlin with Ballets

---

7. *Bacchanale* (1940) is described by Cage as the first piece for prepared piano. The premiere was on April 28, 1940.

Suédois in Paris.[8] Anyway, he played this old piano. In the script there was a wonderful crazy moment when it says "and telegrams flutter to the stage." Well, I got the mad idea that I didn't want telegrams, I wanted dancers to flutter to the stage and I would have to have a fireman's pole, the kind they slide down from the sleeping quarters to the trucks. So I visited a fire department and tried sliding down one, and the firemen thought I was quite mad! They said they got them from a brass foundry, and they turned out to cost five dollars a foot because they were solid brass. But this was the deep Depression, and it was totally impossible to pay for one. They gave me a little piece [of a pole].

I brought it back and handed it to John, who was busily getting composers to write music for *Les Mariés*. Unlike most ballets it called for pastiche, and that meant different composers doing different pieces—the whole thing was a wild send-up. Merce, at the beginning of the second year he was working with me, was taking the leading role. I handed this piece of brass to John just at the beginning of a technique class. And I said, "Well, you can't have a gamelan; I can't have a brass pole." The upshot of this was that John took the piece of metal and put it onto the tray. The tray was a bit wobbly, and when John started to play the first chords for the warm-up exercise it fell off and rolled up the strings as he was playing. Of course, it made the most extraordinary sound, and John, from that moment on, was gone as far as the class was concerned. He began ignoring us, playing different things and experimenting with this metal rolling on the strings.[9]

RB   So is this how he invented the prepared piano—in dance class?

BB   That's right. And then he got tired of that—I had long since said to the students that we'd go on working—and began inserting things from the box full of nuts and bolts into the strings and getting different qualities. By the end of the class he said, "I have a solution to the problem of the gamelan." He went on working with it, but then he realized that he wasn't going to have a grand piano but an upright in the theater. So when he got home, where he had an upright, he began inserting old pieces

8. *Les Mariés*, with a scenario by Jean Cocteau (1889–1963), was premiered on June 18, 1921, at the Théatre des Champs-Elysées, Paris, with music by Georges Auric, Darius Milhaud, and Francis Poulenc. The production at the Cornish School was on March 24–25, 1939, with music by Cage, Henry Cowell, and George Frederick McKay (1899–1970) of the University of Washington. There is an extract from McKay's contribution, "Everyone is deeply moved," in Cage, *Notations* (New York: Something Else, 1969).

9. See Cage, "How the Piano Came to Be Prepared," in *Empty Words: Writings '73–'78* (Middletown, CT: Wesleyan University Press, 1979), 7–9.

of pie plates and things like that. And he went on working with it and that's how the prepared piano came [about]—with *Bacchanale*.

One day in class, I said that raising an arm must be the most beautiful thing in the world. That moment when you raise the arm has to be a thing of beauty, a magnificently shaped arm shaping the space. All of a sudden I said to John, "I wonder if an arm detached from the body would be beautiful?" He looked perplexed, but I began thinking about whether we consider things beautiful if they're detached from the source. It began to be intriguing. John and I had a lot of conversations about it, and finally it led to my having three triangles made, like black flats on feet where a dancer could curl up and hide behind it. Then I had a rectangle made that was six feet tall, and Merce was behind it. If he stood on a step, his head just appeared. I used searchlights from old coast guard ships with a terrifically strong beam to isolate parts of the body. All you saw was white arms moving in space. It was extremely surreal. John and I worked together, and he wrote music for it. It happened that my husband, a psychologist interested in music, had brought home some records of pure tone made by Bell Laboratories. You could play a precise middle C on the turntable. John was intrigued to hear pure tone that could be sustained like this. Then he started playing with the dials so that the turntable went faster and slower so he got extraordinary sliding tones as the pitch changed. He created a piece that was played by manipulating two turntables.[10] The role of the person who played it was to increase or decrease the volume or to shift the speed. He wrote it up as a score. What was intriguing for us was that it had no pulse, and we had never dealt with that before. Since the piece was called *Imaginary Landscape*, there was no reason we shouldn't learn to work with it. We had to listen. It was played live, but because of the turntables it had to be piped in from our radio studio, which was attached to the theater, with the musicians in the studio. It had an extraordinary eerie quality. The piece and the sound absolutely intrigued people, and the audience began to build into it their own script. I was able to create what appeared to be a whole body—legs at one side of the stage, the head at the other, and between the triangles the torso. It looked like one long body. I can't remember the dance completely, but it was a fascinating experiment.

John wrote a number of pieces during the two years we were working together. The second year I did a piece to a poem by Archibald MacLeish,

---

10. *Imaginary Landscape No. 1* (1939) for two variable-speed turntables, frequency recordings, muted piano, and cymbal, premiered March 24–25, 1939. See Miller, "Cultural Intersections," 81, n. 74, for this corrected date.

who was then at the Library of Congress—a remarkably interesting man who wrote a poem about U.S. culture called "America Was Promises."[11] Martha Graham had worked with MacLeish; I knew a bit about him and knew some of his poetry. This poem dealt with the way cultural influences had come to the United States from Europe. It spoke of what had been the promises of a new culture and what had happened during the Depression—we were losing our culture, very [much] like now. I made this work and John wrote the music for it—for piano four hands—and played it with the woman who was head of the Dalcroze training, Doris Dennison, who later became music director for Mills College where there was a fine dance department. She and John became good friends, and he'd always see her when he went to San Francisco.

RB   Was there much collaboration between Cunningham and Cage at this stage?

BB   Not at that time. John and Merce met then, and Merce was in the dances. In 1939, at the end of the first year John was with me at the Cornish School, I took five or six students to Mills College for the summer. I got them scholarships to study with Martha Graham, Doris Humphrey, and Charles Weidman, so I was able to bring Merce and these other students with me. I created a duet for a lovely Canadian girl and Merce, and they performed it in an outdoor theater. Martha had seen Merce in class, and by the middle of that summer she had asked him to join her company. So Merce came to me and said, "I just have to accept this." And even though he had two more years to do to complete the training at the Cornish School, I said, "Of course you have to accept it, and you must go."

John and I worked [together] again for another year, then John decided that he wanted to work with Moholy-Nagy at the Chicago Art Institute—he had come from the Bauhaus, and John was very aware of what was going on in Europe in the visual arts, writing, and music—so he and Xenia went to Chicago for a year. I don't know the history of their time there. I'd get funny little notes from John. And then he went on the next year to New York and began to develop concerts. Merce was with Martha Graham in the company for about five years so they were reacquainted, began to work together, and ultimately [their relationship] actually split up the marriage with Xenia.

RB   Did they come together because they had the same philosophy about experimenting with music and dance?

BB   Merce was very young still. I have charming, funny letters from him in this period because he was beginning to want to do something different

---

11. Archibald MacLeish (1892–1982), Librarian of Congress (1939–44), assistant secretary of state (1944–45). "America Was Promises" (1939).

from what he was doing with Graham—which was called "expressionist dance," which I don't think it quite was. But Merce wanted to move away from that. I think he had been influenced by many different things. One was the association with John in Seattle and the kind of experimentation I was doing too, which was pretty theatrical. We had great fun with the juxtaposition of things, as in *Imaginary Landscape*. Merce wrote me funny letters about writing a play that had one word in the first act—sort of pretty wild, outlandish things. He described living with some friends—they rented a flat together and they couldn't unlock the front door, so they got a hole beside the door and went through that way! It was all rather Bohemian and quite fun.

But Merce always was a serious worker who would pursue things. He left Graham and had a little studio and John began to work there, and that was when they really began together. I think the greatest influence came to Merce from John. He was older and had been pursuing a point of view starting with his work with Schoenberg, who told him he would never be a composer because he didn't understand harmony.[12] So John concentrated on percussion. He gave the first percussion concert in Seattle at the Cornish School, which came about in a very interesting way because John and I both felt the Cornish School was rather square. Most of the concerts that were given were very safe: there was not much experimentation. This was partly because students were brought up through their traditions, which they have to learn. John and I decided there needed to be new breath in the place and thought there should be an exhibit of fine contemporary art. So we took over a room and included Mark Tobey and Morris Graves. Then we asked Nancy Wilson Ross, the novelist and writer whom I introduced to John, who was doing some very interesting work.[13] She'd been to the Bauhaus, and she wrote her first article on modernism in art and delivered it as a paper at the first art exhibit we had.

Then we decided we should be on what was called the "Friday Night Series," [which was] usually music, run by this remarkable woman. She was very correct, a Bostonian, and she had the only music salon in Seattle. She was a close friend of Miss Cornish, who had now gone, and Lady Beck, as we called her, ran the Friday series. We applied to put on

12. See interview with Michael Oliver, chapter 18. 202.
13. Nancy Wilson Ross (1910–86) lived in Washington state from 1938–42. In the Foreword to *Silence: Lectures and Writings* (Middletown, CT: Wesleyan University Press, 1961), xi, Cage says: "One of the liveliest lectures I ever heard was given by Nancy Wilson Ross at the Cornish School in Seattle. It was called Zen Buddhism and Dada. It is possible to make a connection between the two, but neither Dada nor Zen is a fixed tangible."

a concert of percussion music. Earlier that year John had written to composers in Cuba, Mexico, Chile, every place, to see if contemporary composers had written percussion pieces. Amazingly, they had! Pieces by Caturla[14] from Cuba and Revueltas[15] from Mexico were really fascinating but required the most extraordinary instruments. Caturla's piece required an instrument they used in Cuba that is the jawbone of an ass. You beat on one part of the jawbone, and the bones and the teeth rattle and make a very dry, vibratory sort of sound. And a thing called the Bull Roarer is a drum with a hole in it, and you draw through that tight hole a heavy rope and it shudders![16]

RB   So how did you get hold of these instruments?

BB   We had to make them or look for them. John was fascinated by what made gong-like sounds and couldn't get gongs, so he began using brake drums. We would go on Saturdays to used car lots, and John would stand around beating brake drums or parts of old cars—and create the instruments. When it came to writing out the program, we didn't have enough money to advertise it properly. So John went to a printer who would do things very inexpensively and said, "I have a real problem paying for the paper." The man said, "Well, I have leftover pieces; they're long, skinny pieces chopped off the bottom of larger pieces, you can take a look at those."

John was absolutely thrilled. He wrote up the program with no capitals—all lower case.[17] By folding the paper we could mail it as advertising. The audience on that particular Friday night absolutely jammed the hall—they had huge chips on their shoulders because they had received this information and read this strange instrumentation. John looked like a very young boy when he was in his thirties and had a marvelous laugh. It was a big laugh, and he laughed at a lot—sometimes as punctuation at the end of a sentence, where he would turn the sentence by this funny laugh that supposedly wiped it all out.

---

14. Alejandro Garcia Caturla (1906–40) studied composition with Nadia Boulanger in Paris and practiced law in Cuba.

15. Silvestre Revueltas (1899–1940), colorful Mexican composer and violinist with periods of study and work in the United States between 1916 and 1929.

16. Cage mentions his first percussion concert, December 9, 1938, as containing works by William Russell, Gerald Strang, Ray Green, and himself. By the second concert a year later he had asked many composers for percussion works and reckoned that "the literature for percussion instruments alone grew from about three or four in 1934 to about fifty in 1940." In Richard Kostelanetz, *John Cage: Writer. Previously Uncollected Pieces* (New York: Limelight Editions, 1993), 33.

17. Reflecting the practice of E. E. Cummings, whose poems Cage had set as *Five Songs* in July 1938.

The audience came in, and Morris Graves, a remarkable painter who later became a close friend of John's, was at that time in Seattle.[18] He was head of the art section of the Works Progress Administration, which gave employment to painters, a place [for them] to work, and commissions for the city. Morris told me later, "I just thought that all the windows at the Cornish School ought to be opened up and the wind should blow through." So I said, "Well, that's fine, you just chose the wrong night." He had decided that the Friday Night Series should be given this bit of fresh air. Morris earned part of his living by going out into the forest—there were marvelous ones nearby—and finding certain kinds of fern that florists loved. He would cut the ferns and put them into a half-ton truck he had, which was actually an old car with its back chopped off and a platform put in. He and his pals would also go to the garbage dumps to see what kind of furniture they could find, and [on one visit] they found a long roll of carpet.

They came early to the concert and had apparently caused a commotion outside. Morris was sitting in the back of his truck like a king, and his flunkies rolled the carpet up to the front door of the theater, which was a long distance. Morris got out and grandly walked in his dumpy old clothes, followed by his various-sized friends who were equally scruffy. They came in and took a whole row of seats in front. I had done a dance to one of the pieces that was going to be on the last part of the program; it was called *Three Inventories of Casey Jones*. It was based on a folktune, and Ray Green had written the music for it, which was played on toy piano and pop bottles filled with water—all tiny, crazy instruments.[19] People were coming into the theater, and I was sitting in the back of the theater with some of the students who were going to dance later. One of them said that when she saw Morris Graves come in with his group she knew something was going to be up. And they began to eat peanuts—to crack them and drop them on the cement floor—acting as if they were going to a circus. People began to

---

18. Morris Graves (1910–2001), painter and sculptor who met Cage in Seattle in 1937. He was featured in *Life* magazine (September 1953), along with Mark Tobey (1890–1976), as one of four Mystic Painters of the West.

19. Ray Green (1908–1997) studied at the San Francisco Conservatory and the University of California, Berkeley, before leaving for Paris to study with Milhaud. He had probably returned to the West Coast by the time of this concert. He had a varied career and wrote for dance through his marriage to dancer May O'Donnell. His *Three Inventories of Casey Jones* was originally scored for percussion ensemble, but he revised the work as a fantasy for piano and orchestra in 1939. Casey Jones was a railroad engineer killed in a train wreck at Vaughan, Mississippi, in 1900. Green's use of a toy piano may not have been lost on Cage, who wrote his Suite for that instrument in 1948.

look at them and make noises—very middle-class behavior—expressing displeasure that they were dropping stuff on the floor. Morris had taken some paper eyeballs and made a lorgnette through which he looked at them. They didn't think it was funny and were very disturbed. It had a marvelous effect on the concert because all those people who had come with chips on their shoulders were now feeling that Morris was the devil incarnate, that he was disturbing this young man who was giving an unusual concert! They were pushed to John Cage's side, but they hadn't come for that reason.

So the concert began, the curtains opened, and people were astounded. Here were Merce, Doris Dennison, and quite a few people who had been working with Merce to play these very strange instruments. John stepped forward, and they were all correctly dressed in black trousers and white shirts, except they didn't wear any coats. [*laughs*] You didn't do that in music at this time. They had their sleeves rolled up; they were going to be very busy. And Merce was standing in front of a great array of gongs and things, hung on wooden frames. John stepped forward and spoke very charmingly—he's so beguiling—and quite disarmed the audience, which was ready to be furious. He explained what he was doing, and they played the first and second pieces. Then there was a piece in which there was a great silence, and Morris stood up and said "Jesus in the Everywhere" to no point at all [*laughs*] and sat down.[20] John wasn't aware of this from backstage. Lady Beck was so furious that she went to the head of the radio department and some other man and said, "You must take him out of the theater; it's disturbing this program." So they marched down the aisle in the intermission to Morris and said they would like him to leave the theater. It's the first time I ever saw passive resistance. Morris quietly lay down on the ground [*laughs*], so they were faced with having to pick him up! They couldn't pick him because he was like a jellyroll, but he accommodated them by stiffening himself like a board. They carried him out in front of Lady Beck, and as he went by Morris said, "Good evening, Lady Beck; lovely evening." The concert made quite a hit!

---

20. More detail is provided by Cage in "Series re Morris Graves," in *Empty Words: Writings '73–'78*, 99, 104–5: "It was following the third movement of my Quartet for percussion (1935) that Morris Graves said: 'Jesus in the Everywhere!' That was taken as the signal. . . . As they carried him down the aisle, his face upward as though he were on a stretcher, he found himself passing beneath the large bosom (it was she who had given the order). She said: 'I am Mrs. Beck.' Morris replied: 'Good evening, Mrs. Beck.' . . . Mrs. Beck followed Morris and the men carrying him outside to the patio. The fast drumming had begun and was audible through the closed doors. Morris, released, began dancing. 'His dance,' Mrs. Beck later reported, 'was very sinuous.' And it was the day after that event that we first met one another."

RB   Cage has said that if he didn't shock his audiences he'd think there was
      something wrong. Did he always want to be on the edge of acceptability?

BB   I don't think that to be on the edge of acceptability was John's objec-
      tive at all. That happened because of the nature of the things he did—
      it didn't surprise him and he was quite intrigued with the kinds of
      responses people had. And often he would say: "Well, why not? Why
      can't it be done this way?" He would challenge preconceptions about
      music because he was trying to stretch the boundaries and say that all
      sound to him was musical. He went pretty far out on that!

RB   Cage has said his favorite piece is $4'33''$ because he listens to it all the
      time—any noise is music to his ear.

BB   He loved that kind of thing, and that was in a way John's hidden
      agenda. Because he was challenging himself to support his own point
      of view, he liked to challenge other people to think further when they
      came in touch with his work. Of course, it brought many young people
      on his heels because he made them think about things like silence. He
      made them think of the world they actually live in and listen to it in a
      totally other way.

RB   Do you think there was any development in Cage, or is it new each time?

BB   I don't think he thought of things in a developmental fashion, where
      this leads to that. It's partly based on the *I Ching* and the chance oper-
      ations. You don't think that way—it's always new, unexpected associa-
      tions of things. John was extraordinary in that he reached out, whereas
      Merce has concentrated on dance. John got interested in mushrooms
      and became one of the international authorities, so finally he had to
      say, "I have to give it up, the mushrooms are taking over." I remember
      visiting him, and he had a wonderful collection of mushroom books.
      When he was deep into the mushroom business he was living in
      Rockland County in an apartment built on top of another house that
      extended to the hill. You could walk out into the woods. John would go
      out every day with a basket, discovering mushrooms in a place that pro-
      duced quite a variety. There were mushroom growers in the area who
      used dark houses. John was learning about mushrooms and was terri-
      bly organized, as he always was. He had a whole wall covered with
      round white cartons to store mushrooms, with their type and date. He
      was like a collector and also got interested in painting.

RB   And actually exhibited his scores. Do you remember the audience
      reaction to the way Cage and Cunningham put the music and dance
      together without any connection between them?

BB   In every audience there was always somebody who was offended by this
      juxtaposition and others who were absolutely intrigued. There were
      times when I didn't like what came out of John in the way of music—
      it didn't always work for me. There was a period in John's music when

it just got so gratingly difficult—the music, not what Merce was doing on the stage, except that it got bothered, too. In a performance I was having a hard time with at Connecticut College, where Merce's company was in residence, John was doing the music and somebody was doing the lighting. The piece started, and what was John doing? He was scratching the walls, doors, and handles, moving around in the theater and amplifying this. It was the most god-awful sound—the kind of thing that hurts your teeth! Scratching on a blackboard! The dancers were on the stage dancing with a big light on a stand, and suddenly that [light] was swung around and pointed at us in the audience. We were trying to see under the light and wanting to cover our ears—people were walking out. It was a test.

RB The sounds Cage was making must have detracted from the dance?

BB It was like a competition! [*laughs*] The light became a total barrier too.

RB Do any of their collaborations stand out in your mind?

BB I loved *Inlets*, which brought Morris Graves, John, and Merce together.[21] It's a beautiful work. At that time John was experimenting with the sound of water in huge conch shells. What the musicians did was to tilt these [shells] ever so slightly on a time frame. It's the most extraordinary sound, never quite the same, but texturally it produces the sense of water falling through pipes and onto rocks. And it was so right—a very Northwest piece on Merce's part.

RB Was the music composed separately from the dance?

BB Yes, it just came together. But I think possibly those two responded to the fact that they both grew up in a particular kind of landscape—heavily wooded, magnificent waterways, light, sound, mountains, trees, and so on. It's where I grew up too, and it touched something common to the three of us. The relationship to the painters is as fascinating as the music because they were independent too. I remember the beautiful piece with the helium-filled pillows by Andy Warhol.[22] I saw the opening performance, and some of the pillows floated off the stage and the audience just batted them back! [*laughs*] The dancers were in silver and reflected light; their movement was completely luminous.

RB Sometimes Cunningham looks back to ballet but organizes movement in a different way from Martha Graham.

BB I think Merce recognizes that his choices for movement are quite linear: he's interested in line. He is a tall, slender, vertical man, not a

---

21. *Inlets*, first performed by the Merce Cunningham Dance Company in Seattle, Washington, September 10, 1977.
22. This was *Rainforest* (1972), which was done by the Merce Cunningham Dance Company, but the music was by David Tudor.

great one for going off balance at all. There's a kind of classical quality, too, in ballet, which is also vertical, light, and airborne.

RB   Whereas Martha Graham was more aware of the use of the floor?

BB   She was much more an earth-interested person and used the floor as a surface. Now that's not to say that Merce doesn't have his dancers go to the floor, but not at all in the way Graham did where they would fall into the ground or use it like a sounding board to spring off. He's a much more design-oriented person. Quite coolly, abstractly design. What intrigues him are the surprising things that come up that he would never think about. He might, but it would take him years perhaps to cover the amount the *I Ching* throws up through chance operations—and that intrigues me. I don't think I've known anyone who has pursued more steadily a single concept, found it, and mined it for all its richness. Most people get tired of a single concept, give it up, and go to another. But he has been absolutely endlessly fascinated by the same palette.

RB   Have you ever used chance techniques?

BB   Only experimentally for students.

RB   I imagine it must be very difficult for a dancer, especially when the music isn't helping?

BB   The thing is that the dancers were so used to the fact that they had no music that they developed their own, in a sense. They had to count, they had to pulse things, they had to learn a tremendous amount of peripheral vision so they knew exactly when to move. So they literally cut it all out and just as well, too, because they never knew how the opening night was going to assault them! So they moved through it, as if it was not there.[23]

　　During the period when John was working on *Roaratorio*, Merce did a piece called *In Six-four Time* and John wrote the music to go with it.[24] On opening night, when he played, John was so close to the actual rhythmic pattern of the dancers that they couldn't fight it. It drove them absolutely mad and they had a terrible time—and the piece looked unsteady. They had to force John to slow it down or speed it up so it was distinctively different because it was like being sucked down a tube!

---

23. See Carolyn Brown's comments, introduction to Merce Cunningham interview, chapter 2, 53.
24. There is no piece with this title.

Chapter Four

David Tudor

Interview with Peter Dickinson, Ibis Hotel, London, July 26, 1987

Introduction

David Tudor was born in Philadelphia in 1926 and died in New York in 1996. He studied piano and organ from childhood and studied composition with Stefan Wolpe.[1] From his early teens he held traditional posts as an organist, finally at Swarthmore College until 1948, and he then taught piano at the Contemporary Music School, New York, and at Black Mountain College, North Carolina. Immediately after he gave the American premiere of Boulez's Sonata No. 2 in 1950, he was much in demand as the preeminent virtuoso pianist of the avant-garde, which included Stockhausen and many others as well as Cage, with whom he had a long partnership. Tudor was involved with the first happening at Black Mountain College in 1952; he lived at Stony Point with Cage and other artists and spent over forty years with the Merce Cunningham Dance Company, founded in 1953. He taught at various institutions, including the Darmstädter Ferienkurse. From the late 1960s onward he developed as a composer in the medium of live electronics, designing his own equipment. Some of his works were presented as collaborations with other composers, including Cage.

For his own solo performances Tudor frequently made fastidious realizations of indeterminate scores, which led to interpretations of unique authority and distinction.[2] Cage's debt to Tudor was incalculable. In 1965 he discussed

---

1. Stefan Wolpe (1902–72), German-born American composer, pupil of Webern, who moved to the United States in 1938 where his various posts included director of music at Black Mountain College (1952–56).
2. See David Vaughan, "David Tudor: Black Mountain Sounds," *Guardian*, August 28, 1996. The unsigned obituary in *The Times* (London), September 5, 1996, refers to

the different tempos in *Music of Changes*: "David Tudor learnt a form of math-ematics which he didn't know before in order to translate those tempo indi-cations into actual time. It was a very difficult process and very time-consuming for him."[3] In 1973 Cage admitted: "Most of the music I've written has been for individuals who have developed a virtuosity, who've devoted themselves to this work in a way that involved them in discovery and such things as stamina. The perfect example, of course, is David Tudor."[4] And finally, in 1992 Cage said, "He's a very important musician and a very striking one" and referred to Tudor's remarkable ear and his independent career as a composer.[5]

Interview

By permission of the David Tudor Trust

PD   What's your first recollection of anything to do with Cage?

DT   I recall that one of my teachers remarked that she had gone to a con-cert of his music for prepared piano—I think it was the *Sonatas and Interludes*—and she simply remarked that she found it very unusual and interesting. A couple of years later John appeared at my door one day with a work by Ben Weber that Merce Cunningham was choreograph-ing; they needed a tape to rehearse with.[6] So I made that tape. A year later I was formally introduced to John by Morton Feldman—after that, John composed a piece for me. [*laughs*] That would have been 1951.

PD   Presumably *Music of Changes*—four sets of it?

DT   Yes, and I played each one as it came off the press or off the table.

PD   How did the different personalities of the New York School interact then?

DT   There was a real feeling of excitement, that something was happening and we were discovering it. I recall that the first few measures of *Music*

Tudor's "unshakeable commitment to a philosophy which celebrated the numinous potential of any and every sound. . . . It is for this integrity and loyalty to his forma-tive ideals, as well as his magnificent piano playing . . . that he will be remembered." 3. Michael Kirby and Richard Schechner, "An Interview with John Cage," *Tulane Drama Review* 10, no. 2 (1965–66): 68. 4. Richard Kostelanetz, *Conversing with Cage* (New York: Limelight Editions, 1988), 121. See also Joan Retallack, ed., *MUSICAGE: Cage Muses on Words Art Music* (Hanover, NH: Wesleyan University Press and University of New England Press, 1996), 297–29, and John Holzaepfel, "Cage and Tudor," in David Nicholls, ed., *Cambridge Companion to John Cage* (Cambridge: Cambridge University Press, 2002), 169–85. 5. Retallack, *MUSICAGE*, 298. 6. Ben Weber (1916–79), twelve-tone composer mainly based in New York. Cage wrote a touching obituary tribute, "B. W. 1916–1979," in *X: Writings '79–'82* (Middletown, CT: Wesleyan University Press, 1983), 119.

of Changes were on John's work table, and Morton Feldman looked at it very carefully and remarked, "That's it!" [*laughs*]

PD   That's what Feldman said about the *I Ching* as a discovery, which coincides with when you came on the scene?

DT   It does, yes.

PD   You hardly knew John before the *I Ching* days. The *Concerto for Prepared Piano* was the transition?

DT   That was scheduled to be performed and the pianist was ill, and so I did the first performance.[7] *Music of Changes* was already on its way at that time, and I had played the first book in 1951.[8]

PD   Was the whole business of the *I Ching* the result of a crisis in the 1940s for John, after which he used Zen to take himself out of his music and never changed?

DT   Yes, but there has been evolution in his music. Before his use of the *I Ching* he had been working with what are known as magic squares, which, I believe, were first used in one of the movements of the *Sixteen Dances*[9] and later in the *Concerto*. That leads to a kind of tabulation of your sound materials. It's like a directory of access, so it was natural that chance means came about. John had a profound change when he went to Europe and met Pierre Boulez. He heard him play his Second Sonata[10]— or part of it—and was very struck by the disorder and chaos of the music. His way of coming to terms with that was that it was exactly the same as perfect order. Even though the total structure of *Music of Changes* reflects the same symmetry as the *Sixteen Dances* and *Sonatas and Interludes*, the new factor was that the tempo is constantly changing so the time order was, in effect, chaotic. And so things went on from there. [*laughs*]

PD   In the *Sonatas and Interludes* Cage chose his sounds "as one chooses shells while walking on the beach,"[11] but in *Music of Changes* don't they arise solely through the *I Ching*?

7. Premiere: Music in the Making, Cooper Union, New York, January 1952.
8. *Music of Changes: Volume 1*, University of Colorado, Boulder, July 5, 1951; Black Mountain College, August 19, 1951; Cherry Lane Theatre, New York, January 1, 1952.
9. "Sixteen Dances was composed in the series of rhythmic structures of the dances by Merce Cunningham. The sounds are a fixed gamut of noises, tones, intervals, and aggregates requiring one or more of the players for their production. The composing means involved the establishing of this gamut in a chart. Systematic moving upon this chart determined the succession of events. The notation is conventional." In Richard Dunn, ed., *John Cage* (New York: Henmar, 1962), 28. Premiere: Ensemble conducted by Cage, Hunter College Playhouse, New York, January 21, 1951.
10. Pierre Boulez. Piano Sonata No. 2 (1947–48). Premiere: Paris, April 29, 1950.
11. John Cage, *Silence: Lectures and Writings* (Middletown, CT: Wesleyan University Press, 1961), 19.

DT   Yes, but if you look at the charts that were used you can see that he did indeed select the sounds. They were composed on the basis of what was available within the framework of the charts. That is—you'll have to forgive me if my recollections are inexact—there was a system where all the twelve tones had to appear before the next twelve. When the incidence of a sound came about through tossing the coins, he then had to make that sound. So those sounds really are his. They weren't dictated completely by the coins. He had to make, say, an aggregate, which would depend on what sounds were available to him at that time. He then chose the arrangement of the pitches—the equivalent of choosing the sound.

PD   In the way he asked the performer in *Winter Music* to choose the aggregates in various ratios?

DT   Right. It's very much the same, except that in *Music of Changes* it was he who made those choices.

PD   But the continuity of the piece comes from the numbers?

DT   It does, yes.

PD   What has it felt like to be the composer's chosen instrument for so long?

DT   For me it was a great freeing influence because I'd been playing a lot of European music, which I enjoyed—it was challenging and exciting—but when I became known for that, scores would arrive in the mail every week or two. They were all very black [*laughs*], and I began to feel that I'd done this before! [*laughs*] But with Cage's music everything was fresh, and each piece had different features. It was alive—the process of performing and even helping sometimes with the compositional details. I still find it interesting.

PD   How much do you feel that with indeterminacy the performer is half the composer or even more?

DT   I've struggled with that question, and I have to say that for me the differences really disappear. I think that's the change that has come about. Nowadays we have a situation that is more comparable to the Oriental difference between composer and performer. The one doesn't exist without the other. The European tradition has led us to believe that the composer is the only inspiration, whereas it's not true. Anybody's music can only exist when it's brought to life.

PD   How far has your experience with Cage's music propelled you into being a composer yourself?

DT   By doing it and dealing with the problems, you begin to have a feeling for what composition [*laughs*] really is. I recall one work, which was very important for me but not for John, was his *Variations II* (1961). It can be performed on any instruments—or no instruments, actually! [*laughs*] I had been working with amplifying the piano in terms of realizing this score, and I began to see that I had to consider it as a completely new instrument. Therefore if you try to tabulate settings of electronic equipment in relation to ordinary acoustic parameters, you're dealing with conditions that are not precise in the way you're accustomed to think of precision. You're dealing with field conditions where the difference between 3 and 4 is rather the difference between 1 to 5 and 2 to 8. Just recently a young composer came to my home trying to locate materials about that period, and, looking through things, I came across an unsigned manuscript, which I think John wrote for my birthday, called *Haiku*, written in the style of the *Variations*. So looking at that and realizing it was dated 1958, I was astonished that his description of the parameters didn't deal with numbers at all. For instance, in the description of the time of occurrence, the limits of the parameters were "soon: late." There were similar things in the other parameters, indicating a change in his mind. Any determinations you make from his graphic material are made in a field. Similar things happened later on. When he was composing *Music for Piano*, which is in four volumes, I noticed that he wasn't tossing coins or that he was using them very sporadically. I asked him what had happened and he said, "I found that my mind is a chance operation!" [*laughs*]

PD   Is your *Haiku* related to the *Seven Haiku* (1952)?

DT   No. This was done in the style of the *Variations*, which came later. It was called *Haiku* merely because it used graphs containing 5+7+5 events, which is the structure of a haiku.

PD   What was it like when Cage began to make an impact in European new music circles—Donaueschingen in 1954, meeting Stockhausen, and so on?[12]

DT   It was very exciting [*laughs*], very hard work! [*laughs*] At that time I was playing a lot of other things besides John's music. I came next to Europe in 1956, and at that time I was doing all my own writing for engagements. After that, I began to realize that what was very exciting for me was introducing American works, really making a completely new atmosphere for Europeans. I was offering in my programs quite a lot of European music. So I began to drop some of those works because I realized that if I kept offering them I would have to play them for the next forty years—and I didn't want to do that. I wanted to be able to do new things constantly. [*laughs*]

PD   What about Stockhausen?

---

12. See interview with Stockhausen, chapter 9, 129. Donaueschingen was one of the main centers for new music in Germany from the 1950s onward. Cage and Tudor performed *34′46.776″*, commissioned by the Donaueschinger Musiktage, on two prepared pianos on October 17, 1954. The performance created a scandal, and Cage was not asked back until 1972.

DT   I think they appreciated one another very much. During my first years touring in Europe, Stockhausen invited me to put whatever I wanted into the programs in addition to playing his music. Later on he changed when he discovered the American method of doing a one-man show! [*laughs*]

PD   Do you think Stockhausen was influenced by Cage?

DT   He was very struck first by the sounds and then by the continuity. I remember his rapt attention in 1954 when I first played some of the American pieces for him. He welcomed it because it must have been like a kind of identification for him, at least in a social sense. Spiritually, of course, he was quite different. The only concrete reflection, I guess, would be *Klavierstück XI*. I recall when he asked me, in his studio, whether I would be interested in such a work. He was in the process of beginning to compose it. I said, "Of course." And I told him there was a work of Feldman's using similar principles. He said, "Oh, then I shall not do it." [*laughs*] So I had to explain to him that it was really quite a different thing! [*laughs*] Actually, the Feldman piece has never been performed.

PD   You gave the first performance of *4′ 33″*.[13] How did it arise? Did John talk to you about it first?

DT   That's a marvelous example of how history gets deflected. [*laughs*] That piece arose from the method of composition of *Music of Changes*. When John was doing it he spoke of it to me as something that was inherent in the *I Ching* process and that he felt he should do it. That was simply the fact that it could easily happen that no sounds would be tossed by the coins. Since the procedure for *Music of Changes* was that out of 64 possibilities 32 were silence, he simply arranged his chart so it only dealt with the 32 numbers that would produce silence. Then another interesting fact—which has completely disappeared because the score has disappeared—is that the original manuscript was notated in the style of *Music of Changes*. So when I performed it I was looking at sheets of music paper scored for piano—two staves—with measures of four beats and the structural delineations given by the constant tempo. So I was looking at the first movement and I was turning pages because I was reading the score in time. Then later on John decided

---

13. *4′ 33″* (1952) (tacet, any instrument or combination of instruments). "This is a piece in three movements during all three of which no sounds are intentionally produced. The lengths of time were determined by chance operations but could be others." Dunn, *John Cage*, 25. Premiere: David Tudor, Maverick Concert Hall, Woodstock, New York, August 29, 1952.

to dedicate that piece to his friend Irwin Kremen,[14] and he didn't have the score. My recollection is that I gave the score to him because the score contained the rhythmic structure of the piece, delineating the parts. In the process he made a new score for Irwin Kremen, which he has. That one differs because it is not on music paper; there are no staves. The time is simply equivalent to the space on the empty page.

Later on I was asked to revive that work—in 1982, I think—as it was originally performed. The published score, without notation, bears no relationship to that. I recovered the score from Irwin Kremen, but something seemed wrong about it—the time-lengths of the three movements were not the same as when I had performed them. I looked through my programs, which say $4'33''$ and list the movements, and discovered that the times were different. Then I figured out that, instead of trying to reproduce the original score for Irwin Kremen, John must have tossed the coins and come out with three different lengths in the movements.[15] I compared that with the original lengths, and I had to make a new score with the original time-lengths because they asked me to perform it as it was originally performed.

Those things are not known, and I think people don't understand that it was a compositional necessity for John to write that. It wasn't just an idea out of the blue but a continuation of the work with the *I Ching*.

PD   I don't think he's said that.

DT   Well, he doesn't remember. I recall it. [*laughs*]

PD   The implications of $4'33''$ have been so thunderous, if a silent piece can be so described, that the details about how it arose have been

---

14. Irwin Kremen (1925–), widely exhibited painter and professor of psychology, who studied poetry and literature at Black Mountain College with M. C. Richards. When she moved to New York City in 1951 she introduced Kremen to Cage, Tudor, and Cunningham. E-mail from Irwin Kremen, November 9, 2005. Two published scores of $4'33''$ are currently available from Peters Edition, both dedicated to Kremen. The earlier of these two, copyright 1960 but apparently published in 1986, is known as the "Second Tacet Edition," since it replaces the first and has the same catalog number, 6777; and the more recent is described as "Original Version in Proportional Notation," number 6777A, known as "the Kremen manuscript." However, the original score that Tudor used, the "Woodstock manuscript," is lost. These terms come from Larry J. Solomon. For a thorough examination of all aspects of $4'33''$ see his "The Sounds of Silence: John Cage and $4'33''$ at http://solomonsmusic.net/cage.htm. Confusingly, $4'33''$ (*No. 2*) (*0'00''*) (1962) is a different work altogether.

15. Solomon considers this unlikely and favors the idea—encouraged by some of Cage's statements—that Cage may simply have accepted a mistake in the second set of timings. See Cage, *I–VI* (Cambridge, MA: Harvard University Press, 1990), 20–21. The original timings were 30'', 2'23'', and 1'40'' followed by 33'', 2'40'', and 1'20'', making the same total.

completely lost. Do you remember any connection with the all-black and all-white canvasses of Robert Rauschenberg?[16]

DT   It was like a familiar world. The difference between doing it white or black was very close to John. It was all happening at the same time— 1952.

PD   That was the Black Mountain College scene. Did that extraordinary group of people anticipate the sixties?

DT   Oh yes. [*laughs*] Black Mountain was a marvelous place. I think it's being appreciated now because of the declining situation in education.

PD   But what did it feel like to play $4'33''$?

DT   It was very intense and it still is because it is a piece of music that exists in time, and you have to pay attention to what's happening when you perform it. Each performance has memorable moments. [*laughs*] The most obvious one was during the first performance. There was a tin roof and it rained during the second movement—not during the first or third. [*laughs*]

PD   It's been seen as opening up the sounds of the environment, which John says he finds more useful aesthetically than so-called music.[17] Does it do that?

DT   Well, that's John's perception. It would be nice if people understood how that piece arose. It has, rather recently, when people perform John's music, given them the feeling that anything goes. I feel that to be faithful to the spirit of John's music you have to understand how his compositions came about, why they are notated the way they are, and why certain instructions are given and some not given. Of course, I was taught as a performer to be very faithful to a given score. It's important for me to look at every detail and make sure I perform in the spirit of what is indicated. I welcome the freedoms a lot because it has changed the way younger people perform.

I'll give you an instance. A few years ago I was asked to participate in a performance of *Rozart Mix*, which was done in Germany; I believe it was Berlin.[18] The person who was organizing the performance did not arrive until two days before. *Rozart Mix* deals with tape loops, which are made in various lengths, each one run between two machines. According to the length of the loop, the spatial relationship of the

---

16. See interview with Cage, chapter 1, 41n43.

17. John Cage, *A Year from Monday: New Lectures and Writings* (Middletown, CT: Wesleyan University Press, 1967), ix.

18. *Rozart Mix* (1965), for live performers, tape recorders, and eighty-eight tape loops, was originally composed for a concert organized by Alvin Lucier at the Rose Art Museum, Brandeis University. See Kostelanetz, *Conversing with Cage*, 72.

machines changes so that two related machines may be three feet apart, another [pair] twenty feet apart. These loops are made by cutting tapes of any sound material whatsoever into smaller pieces and splicing them together with blank tape. You have to make a supply of these loops, and the process of performance is to change the loops, to take one off and put on another. To make those materials, the man who was responsible held a splicing party, which apparently went on all night. I was busy preparing other performances, so I did not see that. When it came time to do the performance I found something astonishing. [*laughs*] They had taken the tapes and cut them into pieces of two inches, four inches, and six inches. Then the loops were made from these pieces. In the performance the rhythms were completely predictable because of the time relationship between the lengths of the sounds on the tapes. They hadn't seen that, which means they hadn't perceived that the idea was to mix everything up in order to be unpredictable. Instead, they had gone about it with faith and devotion to the activity—they had done their best—but hadn't seen that one little thing that made all the difference to the music. That's an example of not reading the score and trying to understand what it tells you to do.

I'm not criticizing—it's just another experience. Of course, it's perfectly possible to perform *Rozart Mix* with regular rhythms, but I happen to know that wasn't John's intention! [*laughs*]

PD You took part in the New York Town Hall Retrospective in 1958, and on the recording you can hear some audience protest. Is that a necessary part of the Cage aesthetic?

DT I think it's necessary for the audience, perhaps. During the time that I performed extensively in Europe, it happened not only with Cage but in other pieces. I recall a performance of Stockhausen's *Klavierstück VI* in which the audience became extremely restive because it's a long and difficult work to listen to. They began to make so much noise that Stockhausen stopped the performance, which was totally against my nature: [*laughs*] I wanted to continue to the end. When he stopped it there was only one minute left! To me, that is not the way. [*laughs*] It's not only protest. Sometimes it happens because of interest or shock or unfamiliarity.

I recall a performance in Zagreb where I was doing John's *Variations II* in my electronic version. I had no sooner started to perform than the audience began to come onstage. I had to stop after five minutes of my projected fifteen or twenty because I had no room to perform in! They crowded over the piano like flies. I couldn't even reach the controls of my electronic equipment. [*laughs*] There was nothing I could do. It wasn't protest. They were surprised and they wanted to see what was going on.

PD   Some people feel that some of those pieces from the sixties, such as the *Variations*, seem to have lost their power to surprise.[19] Is this something that needed to be done then but is no longer necessary?

DT   I feel that a beautiful performance is a beautiful performance. If those works seem to have lost their surprise, I think the performers should make it their job to make it surprising.

PD   How far has the impact of pieces like *HPSCHD* and *Musicircus* been related to the presence of John himself and his charismatic personality?

DT   I don't think his presence is really necessary if you do it as he would do it. When I've been invited to do seminars or workshops at universities, if I have a group only peripherally involved in electronics, sometimes it's rewarding to do a Cage piece with them. I've done *Variations VI* and *VII*. It feels just like when John was there! [*laughs*]

PD   I'm devoted to John, as you know, but I sometimes wonder how far his reputation is related to his personality and the way it's put across in interviews with the Zen contradictions and so on.

DT   I think it's intrinsic to John's belief that one should do everything. He is a person who answers every letter: he would feel it was improper not to respond. That's one of the most beautiful things about him—he gives access to everyone, no matter what feelings he may have. He gives the same attention to something he anticipates he might not enjoy as to something that excites him because it's a new encounter. It's natural that his presence in a happening like *HPSCHD* or *Roaratorio* contributes a lot. When you see the manner in which he performs, in utter faithfulness to his own ideas, it's a beautiful thing to have him there.

PD   So working with him has not been like working with any other composer?

DT   Oh, definitely. It's a real spirit of freedom and mutual respect.

PD   John wants to change people's minds to make them as sophisticated and creative as he is. Isn't this asking a lot from his listeners?

DT   Since it is a change of mind, it's not difficult at all. If you can open yourself to a point of view like that you'll have an experience—when you leave the concert hall you'll hear the environment differently, as many people have found. Sometimes one goes through a difficult process, but you come out very much richer for having done it. I recall that I had to invent all kinds of new technical procedures for myself to play John's music. I myself went though a change of mind: for me it was disciplinary. For instance, I had to change my feeling about musical continuity, and I had to perform in a manner where I prepared myself for every given instant. And as soon as that instant was released

19. See interview with La Monte Young, chapter 12, 160.

into sound, my mind had to completely forget and not relate the next
incident to the previous one. So it became quite a yoga for a while—
any yoga takes a bit of time. After a year or two I began to realize that
after hearing a few measures of a classical piece I could visualize the
continuity of the piece and the end, giving a whole different perspective on the question of musical style. It became very alive, as if it was a
taste—of Indian or Italian food! [*laughs*] I mean, the differences were
like changes in color perception—that's something that comes about
through a totally different type of musical experience.

PD   You've played some remarkably difficult works. John doesn't always
write his scores in the most practical way. Has this been a problem?

DT   I would say on the contrary! [*laughs*] There's just a difficulty of language in that the language he uses for each work can be different. His
method of notation only comes from his sense of the practical. That's
something you have to look at when you see one of his scores. Why did
he notate it that way?[20]

PD   I think of the space-time notations where you have to get a horrendous
number of notes in. It must be impossible, but somehow you manage
to do it.

DT   [*laughs*] You have to imagine that you're doing it! [*laughs*] For
instance, in *34′46.776″ For a Pianist* (1954), the compositional procedures come directly out of those used for *Music of Changes*. Only the
notation is changed because there is no rhythmic notation. It's done
according to stopwatch time: an inch equals one second or whatever.
When he composed that piece there was a great deal of chart information that he had to take care of, so he did the whole thing on rolls
of graph paper. At that time we happened to be living in the same
house because we had just moved to Stony Point and there was only
one house there. He was living in a very small room in the attic and
these rolls were piling up, and he began to throw them out into the
trash. One day I happened to notice them and asked if he would mind
if I kept one as a sample. So I began to collect these rolls. [*laughs*]
Recently, people are becoming very interested in the history of John's
methods. For instance, university students find it a rich field for their
theses because there's a lot of material that's not understood. They're

---

20. This is a generous response, taking into account the amount of rewriting Tudor
actually had to do. An example is given in Cage's *Notations*, where there is a page of
Solo for Piano presumably done for the recording, *Indeterminacy*, Folkways FT 3704
(1959), where the sleeve-note says: "Tudor plays material from his part of the *Concert
for Piano and Orchestra.*"

seeing these original materials and not understanding them completely. I told John recently that I'd found a number of these rolls and that some students were asking me questions I couldn't answer. Among the remarks he made was that he had noticed that when I was performing *Music of Changes* I was using a stopwatch. The thought occurred to him, "Why do I need to notate all these rhythms?" I was never aware that he had consciously decided that. I thought it was a new method of notation appropriate to this piece.

I think you'll find that practicality is John's middle name in many ways. But it can lead to the opposite condition. In those days I subscribed to *New Yorker* magazine, which was very fond of taking quotations from the newspapers that were absolutely nonsensical and featuring them [*laughs*] for further amusement. One happened to be the program note for *The Seasons*, which went into great detail about the difference between the number one and the number two, with references to three, four, and perhaps five. By the time you had finished reading just one paragraph—total confusion! But the real fact of the matter is that the difference between the number one and the number two is very important to John and always has been. [*laughs*]

PD   Because he works with numbers all the time.

DT   The *I Ching* charts deal completely with the difference between 1 and 2.

PD   Do you feel his influence is as strong now as it has ever been?

DT   I think it's stronger because of his social recognition. His books are very widely read and accessible; they're in every college library. Professors of music who would not normally wish to discuss the changes John Cage has made now have to take them into account, at least in the sense that they have to realize that their students are entirely aware of Cage's point of view and looking out for its manifestations.

PD   What is Cage's principal legacy as we move toward the end of the century? The ideas, writings, the early works, or the indeterminate ones?

DT   [*laughs*] Well, obviously *4'33"*! [*laughs*]

PD   Which he says is his favorite piece!

DT   Does he?

PD   You didn't know that?

DT   Well, [*laughs*] I'm not surprised! [*laughs*] It's hard to pinpoint a single work: there are so many. *Music of Changes* is very important and I think will [continue to] be. But then, I feel that pieces like *HPSCHD* are important in a different way, dealing with different aspects of music. The important thing is that he's changed people's hearing, and that's going to remain with us for the future.

Chapter Five

Jackson Mac Low

Interview with Peter Dickinson, New York City, July 2, 1987

Introduction

Jackson Mac Low was born in Chicago in 1922 and died in New York in 2004. Around 1986 Cage compared him with the New England writer Henry David Thoreau (1817–62), whose account of his two years living in a cabin beside Walden Pond, near Concord, from 1845 to 1847 has become a classic. Cage was attracted by Thoreau's advocacy of civil disobedience.

> Mac Low's Thoreau: he gives exact attention. No added flavor: just it. His poetry sets us ecstatic, though he insists we speak it "soberly and clearly (as in serious conversation.)" Bells ring (Stein, Whitman): others will (Joyce, Ancient Chinese). He was ringing them before we were able to hear. Musician, he introduced poetry to orchestra without syntax. Poet, he "sets all well afloat." That's why his poetry, even though it looks like it, is poetry.[1]

Mac Low returned the compliment by writing about Cage's literary work.[2] Jerome Rothenberg, in a preface, written in 1980, to Mac Low's *Representative Works*, says:

---

1. Jackson Mac Low, *Representative Works: 1938–1985* (New York: Roof Books, 1986), back jacket.
2. Mac Low, "Cage's Writings up to the Late 1980s," in David W. Bernstein and Christopher Hatch, eds., *Writings through John Cage's Music, Poetry, + Art* (Chicago: University of Chicago Press, 2001), 210–33. Also Mac Low, "Something about the Writings of John Cage (1991)," in Richard Kostelanetz, ed., *Writings about John Cage* (Ann Arbor: University of Michigan Press, 1993), 283–300.

Mac Low stands with John Cage as one of two major artists bringing systematic chance operations into our poetic and musical practice since the Second World War. The resulting work raises fundamental questions about the nature of poetry and the function of the poet as creator. For raising such and other questions, Mac Low like Cage has sometimes met with strong rejection and . . . has found less public recognition for work that's often sensed as "abstract" and that seems, by setting "chance" over "choice" in the making of poems, to act against the projection of personality usually associated with "the poet." Still he's widely influential and recognized by many (Cage among them) as the principal experimental poet of his time.[3]

Rothenberg goes on to explain how he found ways into admiring Mac Low's work through performing it—a link with Cage's writings—and Cage himself wrote an appreciation of Mac Low in 1980.[4] Rothenberg stressed Mac Low's musical studies in early childhood—piano, harmony, violin—and later lessons in New York with various piano teachers, including Grete Sultan, for whom Cage wrote his *Etudes Australes*. Mac Low attended Cage's classes in experimental composition at the New School for Social Research from 1957 to 1960, and Cage provided music for Mac Low's play *The Marrying Maiden*.[5] In his article Cage discusses Mac Low's compositions from the 1950s onward with the care he had taken twenty years earlier over the works of Virgil Thomson.[6]

Mac Low studied at the Chicago Musical Institute and Northwestern University School of Music. He went on to study philosophy at the University of Chicago until 1943, when he moved to New York. There he took a degree in Greek, held various teaching posts, and in 1975 studied Indian singing with Pandit Pran Nath. Mac Low was a founding member of the avant-garde group Fluxus and is now seen as a pioneer of sound poetry and performance art whose work bridged the gap between writing and music. He and Cage had much in common—the use of chance, Buddhism, silence, and utopian political views. Cage summed it up: "Mac Low's work, it seems to me, is that of an idealist—or religious-anarchist. Like other such anarchists, he finds through experience the necessity to make laws ('No jumping up and down on the beds!'), but this paradox in which he finds himself does not distract him from his ethical purpose."[7]

3. In Mac Low, *Representative Works: 1938–1985*, v.

4. Cage, "Music and Particularly Silence in the Work of Jackson Mac Low," in Richard Kostelanetz, ed., *John Cage: Writer. Previously Uncollected Pieces* (New York: Limelight Editions, 1993), 147–52.

5. The Living Theatre, New York City, June 15, 1960, through April 25, 1961 (47 performances).

6. Kathleen Hoover and John Cage, *Virgil Thomson: His Life and Music* (New York: Thomas Yoseloff, 1959).

7. Kostelanetz, *John Cage: Writer*, 152. In a 1972 footnote to a discussion about his relationship to contemporary American writers Cage commented: "I have a real

In a 1999 lecture Mac Low described his ways of working in terms very close to Cage's philosophy: "They are almost always ways in which I engage with contingency, and in doing so I am often, to a large extent, 'not in charge' of what happens while I do so. . . . They often surprise me, and they almost always give me pleasure and seem to give pleasure to others."[8]

Interview

By permission of Anne Tardos

JML I first heard of Cage somewhere between 1945 and 1947 and spoke to him for the first time at a concert at Columbia, where he played the *Sonatas and Interludes* and we talked briefly about the preparations.[9] Then I became acquainted through a friend in 1953, and we've known each other since then.

PD That's already the time when he'd become affected by Zen?

JML We both went to the classes of Dr. Suzuki at Columbia from about 1954–55 to 1957–58 when he went back to Japan.[10]

PD What were Suzuki's classes like?

JML They were very quiet. He always said he wasn't a Zen master but a university professor. They were careful expositions, but he would speak in a quiet tone of voice: if people made any sound he was drowned out. The arrangement was that he'd teach at Columbia if anybody who wanted to go would be admitted—there were a number of artists and musicians.

PD It's sometimes difficult to explain how an American composer has been so affected by Oriental thought?

JML I think this is true in Europe too. Stockhausen has been influenced by some form of Hinduism. I don't think it's unusual. There's a large Buddhist society.

PD Do you think this creates difficulties with an audience, which may not have the same background in Zen?

JML Whatever influences have gone into making a work of art are one thing. How the public receives it is another. Let's take the paintings of

admiration for the work of Jackson Mac Low and Clark Coolidge, as well as for any poet who attempts to liberate language from syntax." Cage, *For the Birds: John Cage in Conversation with Daniel Charles* (London: Marion Boyars, 1981), 55, n. 2.

8. Margalit Fox, "Jackson Mac Low, 82, Poet and Composer, Dies," *New York Times*, December 10, 2004. See also Michael Carlson, "Jackson Mac Low," *Guardian*, December 20, 2004.

9. This might have been Maro Ajemian's performance of four *Sonatas and Interludes* at McMillin Theater, Columbia University, New York, on May 14, 1949.

10. Daisetz Teitaru Suzuki: see interview with Cage, chapter 1, n. 32.

Morris Graves, who's very much influenced by Buddhism and Zen in particular. I doubt that people who look at his paintings need to have had a background in Buddhism.

PD   You've had this influence too?

JML Yes. I had been doing a number of kinds of work including avant-garde and more conventional. Three or four influences came together in the middle fifties. One was the music of Cage, Wolff, Feldman, and Brown; I had been reading the *Book of Changes* (the well-known Wilhelm translation came out around 1950); reading Suzuki; and reading Gershom Scholem on Jewish mysticism.[11] These four things came together, and I became interested in using chance operations in literature. At that time Cage and his friends had done their work almost exclusively in music, although M. C. Richards had made a few poems with methods that John had worked out.

At the end of 1954 I began to use chance operations in my *Five Biblical Poems*.[12] It was partly through the thinking embodied in the *Book of Changes* and the notion of selflessness, that the self is an illusion. Also the practice of Cage, Wolff, and their friends. This made me interested in what was possible in language using chance methods I'd devised myself. I used the Bible as a source and methods of permuting the letters of the scriptures and coming to some epiphanies.

PD   This is quite close to the way John has treated *Finnegans Wake*, reading through it five times based on his mesostics.[13]

JML The reading-through method is one I've employed extensively since 1960.

PD   Did John get the idea from you?

JML In the introduction to his piece called *Alphabet*,[14] he said his interest in working in literature again had some input from my work. At about the

---

11. Gershom Scholem (1897–1982), German-born authority on Kabbalah, Jewish mystical writings, who emigrated to Palestine in 1923.

12. Mac Low, *Representative Works: 1938–1985*, 116–34.

13. Cage created reduced versions of Joyce's avant-garde novel using his mesostic technique. (See his explanation in Introducing *Roaratorio*, chapter 20.) These are *Writings through Finnegans Wake* (Tulsa, OK: University of Tulsa Press, 1978); *Writing for the Second Time through Finnegans Wake* (in *Empty Words: Writings '73–'78* [Middletown, CT: Wesleyan University Press, 1979]); *Writing for the Third Time through Finnegans Wake* (not collected); *Writing for the Fourth Time through Finnegans Wake* and *Muoyce* [*Writing for the Fifth Time through Finnegans Wake*], both in *X: Writings '79–'82* (Middletown, CT: Wesleyan University Press, 1983), 1–50 and 173–87, respectively.

14. *James Joyce, Erik Satie, Marcel Duchamp: Ein Alphabet* (1982) was commissioned by Westdeutscher Rundfunk following the success of *Roaratorio*. Cage's text, in the form of mesostics, is in *X: Writings '79–'82*, 53–102. See also Richard Kostelanetz, *John Cage (ex)plain(ed)* (New York: Schirmer, 1996), 154–55, and Kostelanetz, *Conversing with Cage* (New York: Limelight Editions, 1988), 168–69.

same time John and I were asked to do work dealing with Pound's *Cantos*, so I have a whole book where I went through them using a method I called diastic, which I began using in 1963. He produced a series of mesostics. I just used Pound's name to pick out words and ends of words as I read through.

PD   Did you do this before John?

JML I hate to go into that kind of priority stuff. It is true that I began using an acrostic method in 1960.

PD   You've a variety of methods, whereas John uses one. I find the results of some of this suggest Gertrude Stein.

JML I liked the *Biblical Poems*, when I'd finished them, since they seemed to have an affinity with Stein, whom I'd loved since I came across her work in a bookstore when I was in elementary school. I've always had a strong empathy with Stein, along with John and Kurt Schwitters, even where she didn't directly influence my work.[15] John was always deeply involved with Stein.

PD   How would you assess Cage as a writer?

JML In what sense "assess"?

PD   I know you're not comfortable with my terms! [*laughs*]

JML I love the work but don't know what you mean by "assess"! The literary canon? He'd stand alongside practically anything in American poetry.

PD   You really mean those readings through *Finnegans Wake*?

JML Wonderful poems. His chance-operation literary work—*Thoreau*,[16] *Mureau*,[17] and his earlier lectures—are wonderful works of literature

---

15. Kurt Schwitters (1887–1948), German artist, leading figure in the Dada movement who moved to England in 1940. Inventor of collage technique known as Merz, which he also applied to poetry. Cage admired Schwitters: "So a great Dadaist is Schwitters, whose work is actually beautiful . . . and unfortunately remains beautiful . . . because you get caught in art." In Joan Retallack, ed., *MUSICAGE: Cage Muses on Words Art Music* (Hanover, NH: Wesleyan University Press and University of New England Press, 1996), 103–4.

16. Mac Low probably means Cage's *Lecture on the Weather* (1975), which takes texts by Thoreau and subjects them to chance operations to create an incomprehensible collage of twelve simultaneous spoken voices supported by recordings of wind, rain, and thunder. The work was commissioned by the Canadian Broadcasting Corporation for the American Bicentennial, and Cage used the opportunity to express his disgust with all political systems. See Preface to *Lecture on the Weather*, in Cage, *Empty Words: Writings '73–'78*, 3–5.

17. *Mureau* is the first syllable of the word *music* followed by the second of the name Thoreau. Cage wrote it by subjecting Thoreau's remarks about music, silence, and sounds to *I Ching* chance operations and often read the result in his public appearances. See Cage, *M: Writings '67–'72* (Middletown, CT: Wesleyan University Press, 1973), Foreword and 35–56. At The Royal Albert Hall, London, on May 22, 1972,

and will eventually be recognized as such. Generally, something isn't admitted into the so-called canon unless it fits in with a rather narrow tradition. Stein isn't admitted into the canon.

PD   I'd like to ask about the reading-through technique. Why do you need the original?

JML   In chance-operational work there are a number of ways of proceeding. One is to start with a text and to use some kind of sampling technique such as John's use of the *I Ching*, diastic and acrostic treatment, and numerical techniques. One can start with a text and produce another text. This is not only found in chance-operational work today, but throughout American literature there is a large school of writers who have fallen under the somewhat ambiguous name of language-writers. They very often will not just process one text but appropriate material from many other texts into the works. *The Waste Land*[18] and the *Cantos*[19] bring in work from many other sources.

PD   There's a difference of degree. I wouldn't accept *The Waste Land* as the same situation at all.

JML   Yes. The difference is that in works like *Writing through Finnegans Wake* one starts with a single source and sticks with it. That's what I started doing with my *Biblical Poems* based on the Bible.

PD   *Finnegans Wake* is already very complex and is difficult for the reader to come to terms with. It involves a great deal of reference. By abstracting it in the way John does, he's made aspects of it completely unintelligible. Does this matter?

JML   I think this is true of all work of this sort. I don't believe you are dealing with the same sort of meanings. You're dealing with meanings that are there but also ones that are produced by the reader or listener. Even with *Finnegans Wake*, because of its denseness and the fact that the

---

there was a simultaneous performance of Cage's *Mureau* and David Tudor's *Rainforest*. In the program book Cage says: "The chants to be heard (with David Tudor's *Rainforest*), three recorded, one performed live, are improvised on fixed texts. These texts are my most recent attempts to free English from syntax. They are letter-syllable-word-phrase-sentence mixes obtained by subjecting all the remarks by Henry David Thoreau about music, silence and sounds he heard that are indexed in the Dover publication of *The Journal*, edited by Bradford Torrey and Francis H. Allen (New York: Dover, 1962) to a series of *I Ching* chance operations. The personal pronoun was varied according to such operations and the phrasing which corresponds to changes of typography in the printed version." See interview with David Sylvester and Roger Smalley, chapter 16. A version of this interview appears in David Sylvester, *Interviews with American Artists* (London: Chatto, 2001), 109–29.

18. T. S. Eliot, *The Waste Land* (1922).

19. Ezra Pound's extended series of poems appearing from 1917 to 1970.

meaning structure Joyce had in mind is not known to most readers, they're reading in the same way as other work produced by chance operations.

PD Do you think they are?

JML I think in many cases they do because of the denseness of reference.

PD Could I be awkward and say that *Finnegans Wake* is based on Joyce's Irish heritage, his European connections, his play of words in many different languages, and those can mostly be fathomed?[20]

JML They can be fathomed—by the reader who comes armed with all the references and knowledge of the languages and mythology involved, but not by a reader who begins reading it simply for itself, who will get some of the things that Joyce puts in, finding his own meanings as he goes along. What is different about chance-operational work and what's called language-writing is that the writer does not determine all of the meaning. He may determine part of the meaning or none of it. With chance-operational work one makes certain decisions such as choosing *Finnegans Wake*, Hebrew scriptures, or Empson's poem "Let It Go"[21] or whatever. I have done that myself through impulse. John, because of his attraction to *Finnegans Wake*, didn't do it by a chance operation. And he was drawn to and fascinated by Thoreau.

So you get a general universe of discourse when you choose a text to process in this way. Just as during a period of my life I was very involved with the work of Pound—in some ways influenced. So when I came to do this long piece where I read through the whole *Cantos*, using the words and ends method, it was working with a poet with whom I had a very ambivalent relationship. We corresponded for ten years, from 1945 to 1955, and actually blew up over the Jewish question. I didn't push him on it because I thought it was just craziness, but somehow I decided to ask him about certain things.

PD He was in St. Elizabeth's Hospital then?[22]

JML Yes, during that period. When he said he wasn't anti-Semitic I said, "Oh good, then this couldn't possibly mean this?" I broke off the correspondence in a rage! In reading through the *Cantos* a curious thing

---

20. I was being optimistic—see attempted explanations such as William York Tindall, *A Reader's Guide to Finnegans Wake* (New York: Farrar, Straus and Giroux, 1969). See also interview with David Sylvester and Roger Smalley, chapter 16.

21. William Empson (1906–84), British poet and critic: *Collected Poems* (London: Chatto and Windus, 1955), 81.

22. During World War II Pound lived in Italy and gave radio broadcasts favorable to the fascist regime. He was arrested by the U.S. Army in 1945, held at Pisa, then transferred to Washington, D.C., and confined to a mental institution until his release in 1958.

happened. I began to write it as "Words nd Ends for Ez" and it ended up "Words nd Ends from Ez" because I got enraged during the more fascist sections![23] [*laughs*]

PD Even with the difficulties of Pound and Joyce, the reader is responding to their personality. That's what John wanted to take out of his work, and you are in the same position. Do you ever feel you have lost anything by doing that? Do you regret it?

JML No, but I think I am much more mixed. As against someone who thinks there is one right principle—something I got from Aristotle and the other Greek critics—I have consequently written both personally and with chance operations and mixed also. Practicing it for thirty years you realize how much, even if you choose a system where the whole thing is put at a remove, the choice of using a system is a personal thing. To use chance is a choice. The kind of method one uses involves one's personality. The removal of the personality has certain values. You are able to get to views of sound or language that the imposition of your taste, writing completely intuitively, would not have made possible. I have learned a great deal through doing that. I do not see anything wrong with using a number of different methods.

PD John doesn't go along with that: he made a decision about chance.

JML I've never felt there is one right way. I feel strongly that these methods are valid and good ways of working. I've always had this incorrigibly pluralistic way, which I think is typically American. As an example, William James[24] has a book on pluralism. I was at the University of Chicago from 1939 to 1943, and when I met political people—communists, Trotskyists, socialists—I could never get along with any of them.

PD What do think about John's political ideas?

JML Our political ideas are very near. He's a kind of anarchist—I'm an anarchist who votes! In the intervening years I adopted anarchism as my predominant political belief—maybe pacifism is a floor under all of them. Even so, I feel that an anarchist must deal with the short run. For a number of years I've argued with the more doctrinaire anarchists that you have to vote. It would have made a great deal of difference if we'd had someone other than Ronald Reagan in the White House![25]

PD Do you remember John's interest in Mao in the sixties? He's retreated a bit from that, when confronted.

23. Mac Low, *Representative Works: 1938–1985*, 320–25.
24. William James (1842–1910), American philosopher, elder brother of novelist Henry James: *A Pluralistic Universe* (Cambridge: Harvard University Press, 1909).
25. Ronald Reagan was president (1981–89) at the time of this interview.

JML I don't think he was a Maoist in the doctrinaire sense: he seemed fascinated by what was happening in the Cultural Revolution. I think Christian [Wolff] was more influenced than John.

PD What about the four personalities of the New York School?

JML They all seem very different people. [*laughs*]

PD Did they make an impact as a group at the time?

JML I think they rapidly came to assert themselves quite separately. I'm not conscious of them being in a school. I feel very close to Cage, and I've always liked the work of Robert Rauschenberg, Jasper Johns, and— before that—I discovered Jackson Pollock. I feel I'm not in a school of chance operations, even though I'm often identified as such. Recently, I was included in two anthologies of language-writing. I feel a method of writing is appropriate to the work at hand; I don't tend to adopt a principle as a flag. I think that to begin using chance operations at all demands such commitment that John felt it was the only way to proceed.

PD With his work in music, writing, and graphics, is Cage a major figure for chance-operation techniques in all the arts?

JM Yes. Since the early fifties I've always done all three.

PD What was it like collaborating with John on your play *The Marrying Maiden*?

JM We worked quite separately. I didn't collaborate in the making of the play, although I did write some of it while I was visiting next door to his studio. It was after the work had been accepted by the Living Theatre that Julian Beck asked if John would do the music.

Chapter Six

Minna Lederman

Interview with Anthony Cheevers, New York City, 1987

Introduction

Minna Lederman was born in 1896 and died in New York in 1995. Her parents were German-speaking Jewish immigrants who became prosperous. She studied music, dance, and drama—graduating from Barnard College in 1919—and worked as a journalist. She married Mell Daniel, a painter of the Syncronist school who eventually went into business and returned to painting in retirement.

Lederman became the publicist for the International Composers' Guild and in 1923 helped to form the League of Composers and to launch its journal, which became known as *Modern Music*. With remarkable generosity she edited the journal on a voluntary basis from 1924 to 1946. In its pages she presented American and some European composers, writing about the latest developments in serious music at a time when there was very little discussion of this kind elsewhere. When the journal ceased publication, Virgil Thomson wrote: "My own debt to her is enormous. Her magazine was a forum for all the most distinguished world figures of creation and of criticism; and the unknown bright young were given their right to speak up among these, trained to do so without stammering and without fear."[1] In 2005 Wilfrid Mellers recalled, "I'd hazard that it was the liveliest and best-written music magazine ever issued."[2]

---

1. *New York Herald Tribune,* January 12, 1947. In Virgil Thomson and John Rockwell, *A Virgil Thomson Reader* (Boston: Houghton Mifflin, 1981), 287–88.
2. Wilfrid Mellers, "Odd Men In," *Musical Times* 146, no. 1890 (Spring 2005): 111.

In 1992 Cage remembered his debt as a contributor:

If you write something and it's going to be published, you confront an editor. The implication is that the editor knows how the words should be together and that you, as an author, might not be aware (laughter) of these things. This was the position taken by. . . . Minna Lederman. She actually improved the writing of a large number of people in the field of music.[3]

In 1983 Lederman chronicled her editorial experience in an anthology[4] and recognized that the eighty-nine issues of *Modern Music* had admirably fulfilled their purpose. She also recorded her impressions of Cage on the occasion of his seventieth birthday: "I believe that his impact on our time . . . has been wide and deep—even on those who once accepted but now reject him; who out of fear of the unknown may never have faced up to him; who, furiously irritated—'he always steals the show'—wish he would fade away never to return."[5]

Anthony Cheevers has been a producer with BBC Radio 3 for over twenty years. During this time he has worked on a wide range of programs, but he has a special interest in twentieth-century music. He currently edits a variety of speech and magazine programs for the network.

Interview

By permission of Anthony Cheevers and the Minna Lederman Estate

AC When did you first become aware of John Cage?

ML I can't recall how he came to be a correspondent for me from Chicago; he apparently wrote for *Modern Music* before I met him. I assume it must have been at Virgil Thomson's suggestion. When he came to town in 1942, I came to see a great deal of him because he was such a great friend of Virgil's. When my husband and I went to visit Virgil, John would be there and when Virgil came to us, John would be coming with him.

---

3. In Joan Retallack, ed., *MUSICAGE: Cage Muses on Words Art Music* (Hanover, NH: Wesleyan University Press and University of New England Press, 1996), 146.
4. Minna Lederman, *The Life and Death of a Small Magazine (Modern Music, 1924–46)*, ISAM Monographs 18 (Brooklyn: Institute for Studies in American Music, 1983).
5. Peter Gena, Jonathan Brent, and Don Gillespie, *A John Cage Reader: In Celebration of His 70th Birthday* (New York: C. F. Peters, 1982), 151.

I saw the first concert at the Museum of Modern Art with Merce, John, and his former wife, Xenia.[6] It was percussion music, and what made it spectacular enough to catch the attention of Condé Nast Publications were the non-musical instruments in use—some kitchen utensils and carpentry.[7] I recall that John was in a tuxedo and Merce in tails—or the other way 'round. It was a very fancy, select audience and it didn't make, I thought, a great impression on musicians at the time because we had all heard Varèse with his fire sirens and Cowell with his thunder stick.[8] It seemed to us very subdued, but it made a great deal of stylish copy and brought John into prominence at once.

AC　It was a fashionable audience?

ML　Chiefly. I don't think it was aimed at that. None of the performers was so socially sophisticated as to have had such a purpose. There were plenty of musicians and music lovers present, but it did have largely a chic effect.

AC　Why was there such a fashionable audience at that concert?

ML　I don't know what really brought the whole thing about. Virgil had heard about John before he came here, partly, I think, because Max Ernst[9] and his then wife, Peggy Guggenheim, had been patrons of John's in Chicago. When John came here, he had a certain réclame from his appearances in that city.

AC　Were Henry Cowell and Varèse leading New York figures at that time?

ML　Oh no, Cowell was never a leading figure: he was an avant-garde figure. But Varèse, on the contrary, was. Varèse had, to quote John, introduced

6. February 7, 1943. The program included *First Construction in Metal*, *Imaginary Landscape No. 3*, the premiere of *Amores*, and works by Cowell, Roldan, and Ardévol. See *New York Herald Tribune* review by Paul Bowles, "Percussionists in Concert Led by John Cage (1943)," reprinted in Richard Kostelanetz, ed., *Writings about John Cage* (Ann Arbor: University of Michigan Press, 1993), 22–23. The League of Composers was founded in New York in 1923. It commissioned new works, sponsored U.S. premieres by major European modernists, and ran the journal *Modern Music*.
7. Publisher of magazines such as the *New Yorker*, *Vanity Fair*, and *Vogue*.
8. Edgard Varèse (1883–1965), who settled in New York in 1915, uses sirens in *Amériques*, *Hyperprism*, and *Ionisation*. New York premieres Lederman would probably have heard included *Hyperprism* (1923), *Intégrales* (1925), and *Ionisation* (1933). Henry Cowell (1897–1965): *String Quintet with Thundersticks (bull-roarers)* was performed at Aeolian Hall, New York, in 1925.
9. Max Ernst (1871–1976), German-born artist, representative of Dada and surrealism, who took French citizenship and lived in New York between 1941, the year of his brief marriage to patron Peggy Guggenheim (1898–1979), and 1953.

noise into music,[10] and when he was active with his International Composers' Guild he had introduced a great deal of contemporary music that was new to America, not just New York City. So his entrepreneurial skill and then his own very startling music made him a big figure—but I must say a controversial figure.

AC But how did Cage's notoriety spread?

ML Virgil was a great promoter of John in those early years. He wrote glowingly about him—his importance, his daring, and the novelty of the work. Virgil's column was the most important column not only in the city but all over the country.[11] This, it seems to me, had the greatest effect. Virgil's influence was the basic element in building up John's early reputation on this coast anyway.

AC Were your own first impressions [of Cage's music] favorable?

ML It looked very odd on stage with people in their costumes and [with their] instruments, but the sound was nothing compared to the noise released in the Varèse pieces. I wondered what was so new about it. I didn't get the shock effect that was felt in the fashion pages. But as time wore on and John began writing music for other groups and was being very seriously reviewed by Virgil, one began to take notice of the peculiarity of his work. The sound of the prepared piano and the ingenuity involved in using it began to appeal. I must say that I was led to a more serious appreciation of John's music by coming to know him personally. The effect of his temperament and very brilliant mind and the effect of his daring—I use the word *daring* rather than just courage, which lots of people have. He had that or he never would have come here without a penny to his name. I thought I must listen to the work more carefully than I had been doing since it had been produced by this particular persona.

AC Many people have said this. They may even have thought he was a charlatan, but when they met him the personality totally won them over.

ML I never, of course, took him to be a charlatan, although that was, and in many cases still is, an impression it was easy to have. I questioned the advance in the making of sound John was producing in relation to what had already been done. It wasn't until I came to understand him

---

10. Cage said Varèse "fathered-forth noise . . . into twentieth-century music." Cage, "Edgard Varèse," in *Silence: Lectures and Writings* (Middletown, CT: Wesleyan University Press, 1961), 83–84. This is such an unusual description that it must come from the poem "Pied Beauty" by Gerard Manley Hopkins (1844–89): "Glory be to God for dappled things. . . . He fathers-forth whose beauty is past change: Praise him."

11. During the period 1940–54 Virgil Thomson was chief music critic of the *New York Herald Tribune*.

better and perhaps relaxed my mind to some extent to see and to feel what this was all about.

AC   What was it exactly?

ML   There are pieces that are effective right away like *The Wonderful Widow of Eighteen Springs*.[12] But I came to feel about his larger work that the continuity in his music seemed like the flow in a Chinese landscape. This is not something you get out of Western music; at least, I couldn't relate it to anything else. I kept listening for the usual structure of Western music, but I realized it was perfectly hopeless to explore it that way since it wasn't his intention and wasn't what it was about. One had to give oneself to a new experience and find out through the music. That was the important thing—to stop looking for a connection between his music and the music one knew. If you give up that feeling about music in order to listen to him and thereby come to accept that as a form of music, then you can make that transformation. I'm not a born disciple, not even a born-again one after this immersion, but I have a response to his music now. He has my confidence.

AC   Isn't it a problem to ask a modern audience to forget tradition in order to listen to Cage?

ML   One has to bear in mind his approach to the East. He does not recognize the imitations of the East—the incorporation of Eastern tricks and turns. That isn't it. It's the spirit—and he's against harmony and counterpoint. That is where he's marked off from Western music, a specific difference he used to stress a great deal. This began right away with his studies under Schoenberg. He wasn't interested in harmony. It's something Roger [Sessions], Elliott [Carter], and Virgil can't forgive. Virgil's attitude toward John changed with the introduction of the really important thing in his musical development—the silence. John, in a recent interview, still thinks that's the most important work he's done.[13] Philosophically, it is. You can go from there to all the feelings about white on white, black on black, and the destruction of most of the structures we're accustomed to in almost everything and particularly in Western music. I think John attributes his attitude toward the East to the fact that he was born on the West Coast. It took me many decades to realize that I was very provincial about the East Coast! There is such a thing as a West Coast culture, quite different from the East. I became aware of this at the MacDowell Colony where I found hostility toward me from West Coast composers.[14]

---

12. The song for voice and closed piano (1942) with text from Joyce's *Finnegans Wake*.
13. *4'33"* (1952). See interviews with Cage, chapter 1, 41 and Tudor, chapter 4, 86.
14. Artists' colony in Peterborough, New Hampshire, founded by Marian MacDowell in 1907. See Bridget Falconer-Salkeld, *The MacDowell Colony* (Lanham, MD: Scarecrow, 2005).

AC   Some people think his ideas and writings are more influential than his music.

ML   That's a moot point. The New York critics say he's going to survive on the books he's written, the statements he's made, and not the music, and he bitterly resents that. Time will tell. The fact that he's been given the Charles Eliot Norton honor—a very great one—is a tribute a good deal to his writing, but it's also a tribute to his ideas on music.[15] The whole avant-garde of Europe was affected right away by the idea of chance—totally upsetting. But it was on musical grounds that he touched something there.

AC   So even if in twenty years' time people aren't playing John Cage, we'll be aware of his legacy in the works of others?

ML   I can't believe you won't be hearing more of Cage's music. That would be hard for me.

AC   You think there's a renaissance of interest?

ML   Oh yes. I think things will keep coming up and become public favorites. *The Wonderful Widow* and the *Sonatas and Interludes* are done often. The beautiful *Inlets*, for conch shells. The Arditti does his First String Quartet and has commissioned another.[16] These indicate greater acceptance of the music as music. Of course, it still makes a sensation if someone gets up and does *4'33"* at the piano. Nobody is going to deny that, and it always will. Important as that is, it's also a prankster's trick. That's all part of his rather extraordinary nature.

AC   You've described John as a true American evangelist. What do you mean by that?

ML   He wrote *How to Improve the World;*[17] he's constantly talking about work to be done; he's always on time, making appointments two years

---

15. Cage gave the Charles Eliot Norton Lectures at Harvard in 1988–89. They were published as *I–VI* (Cambridge: Harvard University Press, 1990), with a cassette of the fourth discussion. Paperback edition: *I–VI* (Middletown, CT: Wesleyan University Press, 1997), with CD.

16. *Four*, for string quartet (1989).

17. *Diary: How to Improve the World (You Will Only Make Matters Worse)*. Volumes I, II, and III are in *A Year from Monday: New Lectures and Writings* (Middletown, CT: Wesleyan University Press, 1967); Volumes IV, V, and VI are in *M: Writings '67–'72* (Middletown, CT: Wesleyan University Press, 1973); Volume VII is in *X: Writings '79–'82* (Middletown, CT: Wesleyan University Press, 1987). Cage recorded the whole set for the Swiss radio station SSG on June 22–24, 1991, just over a year before he died, and it was issued as eight CDs on WERGO 6231-2 286 231-2 (1992). In an interview at the time Cage explained that the title came from Chuang-Tse in China. It was the response of Chaos to one of the Winds, who wanted to improve the world. Chaos said: "Oh, you will only make matters worse."

ahead. Talk as he will about pluralism, when he's on the circuit he's planning away like the good old-fashioned Yankee tinker. He's a kind of itinerant preacher. He feels it's his function to convert people. I've seen him work on people. I like to come to things more gradually, but there's nothing very gradual about John. The difference between his explorations and most others is that he carries things right out to the extreme. In an interview he said, "You must always go to extremes—there is no other way." Another difference is chance operations. With Boulez a little chance goes a long way. With Stockhausen chance becomes part of a big heavy structure—you chain your chance. It becomes a system once you start working with the *I Ching* with a principle established.

AC   What will happen when John is no longer around?

ML   It's like any evangelist: it will be how much he accomplished. He's created a disturbance, which will remain. That's quite a thing. He wants desperately to have his music survive, believes that everything has its use and that it will all be used. I'd to like to think so too, but I don't know. He's so prolific.

Thomson remembered that Boulanger[18] taught him that composing wasn't something you do under great stress—the German idea—but as a daily function. If you're a composer you compose. This is John's point of view.

---

18. Nadia Boulanger (1887–1979), influential composition teacher based in Paris with whom many American composers, including Virgil Thomson, studied.

Part II

Colleagues and Criticism

Chapter Seven

Virgil Thomson

Interview with Peter Dickinson, Chelsea Hotel, New York City, July 1, 1987

Introduction

Virgil Thomson was born in Kansas City, Missouri, in 1896 and died in New York City in 1989. His upbringing centered on the Baptist Church and its musical heritage. He was an organist and, after a period of army training, he entered Harvard in 1919. There he began a lifetime devotion to French music, accompanied the Harvard Glee Club, encountered the music of Erik Satie and the writings of Gertrude Stein—he said they changed his life[1]— and began to compose. He spent a year in Paris studying with Nadia Boulanger; then, back at Harvard in 1923, he gave the American premiere of Satie's *Socrate*, which would influence Cage. In 1925 he returned to Paris, where he lived until 1940.

Thomson met Gertrude Stein in 1926 and immediately started setting her words to music. Their two operas, *Four Saints in Three Acts* and *Mother of Us All*, were pioneering examples of the nonnarrative musical theater developed later by Philip Glass and others. In view of the impact Stein had on Cage and some of his colleagues such as Earle Brown and the writer Jackson Mac Low, it is worth noting that Thomson said, "It was . . . the discipline of spontaneity, which I had come into contact with through reading Gertrude Stein, that made my music simple."[2] I took this parallel further, with the

---

1. Thomson, *Virgil Thomson* (New York: Alfred A. Knopf, 1966), 46.
2. John Rockwell, "A Conversation with Virgil Thomson," *Poetry in Review* (Spring-Summer 1977): 419. Also in Virgil Thomson and John Rockwell, *A Virgil Thomson Reader* (New York: Houghton Mifflin, 1981), 427–41.

composer's approval: "Thomson comes closer than any other composer to reflecting the literary techniques of Stein in music by means of the same short-circuiting from poetry to music which she herself had experienced earlier from painting to writing."[3]

During his years in Paris, Thomson began writing documentary film scores, anticipating Copland in this medium, and he perfected his own type of musical portraits actually composed in front of the sitter. On returning to New York he became highly influential as chief music critic of the *Herald Tribune* from 1940 to 1954, the period when he met and supported Cage.[4] In an obituary tribute I wrote: "Virgil Thomson was a composer and writer of originality, courage and wit formed by a unique mixture of American and French influences. . . . He came from a generation of American composers which had to find its own way without benefit of university patronage. In that kind of free market he thrived and survived—and so will the best of his music."[5]

Interview

By permission of the Virgil Thomson Trust

VT   Cage wrote to me in the late thirties when I was in Paris. He had a percussion orchestra and asked if I had any pieces or would consider writing one. I don't remember what I answered, but that was my first communication. When he came to New York in 1942 he came to see me, and we became very good friends. I was working on the *Herald Tribune* at the time, and he was invading New York, which he did by way of Chicago.[6] He

---

3. Dickinson, "Stein Satie Cummings Thomson Berners Cage: Toward a Context for the Music of Virgil Thomson," *Musical Quarterly* 72, no. 3 (1986): 409. This article began as a paper delivered in the presence of the composer at the 1982 Special Joint Meeting of the Sonneck Society (now the Society for American Music) and other organizations in Lawrence, Kansas, on April 1, 1982. On March 2, 1988, after reading the article, Thomson wrote to me: "I remember the speech at Lawrence, Kansas, and am still wildly impressed by it."
4. But Cage may have met Thomson earlier. See Thomas Hines, "Then Not Yet 'Cage,'" in Marjorie Perloff and Charles Junkerman, eds., *John Cage: Composed in America* (Chicago: University of Chicago Press, 1994), 92.
5. Dickinson, "Virgil Thomson," *Independent*, October 2, 1989.
6. Cage and his then wife, Xenia, were based in Chicago in 1940–41. In his autobiography Thomson states that in 1939 Cage wrote to him in Paris from Seattle requesting a new work for his percussion orchestra, which Thomson was too busy to provide. "Two years later, in New York, Cage phoned to ask if he could play for me the records of a broadcast just made in Chicago of works by Harrison and himself. He could indeed, I said. And here began a long musical friendship." Thomson, *Virgil Thomson*, 352–53.

was giving concerts there and then he turned up here. When he goes any-where to do what he wants to do, he always does it! He didn't have a dance troupe then as he does now, but he had a repertory of music, so he gave concerts here and got local composers to write pieces for him. I was very much taken by him and by his music. I think the New York com-posers—most of them—rather resisted the invasion. But somehow or other he managed to get the League of Composers to give him a con-cert.[7] This was in spite of Aaron Copland, who was very powerful at the league and not at all enthusiastic. But Cage always gets what he wants. I was domesticated right off, and I used to write about him and sometimes got him to review things for me. I used extra reviewers beyond the per-manent staff on my paper with all sorts of distinguished people apart from Cage—Lou Harrison, Elliott Carter, Peggy Glanville-Hicks.[8] Quite brilliant.

PD   This was the Cage of the percussion music?

VT   He started out with percussion music; that started making him known.[9] He had lived in California and was brought up there. His father came, I think, from Tennessee. Anyway, his background has plenty of Tennessee backwoods or farm memories.[10] His father was an inventor. Cage used to help his father's research in the New York Public Library to find out what was and was not patented and thus available for inven-tion.[11] I knew his parents, who lived out in New Jersey somewhere. I went there with John once or twice.

---

7.   The Museum of Modern Art concert, February 7, 1943, described by Minna Lederman in chapter 6. Aaron Copland (1900–1990) was closely associated with the league and was executive chairman in 1948–50. Later, Copland wrote: "Chance, as a creative principle, has many varied applications. It challenges the intellect, con-vinced it can produce results not otherwise obtainable. The process is amusing to contemplate; but the question remains of whether it can hold the interest of a rational mind." *The New Music 1900–1960* (New York: W. W. Norton, 1968), 181.

8.   Peggy Glanville-Hicks (1912–90), Australian critic, composer, and entrepreneur active in New York from 1942 to the early 1960s.

9.   Percussion was an essential part of early Cage. It released him from conventional sound sources, gave him the impetus to adopt or invent homemade instruments for his own group, and brought him into contact with dancers. His first percussion piece was the *Quartet* (1935) for four unspecified instruments, and his *Constructions in Metal* (1939, 1940, 1941) have become classics.

10.   These memories would have been distant. Cage's paternal grandfather married a girl from Nashville, but they lived in western states. See David Revill, *The Roaring Silence—John Cage: A Life* (London: Bloomsbury, 1992), 17–18.

11.   Cage's father, also named John Milton Cage, invented an early submarine, but, like many of his other ideas, it was not practical commercially and he went bankrupt.

He had known Cunningham when he was out in the state of Washington. Merce danced first with the Martha Graham troupe. He was already a very skilful dancer who could have had a career in musical comedy because he was a good actor and could speak lines. When Cage took him over, he decided he [Merce] was not going to be an actor but he would make a famous dancer out of him—which he did. And before very long Merce was giving recitals and had a school of his own. His chief female dancer was Carolyn Brown, the [then] wife of the composer. Cage early in the campaign had a batch of his own composers who were more or less pupils—there was Morton Feldman and Christian Wolff. I don't think Alan Hovhaness[12] was ever a pupil, but Cage liked his work and they were good friends.

PD⠀⠀What was different about these composers of the New York School?

VT⠀⠀Their concentration on percussion, or something approaching it, was what held them together.[13] Cage had had lessons in California from Schoenberg—he was no percussion composer! I don't think the lessons did much toward forming Cage, except perhaps the idea of a rigorous method.

PD⠀⠀Cage worshipped Schoenberg.

VT⠀⠀All of his students did. He was a good teacher, and his students were always very grateful. Cage's own music was closer in model to Henry Cowell. Schoenberg did not teach his students twelve-tone music; he tried to teach them harmony, if they would take that.

PD⠀⠀You welcomed Cage's percussion music and wrote about the *Sonatas and Interludes* as masterpieces.

VT⠀⠀I remember taking my aged mother to a concert with prepared piano. Her comment was, "It's pretty, but I never would have thought of doing it!"[14] We also went to an occasion where Merce and his troupe were dancing. He had made a ballet called *The Seasons* with music by Cage.[15] There was Merce, squatting on the floor and then suddenly, from the squatting position, jumping very high. My mother turned to me and said, "My, don't you wish you could do that!" She knew what was difficult and what was not! Merce had a strong theatrical presence—still

---

12. Alan Hovhaness (1911–2000), prolific American composer of Armenian descent and influences. See Cage, "The East in the West" (1946), in Richard Kostelanetz, ed., *John Cage: Writer. Previously Uncollected Pieces* (New York: Limelight Editions, 1993), 22–23, for his comments on Hovhaness.

13. Thomson may have been thinking of Cage's *Imaginary Landscape* pieces or works created on tape.

14. Thomson also tells this story in Thomson, *Virgil Thomson*, 405.

15. *The Seasons* (1947), one-act ballet commissioned by the Ballet Society.

does—and although he doesn't jump as high as he used to, all he had to do was walk across the stage and you can't see anybody else.

PD   But the prepared piano music isn't just pretty. Aren't these pieces classics?

VT   The prepared piano is more purely a percussion instrument than the normal piano because, although played from a keyboard, it does not follow the keyboard scales. By pushing and pinching the strings of the piano with little bits of rubber and metal, he manages to get different kinds of sound and related harmonics of the string he is using. The nearest resemblance to other music is the gamelan—sounds a little bit like that.

PD   There are lots of recordings of the *Sonatas and Interludes* now.

VT   Oh yes. I used to know them—some were commercial and some privately made.[16] Cage, as part of his team, had a couple of Armenian girls—the Ajemians. One was a violinist and the other a pianist.[17] The violinist was married to an employee of one of the recording companies. They pushed his music. One of them gave him a piano. I knew them and their parents because their father was a doctor with offices here in the Chelsea Hotel.[18]

PD   What was Cage's wife like?

VT   She came from Alaska. I used to call her the Eskimo, but she probably had a Russian background.[19] She made things by hand—very delicate, fragile, pretty mobiles. The idea of mobiles came from Sandy Calder.[20] Xenia used to make quite beautiful ones, not heavy metal or anything like that. She was an entertaining woman, and we always laughed together a great deal.

PD   I suppose that when his marriage broke up, Merce filled the gap personally?[21]

VT   I knew them both at the time, but I was not a confidant of either one of them. I continued to be friends with both.

PD   At that time of crisis he was going to Suzuki's classes at Columbia. Do you see the influence of Zen from then on?

---

16. George Avakian's recording of the Twenty-five Year Retrospective Concert; now on CD, Wergo WEA 0247-2.
17. Anahid Ajemian (violin) and Maro Ajemian (prepared piano) both performed in the Twenty-five Year Retrospective Concert.
18. Thomson lived at the Chelsea Hotel from 1940 until his death in 1989.
19. Xenia Andreyevna Kashevaroff Cage (1913–95)—Thomson then speculated about her origins in Alaska, which belonged to Russia until 1867.
20. Alexander Calder (1878–1976), American sculptor and painter, pioneer of kinetic art. Cage wrote music for the film *Works of Calder* (1950).
21. The Cages separated in 1945.

VT   Cage began as a modernist instrumental composer of chamber music, percussion, and prepared piano. After Merce Cunningham moved to New York, Cage—who liked rigorous ideas and influencing people to adopt them, including Feldman, Brown, and Wolff—eventually exercised his influence toward a systematic modernism on Cunningham. From that time on Cage did most of his music for him, almost as a house composer. He was very strict like that. He had models in the painting world, chiefly Mondrian or even the standard surrealists.[22] He liked a mathematical approach and knew all about square roots as the basis for the musical form of his pieces—also the whole theory and practice of the accidental approach to composition, which was also systematically based, usually on the *I Ching*. It was kind of a planned accident.

PD   Why did he say he wanted to get himself out of his music?

VT   His reasons are perfectly sensible. He wanted his music to be based on what he called the processes of nature rather than the personalized expressivity that had dominated music since Renaissance times. Of course, musical composition in medieval and late medieval times was also impersonal, but Cage's stated theory was that music took an unfortunate turn with the introduction of personal expressivity. He considered himself the chosen agent, so to speak, to lead us back to the impersonal. He would give you examples from Eastern practice, particularly Indian.[23] He even went so far as to recommend to his students that they should not study harmony and counterpoint.

PD   The theory is clearly established; one can see his point of view, but audiences don't always like it. Does it work? Is the music interesting?

VT   That's up to persons like yourself to find out because "interesting" is a personal judgment. Cage wouldn't care whether you found it interesting or not. He finds it authentic and—a word he used to use a great deal—innovative. What he means by innovation is a little obscure, but the theory behind his admiring, or even requiring of a composer, a large proportion of innovation is that he thinks all the major music of the world is innovative. That is his judgment of authenticity.

    Cage has a whole setup about his beliefs and practice with regard not only to musical but also to visual aesthetics—and even the dancing

---

22. Piet Mondrian (1872–1944). Cage often stated his admiration for the influential Dutch abstract painter who settled in New York in 1940.
23. Cage studied Indian philosophy with the singer and tabla player Gita Sarabhai and perused the writings of Ananda Coomaraswarmy in the mid-1940s, which led to his interest in the permanent emotions of Indian aesthetics. Cage, *Silence*, 127. Also David W. Patterson, "Cage and Asia: History and Sources," in David Nicholls, ed., *The Cambridge Companion to John Cage* (Cambridge: Cambridge University Press, 2002), 41–62.

business because Merce was a natural dancer with a very facile mind. Cage became a kind of conscience imposed on this other artist requiring a strict approach. You could consider Merce one of his pupils. He was easygoing, not rigid like Cage. The game is, in writing music, what is your next note? And if you choose the next note by nonsubjective methods, then you are following what he would call the ways of nature, invention, and novelty. This was practically a religion to him. He could preach it and he could persuade people to follow it.

We used to discuss these things a great deal when he first started writing for orchestra with his ballet *The Seasons*. He was a little bothered by the problem of strings because he could alter a piano with little bits of metal and rubber placed at nodal points on the strings, but the violin has the historic technique that includes many alterations, such as pizzicato or on the bridge. But the technique of string playing as it evolved classically from the seventeenth century contains almost no alteration that you can add as invention or innovation.

PD   If Cage deliberately takes his personality out of his music, what is left when it reaches an audience? Large works such as *Atlas Eclipticalis* (1962) and *Renga with Apartment House 1776* (1976) caused trouble; some players misbehaved, and people walked out.[24]

VT   They used to walk out on Schoenberg too, you know. Walking out on modern composers goes back to Wagner or even earlier. There was nothing shocking about that.

PD   But you wrote in your chapter on Cage in *American Music Since 1910* that you found Cage's music destructive and said he was pulling the whole temple down on top of himself.[25] Do you still believe that?

VT   I don't know. A great many composers, painters, and poets of the earlier part of the twentieth century seemed to be operating with destructive purposes. Once their music becomes popular and accepted, it becomes clear that they have destroyed nothing. They have simply built something else added to the repertory.

PD   In your Cage chapter you imply that his success was a public relations success.

VT   Well, a great deal of it was. He arrived with Cunningham who had a special version of modern dance.

PD   You've called Cage a dynamo. In fact, when he came to New York he was broke. People find him charming, a kind of saintly person. How did this public relations dynamo get going?

---

24. See interview with Earle Brown, chapter 10, 142.
25. Thomson, "Cage and the Collage of Noises," in *American Music Since 1910* (London: Weidenfeld and Nicolson, 1971), 81.

VT   He attached himself to a batch of modernistic painters. He used to fre-
     quent a picture gallery on Eighth Street and would give lectures there.
     He built up his explainable aesthetic with a great deal of help—not
     necessarily from the painters themselves, although he was always sur-
     rounded by them, as [much as] from their work. His ideal of a mod-
     ernist painter would not have been Picasso but Mondrian.[26]
PD   What do you think will be the final estimate . . .
VT   I don't know anything about final estimates. Everything goes into his-
     tory. It's all on the bookshelves.
PD   What I mean is that you occupied a critical vantage point for an
     extremely long time from which to observe twentieth-century music.
     In your book you seem to regret things about later Cage. Are you now
     saying he has an important place in history? Are you changing your
     mind?
VT   I don't know about changing my mind—I haven't read the book for a
     long time. What I regretted at the time were his sermons about mod-
     ern music, so to speak, and his influence on students was on the limit-
     ing side. I remember once giving a course at Trinity College, London,
     where I was guest professor back in 1968.[27] I explained to the students
     that Cage's was not music that moved forward in any way we are accus-
     tomed to in classical or romantic music, films, or plays. You could lift
     up the needle and put it down in another place on the record, and it
     would be playing the same music or something very similar. It's a static
     method of composition—nothing wrong with that. He used to justify it
     with an example from Indian music in which they would choose
     an emotion and continue that by means of their rhythmic and tonal
     procedures.

     I've always questioned, just a little bit, the entire sincerity of anybody
     who makes up a rigid method of anything. We were all brought up on
     rigid Calvinism, the rigid papal domination of the Catholic Church, or
     the Talmudic procedures of our Jewish friends. I myself am much more
     inclined toward what I called the "discipline of spontaneity," which is a
     form of accidental composition—from yourself rather than from arith-
     metical and numerical setups.

     My displeasure with Cage at the time I wrote that was because he'd
     written a book about my music and analyzed it very skillfully.[28] It was

---

26. See Cage, *Silence*, 127, where Cage himself likens his music to Mondrian.
27. Trinity College of Music, London, founded in 1872, now Trinity Laban, at the
Old Royal Naval College, Greenwich.
28. Cage and Hoover, *Virgil Thomson: His Life and Music* (New York: Thomas Yoseloff,
1959). See Tim Page and Vanessa Weeks Page, eds., *Selected Letters of Virgil Thomson*

my answer to his objecting to my music on doctrinaire grounds. I tended to believe, as practically all classically educated musicians do, that in the long run your musical instinct is your best guide to judgment rather than something external following a describable method. [It was] Cage's devotion to innovation I questioned. What the hell is innovation anyway, which he doesn't describe except in his own subjective terms? And on what grounds does he admire innovation as the highest excellence? He had managed a little bit to sneer in this book [about my music] because I had not arrived at the same conclusions he had.

PD   But you had a lot in common: you both liked Gertrude Stein, Erik Satie . . .

VT   Oh yes. We had some differences—not too happy ones—about that book and I told him so. And when it came to writing about him in my book I turned the tables on him, if you want to call it that, and he didn't like it!

PD   He doesn't like criticism, does he?

VT   Who does?

PD   But the whole thing is fascinating, isn't it?

VT   Rigidity is always fascinating. It fascinates certain types of mind. You can get everything arranged that way, and the rigidities of the modern world are to be found in the strict application to politics and sociology of *Das Kapital* of Marx[29] and the techniques of psychoanalysis as practiced by Freud[30]—not by the others. The scientific world has both the spontaneous discoveries expounded mathematically and mathematics itself, which, in the quantum theories and the relativity equations, has been both rigid and imaginative. So one can approach modernism through the extremes of spontaneity, as in Freudian analytical procedures, or the extremes of planned and preachable explanations, as in Marx, which is closer to the rigidities of Calvinist Protestantism than to the freedom of Catholic confession and repentance procedures.

(New York: Summit Books, 1988), 293, for letter to Lou Harrison (1956): "John has finished his book about my music and it is quite wonderful." But Cage was not happy about the way Thomson interfered; see Cage, *For the Birds: John Cage in Conversation with Daniel Charles* (London: Marion Boyars, 1981), 85–86. However, Thomson told Calvin Tomkins: "John and I have always been friends in a real sense, but we're also enemies. He could never understand why I wasn't as far out as he was." And Cage said, "Our friendship is basically so strong that every so often one of us makes an effort to enjoy it." In Tomkins, *The Bride and the Bachelors: The Heretical Courtship in Modern Art* (New York: Viking, 1965), 114–15.

29. Karl Marx (1818–83): *Das Kapital*, 1 (1867), remainder posthumous.

30. Sigmund Freud (1856–1939): *The Interpretation of Dreams* (1900).

So I liked Cage's work and I still do. It's a contribution to music. But his vanity in writing about my music as if it were in some way inferior to his because it lacked his devotion to method had no proper place in a book about me. I thought he was being very rigid there. This was in spite of the fact that he was personally very much taken by the memory elements in my music. He used to sit playing my *Hymn-Tune Symphony* at the piano and saying, "Oh, this is so beautiful!" It corresponded to his memories of southern childhood.[31] There is a remarkable sort of praise passage for my opera *Mother of Us All*.[32] He was much more skeptical about the rigid elements in *Four Saints*[33] because, although he had a certain respect for Gertrude as a modernist, she was far too free for his taste.

PD   We're talking about Cage as rigid when the impression given to a wide public is that anything goes.

VT   [*laughs*] Provided it has no intention!

PD   He talks of the pleasures of chaos.

VT   The necessity of chaos, I should say. Pleasure he sort of omits in his theory.

PD   But you don't find the necessities of chaos in Elliott Carter, Pierre Boulez . . .

VT   Chaos can be a hell of a lot of fun!

PD   Doesn't it get boring after a while?

VT   Well, anything does. I was a friend of Boulez from the very beginning—I was the first person to write about him. It was the Flute Sonatina when he was twenty-one.[34] Boulez, by a rigid method, followed a certain French model, which is actually that of Marcel Duchamp.[35] By a rigid application of your method you make, before

---

31. *Symphony on a Hymn-Tune* (1928). But see n. 10.

32. *Mother of Us All* (1947), Thomson's second opera with Gertrude Stein. See Cage and Hoover, *Virgil Thomson: His Life and Music*, 203.

33. *Four Saints in Three Acts* (1934), Thomson's first opera with Stein.

34. Thomson, *Virgil Thomson*, 374–75. Thomson quotes here his warning to Boulez not to be trapped by his own method. However, sources conflict about which early work of Boulez's he heard. Maurice Martenot (1898–1980) was grateful for the publicity Boulez had given to his electronic instrument the Ondes Martenot and arranged a recital at his house in Paris and invited friends. This is how Thomson heard Boulez play what must have been his Piano Sonata No. 1 in 1946 and not the Flute and Piano Sonatina, which was not played until later. See Joan Peyser, *Boulez: Composer, Conductor, Enigma* (New York: Schirmer, 1976), 53.

35. Marcel Duchamp (1887–1968) was based in Paris and later in New York, where he became a U.S. citizen in 1955. His *Nude Descending a Staircase, No. 2* created a scandal at the Armory Show in New York in 1913. He then invented ready-mades, notably

you're thirty, a half dozen unforgettable works. Your rigidity gets ahold of you, and you're incapable of arriving at forty with freedom. A bit of that applies to Cage. He doesn't have the freedom in his music writing today that he was sort of promising himself. So he's been the tail to Merce's kite—willfully.

PD   The theory is that the freedom comes from the discipline.

VT   It comes after the discipline. There is no freedom unless it's a freedom from or through discipline. Freedom is not a matter of chaos. It's an ability to create imaginative compositions in your life or in your work.

Marcel Duchamp, whom I knew extremely well, became a sort of guru of Cage's in later life. He was jealous of the artist who had free-dom—very jealous of Picasso. He could do anything he wanted to do and it would always come out. Marcel said to me once, "The trouble with Picasso was that he was sexually excited by the smell of turpentine, so he had to work every day!" Marcel was a pretty sexy guy, with women all over the place, but he was deeply excited by planned chaos. But again, as he said to me very frankly, "There was room for two cubist painters, and those spots were occupied by Picasso and Braque who were five years older than I was." So Marcel, being deeply ambitious, had to make a kind of theory of how you became an artist by not work-ing. Cage is very close to that, and I still consider it a heresy. It comes from his facile handling of rigid ideas rather than from his being a musical natural. Now, Pierre Boulez is: he has a fantastic ear. Cage does not have that ear. Pierre is stymied by his ear: it's too good. Cage is forced into arithmetic and doctrinaire ideas by his lack of that kind of musical ear. Many of the great composers in history, such as Mozart and Beethoven, have had extremely good ears.

But I like Cage and I like his music. The career has been spectacu-lar, and very probably a good deal of the music will remain.

---

the urinal signed R. Mutt exhibited in 1917; contributed to defining the Dada move-ment; and largely gave up art for chess, which he played to international standards—and later played with Cage, who first met him in 1942. Thomson may have been referring to the incident with Duchamp and his sisters that Earle Brown mentioned. See chapter 10, 141n14. Also "Marcel Duchamp: True Father of Dadaism Who Was Noted for 'Ready-mades,' " *The Times*, October 3, 1968.

Chapter Eight

Otto Luening

Interview with Peter Dickinson, New York City, July 2, 1987

Introduction

Otto Luening was born in Milwaukee in 1900 and died in New York City in 1996. His father was a graduate of the Leipzig Conservatory and later was director of the School of Music at the University of Wisconsin-Madison. In childhood he studied piano and flute and was largely self-taught until he went to the Staatliche Hochschule für Musik in Munich. In Zurich he played the flute professionally, studied with Feruccio Busoni, made his debut as a conductor, and was an actor and stage manager for James Joyce's English Players Company. Luening returned to Chicago in 1920, established himself as a conductor, and held various university posts.

His output as a composer is extremely varied, often involving amateurs or students in the community. He was a pioneer in electronic music—his first works date from 1952, and several were collaborations with Vladimir Ussachevsky. Together they established what became known as the Columbia-Princeton Electronic Music Center at Columbia University. During a remarkably active career Luening either founded or supported many leading American music organizations and received many honors. His pupils included some prominent American composers.

Interview

By permission of the Otto Luening Trust

PD   Was Cage a bolt from the blue, or is there a context for him in American music?

OL There is a certain sequence in the avant-garde and the futurist movement represented here. The first man I think of was Leo Ornstein.[1] In
1910 or 1911 he was the enfant terrible with *Wild Man's Dance* and
other pieces that were sensational at the time. Then he calmed down
and became a good piano teacher in Philadelphia but continued composing. He was an avant-gardist who didn't carry it out all his life but
moved into another area. I came across him when I went over to
Europe as a boy.

The next thing was the Dada movement in Zurich with Tristan
Tzara.[2] I ran into that when I was at the Academy in Munich, but when
America entered the war I was kicked out as an enemy alien and had
to get to Switzerland. There were many refugees there, including the
Dadaists. In that group were those who were getting away from all the
art of the past—it was a museum that had to be destroyed or they
couldn't function. Some of them went to Paris in 1919 and became the
basis of the surrealist movement. But they had a definite effect on us—
I was eighteen—and you had to take account of them. When I went
back to Chicago, Cowell appeared on the scene. He has a direct tie-in
because Cage and Lou Harrison worked with him. The Cowell world,
which I knew quite well, is an interesting link between the past and
now—a solid one.

PD Cowell was a pioneer who didn't follow all his innovations through.

OL He had an endless curiosity about music and liked to explore possibilities and go on to the next thing. He was not a traditionalist. He studied with Charles Seeger,[3] read a lot, but he lacked the European
conservatory training that Riegger,[4] Varèse, and I got.

PD Cowell may not have developed his work with playing the piano inside,
percussion music, and Oriental influences, but Cage did?

---

1. Leo Ornstein (1893–2002), Ukranian-born American composer, emigrated to
New York in 1907. *Wild Man's Dance*, piano, ca. 1913.
2. Tristan Tzara (1896–1963), Romanian poet who founded Dada with Hans Arp
and Hans Richter in Zurich in 1915. In 1920 he went to Paris and took a leading role
in a group of artists and intellectuals centered around André Breton. The movement
spread to Germany, but New York Dada, centered around Duchamp, Man Ray, and
Francis Picabia, seems to have been independent. The Dadaists' use of accident and
chance in their provocative demonstrations and performances is often regarded as a
link with the happenings Cage instigated thirty years later.
3. Charles Seeger (1886–1979), musicologist, composer, and writer; husband of
pioneering modernist composer Ruth Crawford (1901–53); father of folk musicians
Pete, Mike and Peggy Seeger.
4. Wallingford Riegger (1885–1961) studied in Germany during 1907–10 and
worked as a conductor there from 1914 to 1917.

OL   Cowell followed up *Fuguing Tunes*[5] but was more interested in new scale formations, acoustic relationships, and contrapuntal manipulations.

PD   So what does Cage owe to Cowell?

OL   At one point he studied with Schoenberg, which didn't work too well. He was too much of a heavyweight. That wasn't really Cage's line and, like many people who worked with Schoenberg, he didn't have his background to start with. I think John got the message and saw that Cowell opened doors rather than choking in the Schoenberg world.

   When Cage went to Europe and met Stockhausen, I can imagine him telling Cage that he now had everything fixed up with total serialization of all parameters; I can hear John saying he'd been working on a new system of total disorientation and disorganization! We have two schools [*laughs*]—the German ultimate control, and Cage working it out by hand and tramping through the woods picking mushrooms!

PD   What about Cage's Oriental philosophy?

OL   We had here at Columbia University the distinguished Japanese professor Suzuki. Cage, Feldman, and other downtowners from Greenwich Village used to come up here and attend his lectures. There is a history of Eastern philosophy in this country. Emerson and William James contributed. Mary Baker Eddy's book on Christian Science began with a motto from the Bhagavad-Gita, which was later removed.[6] Swarmi Vivekananda,[7] a disciple of Ramakrishna, spoke at a conference in Chicago in the 1890s and made a great impression. Such Indian influences, like the poetry of Rabindranath Tagore,[8] reached us in the twenties. I remember getting quite involved in theosophy then.

PD   What would a composer need from this non-Western philosophy?

OL   They were looking for a way out of all sorts of areas they'd been trapped in. There was a different scale system. They could shed the weight of industrial living, technological advance, and megalomania. The Asians had things that were quite different from a Mahler symphony. It gave them more of a chance instead of following on from Mahler and Schoenberg—by discarding.

---

5. Cowell's *Hymns and Fuguing Tunes* relate to the work of early American choral composers such as William Billings (1746–1800) and represent his most conservative idiom.
6. Presumably *Science and Health with Key to the Scriptures* by Mary Baker Eddy (1821–1910), American author, teacher, founder of the Church of Christ Scientist.
7. Swarmi Vivekananda (1863–1902), religious leader, represented Hinduism at the Parliament of Religions in Chicago in 1893.
8. Rabindranath Tagore (1861–1941), leading Bengali writer, teacher, painter, and composer whose poems, in translation, have attracted composers including John Alden Carpenter, Frank Bridge, and Alexander von Zemlinsky.

PD   For Cage, even discarding the personal imagination of the composer.

OL   Yes, that's another strange thing. They wanted to be emancipated from the nineteenth-century concept of the artist. To do this, you have to be on pretty good terms with Krishna or God, which is better than being on good terms with Schoenberg—you're on a higher plane! [*laughs*] Almost a religious identification—the self without the trappings of contemporary civilization, with its wars and destruction.

PD   Schoenberg emancipated the composer from pitch problems; Cage abdicated everything through chance?

OL   I think back to the Dadaists and Carl Jung in Zurich during World War I. Jung thought art was an essential way for people to live and if we didn't have that part of us come out, it would be so black and white that we couldn't stand it. We needed that action and color. There's the unconscious and the conscious thing, which means notation, playing, and getting out and communicating with people. Some composers thought they could free themselves from all that by acceptance of this new philosophy-religion. The question is whether, as they probe deeper, they won't find another discipline of a stern kind.

PD   Something an audience can't share?

OL   The audience has to share it by what they hear or see. They don't know the history of Hindu music or the Upanishad.[9] One of the reasons Cage has done so well is that he knew the value of dancing as part of this. He had a good feeling for the combination of the whole imaginative world and freed himself through that.

PD   Has he been successful with dance because applied music is less demanding than a symphony?

OL   That's it. He latched onto the dance as a more direct way of writing than a symphonic work with the whole apparatus of copying, the conductor's green room, the audience finding it different from Brahms, the reviewers. . . . Creativity can get lost. John got tired of it and saw that you can have fun and artistic experiences at this other level.

PD   Often without professional musicians too?

OL   In the Western tradition we've had a way of abandoning our amateurs, who were the great supporters of music. John got things they could handle—he wrote things for people to play.

PD   He even contributed to *Gebrauchsmusik?*

OL   He does [*laughs*]—that's a great tradition.

PD   He often uses the word *useful.*

OL   He developed a philosophy. In trying to explain himself, maybe to himself, he began writing. Some things he went through were amusing. One

---

9. Hindu Shruti scriptures dealing with meditation and philosophy.

evening Cage and I had dinner at Virgil Thomson's, and Cage wanted to know if he could improvise on the RCA synthesizer at the Columbia-Princeton studio. This was the primitive machine where you had to punch in everything before you could get a sound, and there was no possibility of improvising on it. I remember Cage getting very angry and he thought I was trying to block him—but it was impossible in 1953 or 1954.

PD   As a pioneer electronic composer yourself, what do you think of Cage's *Fontana Mix* or *Williams Mix?*

OL   I've heard them. Louis and Bebe Barron[10] were actually very early in doing electronic music. They had done some film scores and had a commercial studio. John and some of his friends got going by fooling around and doing some experiments down there.

PD   Were you at the John Cage Retrospective in Town Hall in 1958?

OL   No.

PD   But you did hear *Imaginary Landscape No. 4* for twelve radios?

OL   That I heard here at Columbia University.[11] It came on in the evening—very late—and the musicians hunted around the radio stations but they couldn't get anything. We heard a cadenza of a Mozart concerto and that was it! John resigned from the New Music Society the next day [*laughs*] because they hadn't arranged the program better. That was one of those things—orchestrating the universe, photographing outer space.

PD   In other words, you have to accept the different radio channels simultaneously regardless of what comes out?

OL   That's right—counterpoint of action![12]

---

10. Louis and Bebe Barron, sound engineers who helped Cage with equipment when he and colleagues were working on the tape piece *Williams Mix* in 1952.

11. *Imaginary Landscape No. 4* for 12 radios, 24 players, and conductor given at McMillan Theater, Columbia University, New York, on May 2, 1951.

12. Cage included Luening's *Rorschach Symphonic Sonata*—simply a one-page drawing on manuscript paper—in his anthology *Notations* (New York: Something Else, 1969).

Chapter Nine

Karlheinz Stockhausen

Interview with Peter Dickinson, Drury Lane Hotel, London, November 28, 1988

Introduction

Karlheinz Stockhausen was the leading German figure dominating the international new music scene during the period when Cage started to become known outside the United States. He was born near Cologne in 1928 and lost both his parents during World War II, when his life was seriously disrupted. In 1951 he graduated with a degree in music education from the Cologne Musikhochschule and went to the Internationale Ferienkurse für Neue Musik at Darmstadt. These courses were started by Wolfgang Steinecke in 1946 to feature the leading European modernist composers, and Darmstadt would become an important base for Stockhausen. In 1952 he went to Paris to study with Messiaen. There he met Boulez and worked at the studio for musique concrète run by Pierre Schaeffer. On returning to Cologne the following year, Stockhausen joined the Electronic Music Studio at Nordwestdeutscher Rundfunk, directed by Herbert Eimert, and he also studied phonetics and communications theory with Werner Meyer-Eppler at Bonn University. By the late 1950s Darmstadt had become the principal focus for the European avant-garde, with Stockhausen as its leading protagonist.

In 1987, looking back at his twenty-one years of teaching at Darmstadt, Stockhausen told Richard Dufallo how he had supported the American composers of the New York School: "I really fought for the invitation of Cage, Brown, Wolff, Feldman to Darmstadt. . . . I said, 'If you do not invite (for example) Cage, then I will not come again.' And, as a matter of fact, it was the only year I did not go because of this problem. After that Cage and

Tudor were invited."[1] This was in 1958 when there was a gap because Boulez cancelled. Tudor realized that Stockhausen then "surpassed Boulez as a power in Europe" and told Joan Peyser: "If the truth were known, it was Stockhausen who turned the tide. If ever a question of negation came up, Stockhausen came to our aid."[2] Richard Rodney Bennett, a pupil of Boulez, observed Cage's impact at Darmstadt: "Until then the school was serially oriented. Serial plans and charts were everywhere. Cage preached a different doctrine. It was so striking. He shook people awfully. Everyone started to think his way. His became *the* forthcoming style. Stockhausen went absolutely overboard. And almost everyone went along with Stockhausen."[3] He had also supported the inclusion of Cage and Tudor in the Donaueschingen Musiktage—apparently against the advice of Stravinsky and Boulez—and Cage helped translate Stockhausen's lectures for his first U.S. tour in 1958. In 1987 Stockhausen told Dufallo that he believed in a multiplicity of approaches to composition, an attitude that brought him into conflict with Boulez and Luigi Nono at the time. Cage had previously enjoyed his friendship with Boulez, as their published correspondence from 1949–54 shows, but it ended when Cage became totally committed to chance.[4]

Cage's visit to Darmstadt had caused a furor. Christopher Shultis claims "no other event in Darmstadt's history ever generated more controversy."[5] Cage was not asked back until 1990: he told Peyser he was "too upsetting." Cage's impact on European composers and creators in other media would continue, even if Cage had served his purpose for both Boulez and Stockhausen. However, by 1972 if not earlier, Stockhausen summed up Cage very much as he does in this interview: "A composer who draws attention to himself more by his actions than his productions. And everything is mixed up with a good measure of philosophical thinking. A phenomenon that seems so completely beyond the pale, Cage represents, in his anarchic protest against the European tradition, the final destination of its own evolution—in a musical no-man's land."[6]

---

1. "Karlheinz Stockhausen," in Richard Dufallo, *Trackings: Composers Speak with Richard Dufallo* (New York: Oxford University Press, 1989), 205.
2. Joan Peyser, *Boulez: Composer, Conductor, Enigma* (London: Cassell, 1977), 139.
3. Ibid., 140.
4. Jean-Jacques Nattiez, ed., Robert Samuels, trans., *The Boulez-Cage Correspondence* (Cambridge: Cambridge University Press, 1993).
5. Shultis, "Cage and Europe," in David Nicholls, ed., *The Cambridge Companion to John Cage* (Cambridge: Cambridge University Press, 2002), 38.
6. Karl H. Wörner, *Stockhausen: Life and Work*, introduced, trans., ed. by Bill Hopkins (London: Faber and Faber, 1973), 236.

Interview

Approved by Karlheinz Stockhausen

PD Do you remember when you first heard of Cage?

KS I heard of Cage for the first time in 1952 in Paris where I was working in the musique concrète studio and became friends with Pierre Boulez, who had been in New York with Jean-Louis Barrault and his theater company and met Cage there.[7] He said he had corresponded with Cage, and they had even performed in New York together—a piece by Boulez and, in the same concert, a piece by Cage. And a student of Cage, Christian Wolff, had made an analysis of a Boulez composition.[8] So that was the link, and Boulez talked about what a funny man he was—completely unorthodox. He talked about him more like a clown than a colleague in composition.[9] And then I went home, and in about 1954 David Tudor came to Europe and we became friends—people were talking about this brilliant pianist. Tudor had written to me. I wrote back, and I arranged a few concerts for him where he played for the first time some pieces by Cage in private houses in Cologne. When my *Gruppen* was first performed in 1958, I arranged a concert of Cage's music in the house of Ernst Brouschaud, the publisher at DuMont in Cologne. I also arranged the European premiere of Cage's *Concert for*

---

7. Pierre Boulez (1925–) was appointed musical director of the Compagnie Renaud-Barrault in 1946. But Cage first met Boulez when he went to see him in Paris in 1949.
8. Christian Wolff points out that he did not analyze anything by Boulez, but Cage required that he analyze the first movement of Webern's Chamber Symphony, op. 21. E-mail, September 20, 2005.
9. Eric Mottram interviewed Cage in London on August 17, 1972, the week after the performance of *HPSCHD* at the Round House. Mottram referred to Cage's sense of humor, saying the jokes in his lecture "Indeterminacy" made him think of Cage as "a sort of Buster Keaton of indeterminacy."
JC Yes. When David and I first came to Europe to give concerts, particularly in Germany we were thought of as clowns.
EM That didn't offend you?
JC Well, no—the clown can be seen as useful. But, on the other hand, even though I love humor, I must say that I am perfectly serious! (uproarious laughter).
    Eric Mottram, "The Pleasures of Chaos," *Spanner* 1 (November 1974): 3, private publication. The Eric Mottram Collection is at King's College, London, but this first number of *Spanner* appears to be missing. See also *Die Reihe* 5, 115; John Cage, *Silence: Lectures and Writings* (Middletown, CT: Wesleyan University Press, 1961), 260; also on Folkways Recording FT 3704 (1959).

Piano and Orchestra, played in the radio small hall in Cologne with David Tudor as soloist.[10]

PD   In 1954 Cage's *34'46.776" for a Pianist* was done at the Donaueschingen Musiktage.[11]

KS   I had nothing to do with that.[12]

PD   And it was in Cologne that David Tudor played *Water Music* at the Galerie der Spiegel in 1956?[13]

KS   I never heard that, but I arranged with David Tudor that he play my pieces—*Piano Piece XI* at the end of 1956 in New York in a concert with Cage's music. Then he played some Cage pieces in my house—in particular, several parts of *Music of Changes*.

PD   It's sometimes said that Cage's music may have affected your approach to flexible form in *Klavierstück XI*. La Monte Young remembered that you were often talking about Cage at this stage.[14]

KS   La Monte Young was unknown to me until he was in my composition course at Darmstadt in 1959—that was much later.

PD   Do you feel, though, that Cage had something interesting that you were able to pick up?

KS   Yes, he's as interesting as all the happening people in New York. I lived in New York in 1962–63, teaching in Philadelphia, and that was the time when the happenings were on almost every night—Oldenburg, Kaprow,

---

10. September 19, 1958, following the premiere at the Twenty-Five Year Retrospective Concert at Town Hall, New York, on May 15, 1958.

11. *34'46.776" for a Pianist* (1954), prepared piano. The two parts for pianists were commissioned for the Donaueschingen Musiktage and played, together with *31'57.9864"*, by Cage and Tudor on October 17, 1954. They were broadcast two days later on Nordwestdeutscher Rundfunk, Cologne. The two men gave further performances on tour in Paris, Brussels, Zurich, Milan, and London. This was Cage's third trip to Europe.

12. This is not what Stockhausen told Richard Dufallo. See n. 1.

13. On November 24, 1956, and at the Atelier Mary Bauermeister, Cologne, on June 15, 1960.

14. *Klavierstück XI* (1956), premiered by David Tudor in New York in 1957, consists of a set of fragments on a single large page. These can be played in any order, they need not all be used, and the piece ends when one fragment has been played for the third time. Stockhausen's innovation was much discussed at the time, but, in the second of his 1958 Darmstadt lectures, Cage dismisses the indeterminate aspects of *Klavierstück XI* as not removing it from "the body of European musical convention" (*Silence*, 36) and consequently as unnecessary and ineffective. However, as comparison between *Klavierstück XI* and Cage's *Music of Changes* shows, the two composers sound closer to each other than either was prepared to admit. See interview with La Monte Young, chapter 12, 156.

Jim Dine.[15] Cage seemed to be in the same spirit. He liked these unconventional forms of concert where there were a lot of toys. When his *Concert for Piano* was performed in Cologne I said, "This is a real flea market!" Almost ironically, he laughed at this reaction and said, "What a strange kind of collection you need to make music!" There was always this humoristic and clownish aspect of his music and his performances.

PD   I wonder if Cage's *Theatre Piece* affected your *Originale*?[16]

KS   I have never seen it, but I experienced happenings in New York lofts and Tudor told me what they would do. For example, Rauschenberg would come down with a parachute in a big hall in New York and perform to my *Kontakte* on roller skates in a kind of ballet he had made. That was in the air: many people did similar things.[17]

PD   Do you feel the visual and theatrical aspects of your own music owe something to all that?[18]

KS   Maybe. Because everything I have experienced in my life somehow comes out in a transformed way. But I think more, much more, from the *Ramayanas* in Bali[19] and the monastery performances of monks in Japan—in *omitzutori*,[20] for example, or the Sumo fighting in Japan, or rituals and temples in India—far more because I think these happenings in the United States were extremely dilettante. Don't forget that we had a Korean living in Cologne who called himself my student, and I found him somewhere to live nearby, Nam June Paik.[21] He was a

---

15. Claes Oldenburg (1929–); Allan Kaprow (1927–2006), whose *18 Happenings in 6 Parts* at the Reuben Gallery, New York, in 1959 reflected his studies with Cage; Jim Dine (1935–).

16. *Theatre Piece* (New York, May 7, 1960); *Originale* (Cologne, October 26, 1961).

17. Carolyn Brown, e-mail to me of July 11, 2005, confirmed that this was a ballet called *Pelican*, first given at the Pop Festival in the America-on-Wheels Roller Skating Rink, Washington, D.C., on May 9, 1963. Brown danced with Per Olaf Ultveldt and Rauschenberg, who were both on roller skates and had parachutes. She thought Rauschenberg was responsible for choreography, costumes, and music and emphasized Stockhausen's debt to Cage, Brown, and Feldman.

18. Otto Tomek, who worked with Stockhausen at Cologne, told Joan Peyser: "Cage had a tremendous influence on Stockhausen. But Stockhausen always refused to confess this. Sometimes he would say: 'One has to help Cage. He is such a big man.' Then he would be very hard: 'Let's do nothing. It's not music at all.'" Peyser, *Boulez: Composer, Conductor, Enigma,* 167.

19. Indian-derived epic used for Balinese shadow puppet theater where a sung melodic line is accompanied by chanted syllables.

20. Buddhist New Year chanting rituals dating back to the thirteenth century or beyond, which Stockhausen attended at the Temple of Nara.

21. Nam June Paik (1932–), Korean composer and video artist living in Germany. He met Stockhausen in 1957 and Cage the following year at Darmstadt. In Cologne,

clownish person, very much like Cage—they were friends—and this was before I met Cage the first time. Paik would have raw eggs in his pocket and at gallery openings, when nobody expected anything unusual, he would smash them against the wall! All the yokes would run down, and people in their tuxedos and nice dresses to look at new paintings were revolted by this attitude. Paik liked that. I used him in my theater piece *Originale*, which is more the result of our Cologne situation. We also had some happening people—a director of theater, who directed my piece, and Hans Helms the poet,[22] who made strange nonsense poetry, and Mary Bauermeister, whom I later married.[23] She was very much involved with that happening scene, and she was the first one to bring Cage with Cunningham to her painting gallery in Cologne. There were a lot of others who were far more extreme than Cage himself—there was Henry Flynt and George Brecht. These guys were even crazier that he was![24]

---

at the Atelier Mary Bauermeister, he enacted a frightening homage to Cage during which he cut off the composer's tie and started to shred his clothes (Cage, *For the Birds: John Cage in Conversation with David Charles* [London: Marion Boyars, 1981], 167). Paik's "Zen for Film" (1964–65) is a film reel consisting of 23' of leader and hence no visual images at all, other than the dust that may have collected on the film. In 1992 Cage said: "I remember being greatly entertained and preferring it really to any film I've ever seen before or after. It's one of the great films." In Joan Retallack, ed., *MUSICAGE: Cage Muses on Words Art Music* (Hanover, NH: Wesleyan University Press and University of New England Press, 1996), 135. Cage included Paik in his *Notations* (New York: Something Else, 1969). The work is entitled *Danger Music for Dick Higgins* and carries the instruction: "Creep into the VAGINA of a living WHALE." In 1982 Cage said: "*Danger Music* is pure fiction, not music, not danger, at all. That is to say, never to take place." In Richard Kostelanetz, ed., *John Cage: Writer. Previously Uncollected Pieces* (New York: Limelight Editions, 1993), 156.

22. Hans G. Helms (1932–), German writer and broadcaster who produced a documentary film on Cage for Westdeutscher Rundfunk in 1971 and acted as one of the translators for his 1958 Darmstadt lectures. Cage, *Silence*, 18–56. See Shultis, "Cage and Europe," 31–40, for details. Helms's translation of "Indeterminacy" appeared in *Die Reihe* 5, 83–120 (also, in part, in Cage, *Silence*, 260–73), but readers of the German edition of this periodical, edited by Eimert and Stockhausen, would previously have come across Cage's "To Describe the Process of Composition Used in Music for Piano 21–52," in *Die Reihe* 3 (German 1957; English 1959): 41–43 (also in *Silence*, 60–61).

23. She became Stockhausen's second wife in 1967.

24. Henry Flynt (1940–). See "Concept Art" in La Monte Young and Jackson Mac Low, eds., *An Anthology* (New York: Heiner Friedrich, 1963–70). George Brecht (1924–)—an example of his work is included in Cage, *Notations* (1969). See also Brecht, *Chance Imagery* (New York: Great Bear Pamphlet, 1966), where his "After-note" points out that he wrote the text in 1957 and only later realized the full significance

PD   It's not just the happenings in Cage that suggest comparison with your own work but perhaps the spiritual side represented by his involvement with Zen.

KS   I feel that many artists, philosophers, poets, and painters whom I know have become involved with Zen and are spiritually wonderful people, but that doesn't necessarily mean they are great artists. What I'm trying to say is that Cage is certainly spiritually a very consequent person, but for a musician it is not the same to be involved with Zen and have great sound-vision. I have always doubted his musicianship since I knew him. He has no inner vision: he doesn't hear. For me a musician begins to be a musician when he hears something nobody else hears.

PD   So what you're saying really is that Cage is more important for his ideas than for his works?

KS   Yes. He is a great talent as a graphic designer, and he knows that any kind of graphic design in the second half of the twentieth century can be interpreted in terms of sound instruction. You can transform any kind of design into a sound texture. In 1972, as head of the Studio for Electronic Music at the Westdeutscher Rundfunk in Cologne, I organized an international competition for electronic music with more than four hundred entries. There was a jury, and we decided that an American from Buffalo, James Whitman, should have the first prize.[25] It was a short piece but extremely poetic. I arranged for him to be invited to Cologne, and he came and we performed his piece. We became friends, and I said he could even become a collaborator in my studio. When I asked him how he had made his piece, he said there was a rug hanging above his bed in Buffalo with all kinds of threads in different colors. He decided to identify each color and the number of vertical and horizontal threads with timbre in a computer. His piece was the tapestry converted into sound! I said he was a very lucky man to have found something without even hearing anything! It turned out that he never composed again—maybe he didn't find another carpet

---

of Cage's work. See also Michael Nyman, *Experimental Music: Cage and Beyond* (London: Studio Vista, 1974; 2nd ed., Cambridge: Cambridge University Press, 1999), for many references to Brecht; and see Flynt, "Cage and Fluxus (1990)," in Richard Kostelanetz, ed., *Writings about John Cage* (Ann Arbor: University of Michigan Press, 1993), 279–82.

25. The dates cited do not coincide, but James Whitman's dissertation composition at Buffalo was *Dance of Shiva* (1977) for four-channel tape. It was commissioned by Westdeutscher Rundfunk, Cologne, and was based on a variety of fragments from recordings. Whitman also had a performance by the Contemporary Music Ensemble, Northwestern University, in 1979.

or any other object that suited him. As a matter of fact, we have found in the twentieth century methods of making sound agglomerations with graphic designs that don't necessarily need to be musical notation. The same is true for Xenakis,[26] though he has learned through the years to build his own kind of sound environment. He has become involved with the sound, but Cage doesn't want to.

PD Many younger composers have regarded Cage as a kind of liberator cutting them loose from European notions. Is this a good influence ultimately?

KS I have had over a thousand students in thirty-five years—twenty-one years in Darmstadt, and then seven years in Cologne at the State Conservatory; I founded courses in Cologne from 1963 to 1969 with always thirty-five to forty students in my class; many of them were highly influenced at a certain time by this unorthodox way of producing sounds—with graphic designs leading to something the composer didn't even know—and the interpreters had to interpret this in terms of sound. After having been "cut loose," as you said, they were loose and couldn't find their way back to a more musical inner sound-vision because they trusted all of a sudden the graphic designs. They thought that would bring up something interesting, and then many of them were extremely deceived and have stopped composing.[27]

PD Do you think some of them may have been impressed by Cage's standing in art and literature as well?

KS Yes: it is just a shock in the history of the European tradition that someone like him can be called a composer. This is something totally new. He would never have had a chance until the middle of the twentieth century anywhere because one always expected musicianship, a very special kind of craftsmanship—*Handwerk* in German—and imagination and skill to perform, conduct, or play. That's why newcomers like him, coming from a different direction all of a sudden, are considered "red dogs."

PD Aren't there some equivalents in avant-garde literature, such as Gertrude Stein or James Joyce's *Finnegans Wake*?

---

26. Iannis Xenakis (1922–), Romanian-born Greek composer who pioneered the use of computer and mathematical techniques in composition.

27. Franco Donatoni (1927–2000) attributes his crises as a composer to the influence of Cage. Gerard Brophy explained: "He'd been interested in Cage, and he got to the point where he tried to exclude his ego from the music he was writing to such an extent that he thought, 'Well, why write music at all?' And that was the crisis." See Ford, "A Man without Imagination: Franco Donatoni," in *Composer to Composer: Conversations about Contemporary Music* (London: Quartet Books, 1993), 117–18.

KS   I'm talking about the musician who hears and makes other people hear the unheard. That was the great tradition of the whole planet. In India it's the same, in Africa, everywhere. What is new in the Western world is that an intellectual can come and break into a different realm of spiritual activity. Like we have had Kandinsky all of a sudden writing a theater piece; Picasso wrote a play.[28] These things happen.

PD   You dedicated one region of *Hymnen* to Cage.[29]

KS   We were real friends for a while. The friendship underlying all the differences of musical concept is still there because he's a wonderful person, always very friendly, positive, and helpful. He is morally a great example for many artists.

---

28. Wassily Kandinsky (1866–1944), Russian-born painter and writer, pioneer of abstraction; Pablo Picasso (1881–1973), *Le désir attrapé par la queue* (1941).

29. This is the third region of *Hymnen* (1967), a composite work based on various national anthems. There are versions for four-track tape, instrumental ensemble, and orchestra and four-track tape, premiered by the New York Philharmonic under Stockhausen on February 25, 1971.

Chapter Ten

Earle Brown

Interview with Peter Dickinson, Rye, New York, July 1, 1987

Introduction

Earle Brown was born in Lunenberg, Massachusetts, in 1926 and died in Rye, New York, in 2002. He was one of the four principal members of the New York School of composers centered around Cage in the 1950s. He grew up playing the trumpet, largely jazz, and he studied in Boston—engineering and mathematics at Northeastern University, composition at the Schillinger School, and privately with the twelve-tone composer Roslyn Brogue-Henning. In the early 1950s, through the influence of artists such as Pollock and Calder, Brown pioneered graphic notation and open form, and, as his career developed, he was recognized as a leading avant-garde figure in both Europe and America. He worked in production and engineering for Capitol Records (1955–60) and Mainstream-Time Records (1960–73) but also lectured at Darmstadt, taught at the Peabody Conservatory in Baltimore, and held visiting posts with American universities and organizations in Germany, Switzerland, and Holland.

Brown first went to Darmstadt in 1958, before that David Tudor had played some of his earliest open-form pieces there.[1] During 1958 Cage gave his three lectures at Darmstadt, the second of which included discus-sion of works by Brown, Feldman, and Wolff. In "Indeterminacy" Cage dis-cusses Brown's *Indices* (1954) and *Four Systems* (1954) for unspecified instruments. The latter has no score but is a diagram of rectangles that can also be read upside down or sideways. Cage must also have been intrigued

---

1. For details about Darmstadt in the 1950s see "Earle Brown," in Richard Dufallo, *Trackings: Composers Speak with Richard Dufallo* (New York: Oxford University Press, 1989), 103–5.

to discover that performances could be superimposed and that there was no specified time-length.[2]

In 1985, looking back at their association, Cage thought it was his love of theater that distinguished him from Brown, Feldman, and Wolff. He said Brown's music "seemed to me, oh, more conventional, more European. He was still involved, you might say, in musical discourse (or soliloquy), whereas I seemed to be involved with theater."[3] It now seems hard to regard Brown's work as in any way European, except in the serial techniques of his earliest pieces. Further, his derivation from the New York abstract expressionists and from jazz makes him a distinctly New World phenomenon.

Interview

By permission of the Earle Brown Music Foundation

PD When did you first become aware of John Cage?

EB My first wife, Carolyn,[4] and I were in Denver, Colorado, and I had a studio for arranging and composition teaching—Schillinger[5] techniques as well as jazz and pop. Carolyn was dancing with Jane McLean, and Merce Cunningham and John came through on a tour. I had heard about John before that but had no musical information at that point. Jane's pianist had gone to New York, and he came back to Denver saying he'd met this weird composer and had been to a concert of really strange music. Merce gave master classes, which Carolyn took, and she impressed him mightily. We went to a concert of John playing his *Sonatas and Interludes* for prepared piano: that's the first music I

---

2. John Cage, *Silence: Lectures and Writings* (Middletown, CT: Wesleyan University Press, 1961), 37–38, 52.

3. In Richard Kostelanetz, ed., *Conversing with Cage* (New York: Limelight Editions, 1988), 105.

4. Carolyn (1927–) and Earle Brown met Cunningham and Cage in Denver in 1951. She then studied with Cunningham in New York and first danced with his company in 1953. She took part in the premiere of Cage's *Theatre Piece* at the Circle in the Square, New York, on March 7, 1960. Some sources cite this performance wrongly as May and not March, including Richard Dunn, ed., *John Cage* (New York: Henmar, 1962), 42. March is correct—I was there and reviewed that concert in the *Musical Courier* (May 1960, 36). Brown recalls his first meeting with Cunningham and Cage in Denver in James Klosty, *Merce Cunningham: Edited and with Photographs and an Introduction* (New York: Limelight Editions, 1986), 75–77.

5. Joseph Schillinger (1895–1943), Russian-born theorist and composer who moved to the United States in 1928. Brown studied at the Schillinger School of Music, Boston, from 1940 to 1946. See "Earle Brown," in Dufallo, *Trackings*, 103–24.

remember hearing. I was working with various notations, including the beginnings of my open-form developments. I thought the *Sonatas and Interludes* were gorgeous, but they had very little to do with what I was doing. There were a couple of parties at Jane's studio where Carolyn and I met John and Merce. I remember the very first thing I said to him was, "Do you think your music has anything to do with Anton Webern's music?" He looked at me and said, "What do you know about Webern?" Evidently, in 1951 it was very unusual for him to run into somebody in Denver who knew about Webern![6]

PD   You were ahead of John in providing notational opportunities at this stage?

EB   Yes, that's right. For one thing, I came out of jazz, so improvisation and flexible relationships among scoring, performers, and notation were very natural to me. I had done a graphic score in 1949–50 in Denver and had already been influenced by Calder's mobiles, and that was the key to what became my open-form scores.

PD   What happened to Cage around 1951—the upheaval when he wanted to get himself out of his music?

EB   I don't really know, and I've thought about it a lot. He once said to me that he came to a kind of crisis, not only in his music but also in his life.[7] He had to accept either psychoanalysis or Zen Buddhism, and he didn't believe in psychoanalysis [*laughs*] so he accepted Zen, and I think that was the whole turnaround point of his development of chance composition. I can't say that definitively, but I don't think he was joking. His earlier music up to the String Quartet shows choice, finesse, care, and detail until the acceptance of a philosophical point of view. When I first met him in Denver he was talking Zen and working on *Music of Changes*. Then he went deeply into bringing about music rather than composing it. That's what you do when you don't choose.

PD   That's the time when he was going to Suzuki's lectures.

EB   He started probably before I met him. Merce was struck with Carolyn's dancing and John was really astonished at my music, so I think there was a kind of bipartisan desire to have Carolyn dance with Merce and me work with John. We came to New York in 1952, and I started

---

6. Anton von Webern (1883–1945), Austrian composer, pupil of Schoenberg, whose works, with their fragmented aphoristic brevity, inspired both the post-Webern modernists and the avant-garde. In 1980 Cage told Joan Peyser that he would go to a Webern concert in the late 1940s "with my hair on end and sit on the edge of my seat. It was so completely different from anything I'd ever heard . . . he shook the foundation of sound as discourse in favor of sound as sound itself." In Kostelanetz, *Conversing with Cage*, 46.

7. See interview with Cage, chapter 1, 35.

immediately working on the electronic music project that we called *Project for Music on Magnetic Tape*, because we wanted to include all possible sounds.[8]

PD I don't think you wanted to take yourself out of your music. Were you under any pressure to follow Cage's views?

EB Oh no. He disagreed with me a lot. My music has a history through me being a trumpet player working with jazz combos, with a feeling of warmth toward the musicians. I believed it was possible to make scores that would allow flexibility and improvisation that would not be shoddy. John disagreed and thought you couldn't trust the musician, who would play his favorite tunes. But he'd never been in an improvisation situation, and I knew there was a stage beyond quotation that was real creative music making at an instant level.[9]

PD If you get an Ornette Coleman, but for most people . . .

EB I was very idealistic and thought I could bring it about with classical musicians, and I have. I could play you things in my own music and not tell you whether they were written or not and you won't be able to tell the difference. But I have guided rehearsals, and classical musicians react brilliantly. John didn't believe that.

PD With the advent of chance in his works from around 1950, where is his personality?

EB I think Virgil [Thomson] said that no matter how John does it, it always sounds like John Cage. Lou Harrison was asked what he thought of Cage's chance music. His reply was classic: "Personally, I'd rather chance a choice than choose a chance!" Very profound.

John chose the elements like setting up a program, which is then activated by his chance procedures. The program describes the kind of outcome you will get. At that point the musical personality became more a sociological or philosophical one, but he still chooses the potential, the statistical outcome.

PD Another way the personality is assessed is through the public relations: he's been news for a long time.

EB Yes. He's a great publicist himself—I'm not saying that in a derogatory fashion. He makes news in a certain sense of being very audacious. If he were not in music but in sociology, it probably wouldn't be quite so extraordinary. I think all the hullabaloo is because it's so shocking in

---

8. Cage describes their laborious method of working in "Edgard Varèse," *Silence*, 85.

9. Brown was consistent: "There's no real freedom in John's approach. I think that a really indeterminate situation is one where the self can enter in too. I feel you should be able to toss coins, and then decide to use a beautiful F sharp if you want to—be willing to chuck the system in other words. John won't do that." In Calvin Tomkins, *The Bride and the Bachelors: The Heretical Courtship in Modern Art* (New York: Viking, 1965), 74.

the art world that an artist does not choose to control the details, shape, and poetic aspects.

PD   He's gone so far as to say that art's day is over.

EB   He's speaking for himself. Even though I respect and admire him and look back with fondness, we did argue and he would get angry with me because I'd tend to push him on a point of view I didn't agree with. We never became unfriendly and still are good friends. We don't see each other very often because we both travel so much. Since I first met him I've gone very much my own way. One of things that brought us together—Feldman, John, and myself—was a deep interest in the other arts. I've always been tremendously influenced by visual arts and literature. But we all have very distinct personalities. We differed at the beginning and continued to differ, but we still maintained this friendship.

PD   What did it feel like to be part of what we now call the New York School in the 1950s?

EB   There were the three of us—Christian Wolff was not around much. He was at Harvard studying classics. Morty, John, and I were together nearly every evening. John and I worked on opposite sides of a long table from ten in the morning until about five in the afternoon. John and I would talk. I'd push him a bit about my interest in my kind of thing, and I'd challenge him about chance. He used to say about the tape library we were working with that any sound in the world could go into the piece. I used to argue and say I'd think about sounds that couldn't possibly go into these pieces! [*laughs*]

    In the fifties it felt like we were in this alone. John—fourteen years older than Morty and myself—already had some kind of reputation, but at that point his reputation in the standard academic world of composition in New York was very low. He was not getting invited to a lot of places like he is now. A lot of people just thought he was off his rocker!

    There was the feeling that we were doing things nobody else was doing—all three of us were on different tracks, which were compatible. Morty was never interested in chance composition or Zen; I was interested in Zen philosophy—Carolyn majored in philosophy at college—but Zen never influenced me. Most of the things I did were done for aesthetic experimental reasons to see if classical musicians could be brought into a more spontaneous world of music making. I had already written severe twelve-tone serial music, which Boulez saw and admired when he came to the United States in 1952. But I always wanted to bring about a balance between calculation and spontaneity, which is still the story of my life as a composer.

    We also felt very close to painters we admired. I was powerfully influenced by the immediacy and spontaneity of Jackson Pollock and Bill de Kooning.[10] I wanted to bring the spontaneous gesture into music, and I finally did with the open forms. We were looking for a new way of musical expression.

PD So were you New York abstract expressionists?

EB Somebody called Philip Guston[11] an "abstract impressionist," and that's certainly what Feldman is—sort of. Morty's very quiet, very gentle, slow-moving, gorgeous things were completely different from what I was doing at that time, with broad gestures and intricate weblike musical results. John was influenced by Duchamp, who did chance music in 1913;[12] Morty was influenced by Philip Guston; I was more influenced by Calder, Pollock, and de Kooning—the singular moment of the instant making of a sound-piece. We felt we were the sonic extension of potentials we inherited from James Joyce or Gertrude Stein, and I was much connected to Ives and Varèse. We were doing something that had to be done—to hell with it if nobody really pays attention at the moment!

PD There were other painters such as Rothko?[13]

EB We all had connections with Rothko, Feldman especially. In a certain sense it strikes me that Feldman's music is the music of an imagist. His music from the early fifties until now has—kind of—the same image as Rothko's paintings, working with different colors and orchestrations of a singular and single image. Whereas I want to try a lot of different things and go off in a lot of different directions. And John has stuck to composing music by chance all that time.

PD Are there any particular writers who were important?

EB To me the writings of Gertrude Stein—not so much her essays like *Composition as Explanation* or *What Are Masterpieces and Why Are There So Few of Them?* But her piece called *Tender Buttons* was one of the first things I ever set.[14] We were all caught up in James Joyce, who was like

10. Jackson Pollock (1912–56), leading figure in American abstract expressionism; Willem de Kooning (1904–1997), Dutch-born abstract expressionist painter who moved to the United States in 1926.

11. Philip Guston (1913–80), American painter, initially and finally figurative, with an abstract phase in the center of his career.

12. Marcel Duchamp and his two sisters drew the notes of the scale at random from a hat and called the resulting composition *Musical Erratum*. Cage remembered this incident in 1989 as "a fairly simple but interesting way of working." See John Cage, *I–VI* (Cambridge: Harvard University Press, 1990), 50–51. However, Duchamp stressed, "Your chance is not the same as my chance, just as your throw of the dice will rarely be the same as mine." In Tomkins, *The Bride and the Bachelors*, 33–34.

13. Mark Rothko (1903–70), Russian-born American abstract expressionist painter.

14. Stein's *Tender Buttons* (1914); Brown's *Tender Buttons* for speaker, flute, horn, and harp (1953). Stein's *Composition as Explanation* (1926) starts: "There is singularly nothing that makes a difference a difference in beginning and in the middle and in

a twentieth-century revision of the whole concept of continuity. I could make open form and John could compose by chance: one thing we shared was that anything can follow anything. In other words, you can start *Finnegans Wake* at any point and read around back to that point. What you get is a kind of circular whirl. We were the first musicians, maybe, to think of our sound worlds as an environment.

PD   You mean it's got to be circular to allow for something like the timescale of Stein's *The Making of Americans*?[15]

EB   That's exactly it. Gertrude Stein once said, "Life is not built around a beginning, a middle and an end." You'd never know when the middle is and when the end is. That influenced me in the whole concept of time. In my early notebooks I have written that the next thing to happen interestingly in music is a revision of the nature of continuity, rhetoric, and time.

PD   None of the three of you went as far as La Monte Young in his *Composition 1960* series—extreme gestures on a long timescale.

EB   I think there are aspects of that in John and Morty and in my music too. The early 1952 and 1953 *Folio* graphic works of mine really are timeless. The instructions say they can be played by any number of instruments, any kind of instruments and/or sound-producing media, for any length of time. This fractures the idea that we have to have a beginning, middle, and end. We were quite consciously convinced that the Tchaikovskian, Wagnerian, and Schoenbergian way of speaking was not necessary. We didn't need a telegraph or a message.

PD   How does this affect normal concert giving? Some of John's pieces have had a rough ride—the New York Philharmonic playing *Atlas Eclipticalis* in 1964, for instance?

EB   I was there, and my *Available Forms II* was in that concert too.

PD   What was the audience hostility like?

EB   I was critical of John and used to argue with him. Up until 1958 I think John didn't do anything that allowed the performer any latitude. He says he started doing indeterminate music with the *Concert for Piano and Orchestra.* Coming from a background of jazz and orchestral playing, I had a feeling that John was not giving enough information to the musicians to allow them to have the confidence to do what he imagined they might do. I told him they could take advantage of him tremendously—and they did. I've seen John so upset about orchestras

---

ending except that each generation has something different at which they are all looking." *What Are Masterpieces and Why Are There So Few of Them* was delivered at Oxford and Cambridge in 1936 and published in 1940.

15. Written 1906–8 but not published until 1925.

in Europe and in this country. From my point of view, the conditions he presents to the musicians are ambiguous and in a certain way some of the things he does are insulting. I've seen the musicians revolt, as they did in that performance with the New York Philharmonic.

I'll tell you why. One of the things John did in *Atlas Eclipticalis* was give the musicians clusters of notes—maybe seventeen or twenty—and say "choose any five and play them." The big mistake was his thinking, because he'd had so much experience with David Tudor, who was really a Buddha, that he was going to get eighty-five Buddhas in an orchestra. He was not dealing with what I knew to be the psychology of a group of musicians—and he didn't recognize the acoustic difference between a viola and a trombone. What happened was that Jim Tenney[16] was in front of the string section doing chance operations by manipulating potentiometers. Each player was miked with, say, five contact mikes going into one box. The rehearsal started out with the musicians being very careful and concerned. Then, after a little while they discovered that their microphone might be on or off according to a chance procedure. So the player could be playing his five notes with diligent application, then find his microphone was turned off! Over a period of time at that rehearsal, the players wondered why they were trying so hard if nobody could hear them, and they really got angry. It was naive to assume that the orchestra would go along with a philosophical idea that either you are heard or not and it doesn't make any difference! He set up a contradiction. If you're a Buddha you don't care whether your selections are heard or not, but if you're a musician . . .

PD   He's gone on doing it in other pieces such as *Cheap Imitation,* where he deliberately specifies a rehearsal schedule that would be impossible within the budget of a professional orchestra. Why does John attack the administrative structure like this? Or is he trying to convert people?

EB   I don't know if he's that conscious of trying to convert them. He really wants to change the world, but, as he said in the subtitle to his *Diary: How to Improve the World,* you will only make matters worse.[17] That's what we used to argue about. Psychologically speaking, are you making rules and regulations that are compatible with the nature of a performer? You can't be angry with them if you do not deal responsibly with their professionalism. There's a big difference between John and Morty and me in that they both play the piano, which is not an orchestral instrument. I've sat in all kinds of orchestras playing the trumpet, and when I write my scores I do it from my knowledge and

---

16. James Tenney (1934–), composer, pianist, and theorist.
17. For a list of components see the interview with Lederman, chapter 6, 107n17.

background as a performing musician, not as an idealist or a philosophical revolutionary.

PD John does want to change the world, but he's obsessed with political issues and at the same time says he likes chaos. How does all this fit together?

EB Years ago I thought John would get away from writing music. Dealing with an orchestra is such a social institution. I like to work within their terms rather than put them in a situation that gets their backs up. He promised Schoenberg he'd be a composer so he applies these things to music, whereas chance procedures could be involved with a lot of things that didn't involve eighty-five people.

PD His use of chance has also been applied to virtuoso pieces like the *Etudes Australes.*

EB And the *Freeman Etudes* for Paul Zukovsky[18]—one of the toughest pieces I ever had to sit through! But chance procedures can point to extreme virtuosity or ultimate simplicity—a piece that could be played in grade school.

PD Could one say that if sections of a composition are done by chance this can be absorbed, but if the whole thing is chance, then something is lost that is essential to communication?

EB No. I agree with John that communication is not only in the hands of the artist but also in the ear of the beholder. The mental inertia of most music-goers' mentalities stands in the way of really understanding and appreciating my music—and John's, Christian's, and Feldman's.

I think it's very difficult to integrate in a deterministic composition an area where the results are obtained by chance. Chaos is easy, but we have to realize that open-form and improvised music is not chance music. Otherwise all jazz would be chance music, and it's not true. You are making a very fast decision in improvisation. When you hear a jazz solo, the next note you hear is not by chance, it's through a whole web of procedures—history, imagination, extension, development, and taste. In my open-form pieces, when I lay out forty-eight possible sonic elements, which I have written, and the conductor can play element 33 followed by element 1, he is making a decision. I am very adamant that those things are not chance music. Chance has to have an exterior technique to eliminate the composer's and the performer's choice.

PD Would you, like Virgil Thomson, see this as very rigid?

---

18. Paul Zukovsky (1943–), American violinist and conductor. See interview with him, chapter 15, 175.

EB   John sets up these processes and is very disciplined and pure. But I think he made a miscalculation in 1957.[19] Before that, the pieces were fixed by flipping coins, which operated on a chart of possibilities. Once the chance operation with the coins indicated that this sound will go here, that sound went there and the performer played it there.

PD   What about the extreme of indeterminate spectaculars like *Musicircus,*[20] where all those independent concerts are simply assembled under one roof? Is that liberating?

EB   I don't see that as very important. I think John's most distinctive music is when he was really doing music by chance, before he allowed the performer's subjectivity or aggression to come into the piece. Once he did that, the music becomes a little anonymous. I've heard such radically different performances of *Concert for Piano and Orchestra* that they are totally unrecognizable from place to place. People think, "He's not serious about that, he just gave us this stuff and we can do anything we want with it." Whereas actually John is very pristine with his concept of how this piece should be realized.

PD   Is it at all like Stockhausen in *Aus den Sieben Tagen,* where he expects his players to fast for four days but doesn't provide a single note?[21]

EB   Well, I think that's very pretentious. [*laughs*] Before John or Karlheinz or anybody else, I had these graphic scores and there are certain ways to bring them about. There are certain things I can control and some I can't. I don't make the mistake of criticizing the musician because he is doing something I didn't prohibit him from doing. I think meditating or fasting, like a lot of John's things, has more to do with psychology or sociology. One of the last serious discussions John and I had was at the time of my *Available Forms 1* (1961), the first orchestral open-form piece. I said to John, "What you're saying is that you're not really interested in music but are writing experimental psychological and sociological works, experimenting with people's minds." And he said, "Yes, but you keep telling people what to do. You're still interested in art, aren't you?" I said, "Yes." Everything I've done is about modifications of the way music is composed, performed, and conducted from an aesthetic point of view. John is more involved with the potentials of performers' minds: whether he can get them to do what he wants them to do. His means are very inefficient—in some cases.

19. With the indeterminacy of the *Concert for Piano and Orchestra.*
20. See "About *Musicircus,*" chapter 19, 211.
21. Stockhausen, *Aus den Sieben Tagen (From the Seven Days),* Vienna: Universal Edition UE 14790, 1968. The score consists of fourteen separate pieces, with indications about the attitude the performer should adopt toward playing but no musical notation.

Chapter Eleven

Kurt Schwertsik

Interview with Peter Dickinson, BBC, London, June 17, 1987

Introduction

Kurt Schwertsik, one of Austria's leading composers, was born in Vienna in 1935[1] and studied composition and horn at the Vienna Music Academy. He became a professional horn player and in 1958 started, with Friedrich Cerha, the new music ensemble Die Reihe. In the years 1959–62 he studied with Stockhausen in Darmstadt and Cologne, but in 1965 he cofounded the Salonkonzerte "to liven up the stifling academicism of new music" and attacked aspects of the avant-garde, for which he was ostracized by Darmstadt as he moved toward Dada under the influence of Cage. Since then he has had a steady stream of international commissions and has taught at the Vienna Conservatory, the Vienna Hochschule, and in California. In 1987 he said: "I believe the function of art is to denounce seriousness. It should be fun. There's a halo of awe around modern music. You achieve more if you're *not* serious."[2] Photographs of Schwertsik in youth and maturity look remarkably like Erik Satie, whose work and philosophy he has admired for many years. His *Strenger Engel* was included in Cage's *Notations* (1969).

---

1. Schwertsik is incorrectly listed as deceased in *The New Grove Dictionary of Music and Musicians, Second Edition* (London: Macmillan, 2001), 22: 879. In a letter to me in March 2005, after being sent the text of his interview, he confirmed: "I also agreed with all my comments. Cage the Zen composer who disappears!"
2. "Serious Mischief. INTERVIEW/The Austrian composer Kurt Schwertsik once had sugar lumps thrown at him by Stockhausen. Fiona Maddocks talked to him about sweetening the taste of contemporary music." *Independent*, May 29, 1987.

Interview

Approved by Kurt Schwertsik

PD Do you remember when you first came across Cage's work?

KS It was a concert by David Tudor—I think it was 1957 in Vienna—with all the beautiful features of that time, such as a drumstick in the piano and all sorts of sounds.[3] People were flabbergasted. Tudor was very nice; we didn't speak very good English then. [*laughs*] It was the first listening experience I had with the music of Cage and, of course, Feldman and Christian Wolff too. I also saw Cage at Darmstadt where he gave three lectures, including the "Lecture on Nothing"[4] where he has those beautiful pauses. And he gave another lecture during which he lit cigarettes. Each one was somehow handled differently—smoked once, twice, not at all, or smoked to the butt. [*laughs*]

He also gave a course where he explained what he had published in the periodical *Die Reihe* about his *Music for Piano,* where you take a sheet of paper and you mark the points and the irregularities on the paper according to the number you got from the *I Ching* and then you draw the lines over these little points.[5] He said he'd tried to make this very clear in his article but there were always misunderstandings, so he wanted to demonstrate again. He started by actually doing it—throwing the pennies for the *I Ching* and everything. When he came to the line bit he said, "If somebody has questions this is a very good stage in the composition to answer them." [*laughs*] His translator was Heinz Klaus Metzger. People were very upset. I remember Ligeti[6] asking him if he would use chance operations and then select something that pleased him. He mentioned Kurt Schwitters, who used to look at the landscape through a little frame and then say, "Oh look. This is a typical Schwitters!"[7] [*laughs*] He thought Cage might have been involved

---

3. This would have been Tudor's performance of *Music of Changes* at the Internationale Gesellschaft für Neue Musik, Sektion Oesterreich, Vortragssaal der Akademie für Musik, November 30, 1956.

4. John Cage, *Silence: Lectures and Writings* (Middletown, CT: Wesleyan University Press, 1961), 109–27.

5. Cage, "To Describe the Process of Composition Used in *Music for Piano 21–52,*" *Die Reihe* 3 "Reports Analyses" (German 1957, English 1959): 41–43; also in ibid., 60–61.

6. György Ligeti (1923–), Hungarian composer who left Hungary in 1956 to work mainly in Germany and has become a major international figure in modernism. His contribution to a seminar on "The Future of Music" at Alpbach in 1961 was to say nothing but write single words, including silence, on a blackboard. He wrote his *Trois Bagatelles* for David Tudor in that year.

7. See interview with Jackson Mac Low, chapter 5, 97n15.

in an objet trouvé venture, which was not true—obviously. [*laughs*] Most people were upset that the compositional process was so easy. Cage's reaction was that in composing *Music of Changes* the method was very difficult, and so he felt the need to invent a process that was very easy. That was *Music for Piano*! [*laughs*] The beautiful thing, really, was his laugh—that was why I admired him immediately, although I didn't understand half of his English.

When he threw the *I Ching* the first number he got was a 1, and he stopped at this point and turned to the audience and said he was very happy that he got a 1 because it seemed propitious to the venture. [*laughs*] He said this was the number of luck! Somebody asked him— an important point for me—if the introduction of the *I Ching* was bringing mysticism into the compositional process. He argued that the aim of the inventors of the *I Ching* was to get mysticism out so there are no mystic elements in throwing the *I Ching*. [*laughs*]

A lot of the tension, which had built up in Darmstadt and within myself concerning the new music movement in general, was somehow cut through by his very straightforward attitude. There was no ideology in him, which is the main point for me. He had very precise views, but there was no sales talk. At that time Darmstadt was full to the brim about how you should react to something—what you should and should not think—and all this, somehow, fell away. I felt very happy at that time.

PD   You're talking about Cage as a liberator: it's not the music, it's the attitude?

KS   I think this is the main thing about him. It doesn't mean I didn't enjoy the music very much, but you have to say that the idea of Cage's music was not to be involved. That was his outspoken aim: to get the sounds to be themselves. Which is, as he once explained to an orchestra, a concept of Buddhism—that sounds are also beings, which he didn't want to restrain or force in any way. This is a very nice idea. It's hard to talk about his music because he virtually didn't want to make music— he wanted people to realize that the sounds are beings in their environments and to get an affinity for understanding them.

PD   But there are many fully notated works in Cage's earlier period that people don't know.

KS   Yes, but this was not relevant at the time of that encounter. The performances of Cage and Tudor were very specific interpretations of the signs in the scores, which had a definite aesthetic appeal. I would say the interpretation was the composition—the arrangement, so to speak—which was very characteristic and stylistically very influential. It contradicted to some degree his view that the composer shouldn't have any influence over the sounds. He worked very hard to overcome this influence by using contact microphones and having somebody else handling the sounds. Whoever did the sound never knew if it would be audible or not! [*laughs*] This was one thing; the other was the prepared piano music, which I think became important later. At that time nobody paid attention to it, but I think they're probably the most poetic works of the twentieth century—the *Sonatas and Interludes* and the *Three Dances for Two Pianos*. They're most original, with high craftsmanship in everything. I adore them.

PD I agree, but we've got to confront some things that aren't so easy. It's all very well to have open, liberating ideas, but if that means that nobody is in control and anything can happen, then the listener can find it very boring, especially at great length?

KS [*laughs*] I remember a story I was told about La Monte Young giving a performance of his work "Draw a straight line and follow it."[8] Everybody had left except Cage, who always sat on to the last second. It's his attitude toward life, I would say. What he really wants is not for people to enjoy his music—I don't think he's that sentimental or ever was—but to enable people to be aware of sounds. I think if he got people to be patient enough to listen to whatever is happening around them, it wouldn't matter to him if this was during a performance of his music or outside. He wouldn't mind if somebody stood up and went out, but he doesn't like the listener to get angry with him. There was a nice concert given by Tudor and Cage in that first year at Darmstadt. The public laughed in the usual chaotic atmosphere, but the peak was reached not in the noisy, spectacular pieces by Cage but in the very soft and almost inaudible pieces by Feldman. I think people get really riotous when they are thrown back to their own musings or stream of consciousness. This is very hard for anybody to accept—to sit there and be confronted with his own ideas.

PD Cage wants us to regard the sounds of the environment as just as interesting as music. You don't compose like that. Is it going to work, or will it be disposable along with much of the 1960s?

KS His attitude is basically a religious one. He wants to raise somebody's awareness to a level where nobody has to take care of him. In a way, I feel this asks a little too much. Consider the state of a person who goes to a concert after a day of emotional restriction. They have boring things to do at the office, maybe unfriendly reactions; and I would say that they expect to have a broadening of their emotional spectrum in a concert. Or they go to a movie to see crime or something tragic so they feel they are alive again. This is hard—you have to be in very good shape to listen to Cage! I don't think people normally are in that shape when they go to a concert. [*laughs*]

---

8. La Monte Young, *Composition 1960, No. 10*, to Bob Morris—"Draw a straight line and follow it." That instruction is the entire score.

PD Are you aware of Cage's impact on the other arts?

KS He is multimedia. Whatever he did always had a high quality. When I came into modern music I always thought of an artist as somebody like Gandhi, fighting insincerity in art and life. I think Cage has this quality. I really admire him. His attitude toward life was a model for me; his attitude toward artistic or human questions gave me the strength at the time I started to compose tonal music again; so that was it, and I thought it was a very Cageian decision.

PD Why did we need Cage in this role when there was plenty of tonal music in the pop scene and even composers who hadn't stopped writing it?

KS I think it gave us a fresh look at everything. My first personal meeting with Cage was in Venice in the summer of 1960. An American composer arranged a festival of music there; I went there with Cornelius Cardew, and we made a variation arrangement.[9] I played the French horn and he played guitar. There was a very nice scene where Cardew tried to break a string by winding it up and it didn't break. [*laughs*] Cage was, as usual, enchanted by our performance—he liked it very much—and we also performed La Monte Young's piece for chairs, tables, and benches with Cage during the night in the streets.[10] Tables and benches were standing around. Then there was a reception at Peggy Guggenheim's. I had already conducted his *Concert for Piano and*

---

9. They played *Variations I* (1958) in Musica d'oggi at the Accademia di Bella Arti, Venice on September 20, 1960. Twelve years later Cardew, now dismissing Cage on Maoist ideological grounds, wrote: "Once Kurt Schwertsik and I, overcome by Cage's 'beautiful idea' of letting sounds be sounds (and people people etc—in other words, seeing the world as a multiplicity of fragments without cohesion), decided to do a pure performance (no gimmicks) on horn and guitar, just reading the lines and dots and notating the results. It was a desert. Contrary to his 'beautiful idea,' Cage in his performances of this piece with Tudor, never let the sounds be just sounds. Their performances were full of crashes, bangs, juicy chords, radio music and speech. And musically they were right. Without the emotive sounds, the long silences that are a feature of the piece in its later stages would have been deprived of their drama and the work would have disintegrated into the driest dust—as Schwertsik and I found out by painful experience." In "John Cage: Ghost or Monster?" *The Listener*, May 4, 1972, 597, reprinted in Cornelius Cardew, *Stockhausen Serves Imperialism and Other Articles* (London: Latimer New Dimensions, 1974), 46–54. See also John Cage and Geoffrey Barnard, *Conversation without Feldman* (Darlinghurst, NSW: Black Ram Books, 1980), for their strictures on Cardew's political involvements. The interview took place at Cage's apartment in New York on November 28, 1978, when Barnard was interested in the political direction composers such as Wolff, Rzewski, and Cage were taking. See also the discussions with Cage, Wolff, and Hans G. Helms on the three-LP set *Music before Revolution*, EMI (1972), 1 C 165-28 954 Y.

10. La Monte Young, *Poem for Chairs, Tables and Benches* (1960).

Orchestra in Vienna[11] and he wanted to talk to me, but my English was not very good, which he realized. So he spoke to me in a very simple manner, asking how old I was—twenty-five—if I was married—no—whether I smoked—unfortunately, a little. Then he said that one should smoke and even admitted he got up in the middle of the night to smoke! Then he laughed his special laugh. [*laughs*]

There was also a big concert in La Fenice.[12] It was again riotous, but I was always on his side and hoped he would be funnier than the audience—and he always was. After the performance we went backstage and congratulated him, and he had one of those rubber things, which he blew up and said, "Isn't that an ugly noise?" It was the sheer joy of being there.

PD   Did you know anything about other experimental composers in American music then?

KS   I was aware of Ives to a certain extent, but my understanding of him came much later. I knew about Cowell, but it was more word of mouth than music, more about what he did than how it sounded. I knew about the background of Cage—his studies with Schoenberg and his percussion orchestra.

PD   What do you think will survive of Cage's work?

KS   The *Sonatas and Interludes* and all the prepared piano works. I think the history of music has definitely been changed. I can't go through the streets without a musical awareness of what happens. This is a very important feature in my life. I just don't think you can stage it very easily; you can't do it artificially. I always found it less interesting in concerts than in real life.

PD   Cage said he wants his work to be like the weather or the landscape.

KS   Yes—when he defines the form of a piece as certain lengths of time and a place [*laughs*] and you don't have to define the piece any further! This is a very bold statement. The most important thing is the Zen Buddhist quality, so he can give you—almost like a koan—something you have to chew on.[13] What will survive of a personality like Cage is completely beside the point. He wanted to make his impact; survival is a sentimentality he's not really interested in. [*laughs*]

---

11. November 15, 1959, with Tudor and Ensemble Die Reihe for the Internationale Gesellschaft für Neue Musik at the Mozartsaal, Vienna.

12. At the Venice Biennale on September 24, 1960, when Cage and Tudor performed *Winter Music*, *Music Walk*, and *Variations 1*.

13. A koan is a Zen problem set by a master for extended meditation toward enlightenment but to which there is no rational answer: "Some anecdote of an ancient master, or a dialogue between a master and monks, or a statement or question put forward by a teacher, all of which are used as the means for opening one's mind to the truth of Zen." Daisetz Teitaro Suzuki, *An Introduction to Zen Buddhism*, Foreword by Carl G. Jung (London: Rider, 1983), 102.

Chapter Twelve

La Monte Young

Interview with Peter Dickinson, New York City, July 2, 1987

Introduction

La Monte Young was born into a Mormon family of Swiss origins at Bern, Idaho, in 1935. He has said that one of his earliest memories was the continuous whine of the wind going through the chinks in their log cabin, which he found beautiful and mysterious. As a child he learned the guitar and saxophone and, at the Los Angeles Conservatoire, the clarinet. He played with bands during the 1950s but also studied counterpoint with Leonard Stein, who had been a colleague of Schoenberg's, and he became fascinated by Webern. But he soon carried this into his own territory and became obsessed with drones. A landmark in his development was the *Trio for Strings* (1958), later regarded as a classic of minimalism through its slow pace, long notes, and silences. This interest in the simplest materials was also reflected in concept pieces based on a single instruction such as *Composition 1960, No. 10*: "Draw a straight line and follow it."[1]

Young soon became involved with Indian music and musicians, studying seriously as a performer. His *The Well-Tuned Piano* is an extended work—over six hours—using just intonation. He was determined to "get inside a sound." Some of his activities have been multimedia, especially drawing on the beautiful light-sculptures of his wife, Marian Zazeela. In 1963 Young and Jackson Mac Low edited *An Anthology* of the American avant-garde.[2] Cage was represented by an excerpt from *45' for a Speaker* (1954).

---

1. See La Monte Young, "Lecture 1960," *Tulane Drama Review* 10, no. 2 (1965–66): 73–83.

2. Young and Mac Low, *An Anthology*, was reviewed anonymously by the *Times Literary Supplement* ("Chance and Spec," August 6, 1964, 688): "In our stage of development

As early as 1961 Cage paid tribute to him:

La Monte Young is doing something quite different from what I am doing, and it strikes me as being very important. Through the few pieces of his I've heard, I've had, actually, utterly different experiences of listening than I've had with any other music. He is able, either through the repetition of a single sound or through the continued performance of a single sound for a period like twenty minutes, to bring it about that after, say, five minutes, I discover that what I have all along been thinking was the same thing is not the same after all, but full of variety.[3]

In 1973 Cage admired Young's involvement with Indian music and added: "I'm convinced that La Monte Young is a great musician. . . . The reason I value [him] so much is that he has changed my mind; he's one of the ones who has."[4] Much later Young himself said, "Zen meditation allows ideas to come and go as they will, which corresponds to Cage's music: he and I are like opposites which help define each other."[5]

Interview

Approved by La Monte Young

PD   When did you first come across the work of John Cage?
LMY   I believe I was introduced to the work of Cage by Terry Jennings.[6] It
           was a recording of the *String Quartet*, which I love dearly, and Dennis

music gets standardized and rigidified more markedly than any of the other arts. Perhaps this is why Mr. Cage's aurally tedious works seem nonetheless to be influential. He has devised a very roundabout, highly sophisticated means of reintroducing something of the unpredictable spontaneity natural to unspoiled musicians. . . . Unfortunately his followers seem so impressed with the means as not to ask whether the object is achieved, or discredited and made ridiculous."

3. In Richard Kostelanetz, ed., *Conversing with Cage* (New York: Limelight Editions, 1988), 203. Stockhausen gave a lecture at the Institute of Contemporary Arts in London on December 2, 1965. He said he had recently played three tapes of pieces by Young to friends and that he thought he was very important. See Peter Dickinson "London Meets Stockhausen," *Music and Musicians* (February 1966): 24–25.

4. John Cage and Alan Gillmor, "Interview with John Cage," *Contact: Today's Music* 14 (Autumn 1976): 18–25.

5. Kyle Gann, "La Monte Young: Maximal Spirit," *Voice*, June 9, 1987, 70.

6. Terry Jennings (1940–81), composer and performer who met La Monte Young in Los Angeles in 1953 when they played jazz together. In 1960 Young brought Jennings to the attention of the New York avant-garde with two programs in his series of concerts given at Yoko Ono's apartment.

Johnson[7] introduced me to the *Sonatas and Interludes* for prepared piano, which I came to appreciate more later. I think it was in the summer of 1958, before I went to Berkeley; then, at Darmstadt in 1959, I was introduced to a broader perspective of John's work through David Tudor, and I heard a tape of the performance of *Concert for Piano and Orchestra* from the 1958 New York Town Hall Retrospective.

PD   What impression did these works of Cage make on you?

LMY   My *Vision* (1959) and *Poem for Chairs, Tables and Benches* (1960) show the Cage influence most directly. In *Vision* I was working with very unusual sounds played on conventional instruments, in the way David Tudor produces not at all what you'd expect to hear from a piano. In *Poem* I was taking normal chairs, tables, and benches and using them in a way that was uniquely my own in the time structure. I'm interested in long, sustained tones with independent exits and entries. In *Poem* you take a period of time determined by chance operations—that was the Cage influence—and then you determine the number and duration of events and within the events which table, chair, or bench will be used. Then these items of furniture are drawn across a good-sounding concrete floor.[8]

---

7. Dennis Johnson, composer and mathematician, who met La Monte Young at UCLA in 1957. Along with Jennings and later Terry Riley, Johnson was one of the first composers to understand and follow Young's early work with sustained tones. In 1959 Johnson produced a six-hour piano piece called *November* that anticipated Young's later magnum opus, *The Well-Tuned Piano*. For the recording of the *String Quartet in Four Parts* (1950), see interview with Frank Kermode, chapter 17, 1992n2.

8. The New York premiere of *Poem for Chairs, Tables and Benches* was given in the last of three programs at the Living Theatre on April 11, 1960. I was there and reviewed the series "The Living Theater," *Musical Courier* (June 1960): 26: "The final work—*Poem for Chairs, Tables and Benches* by La Monte Young—provided a light concluding number, with the performers outside the hall and the audience inside. It was the *reductio ad absurdum* of the new style." See also Dickinson, "The Avant-garde in New York: Spring 1960," *Musical Times* 110, no. 1408 (June 1960): 377–78. The three programs were focused around David Tudor and provided an introduction to new techniques involving live electronics, extended uses of the piano, and aspects of music theater. Tudor shared the last program with the Japanese pianist and composer Toshi Ichiyanagi, but Cage was the presiding guru and I recall his enthusiastic participation in the subversively entitled *Poem*. The first of the three programs was reviewed by Eric Salzman ("Recital Is Given by David Tudor," *New York Times*, March 29, 1960) and Paul Henry Lang ("Long-Hair Critic Reviews a Glove-Wearing Pianist," *New York Herald Tribune*, March 29, 1960, 14). Sylvano Bussotti's *Five Pieces for David Tudor*, played partly with gloves, came in for attack. Lang was totally baffled, and Salzman called it "an obvious intellectual swipe from John Cage. . . . Real sound content: almost nil."

PD   Cage welcomes the sounds of the environment; he likes noise and, like you, he likes things that go on for a long time. How important is Zen in all this?

LMY   It's very important in his work, and I also feel that John was a source of inspiration for my work. For instance, the beautiful way the sounds are sustained in the *String Quartet*. Not long, as in my work, but I found the modal character of the tonal relationships in the *String Quartet* and the fact that the tones are played without vibrato very interesting. Also, his writings were very important to me. Western musical history was reshaped through John's work, which set me thinking. In my *Trio for Strings* (1958) I feel I had already started off in my own direction and Cage's ideas gave me support—unusual sound sources in *Poem* and *Vision* and then the 1960 series of conceptual works.

PD   Cage can be seen as a pioneering American figure like Ives and Cowell. Why did he need Japanese traditions?

LMY   As the globe shrinks we find that East needs West and West needs East. This need is on a larger level than positive and negative poles, night and day. Opposites attract. The East has needed the technology of the West and the West needed spiritual reinforcement on a believable level. We were beginning to question our own religious backgrounds but found that through Oriental philosophy we were able to tie in with a much more ancient tradition. Remember that America is a very young country. We pride ourselves on our inventiveness, but we have to find our roots. European ones are extremely strong and important but comparatively young compared to the Orient. John found in Zen a philosophy that really tied in with his way of making music. In the same way, I became interested in yoga and Indian classical vocal music. Even there, John has pointed out that he and I are opposite sides of the coin—two Eastern philosophies that are different approaches. In yoga the focus is on concentration—in my case finely tuned intervals—whereas in John's work everything goes, with this Zen concept of clearing the mind.

PD   It's not quite true that everything goes, since chance procedures are applied rigidly. But when it comes to hearing Cage, can the listener prepare for it?

LMY   I think this is true in any music. In our classical repertoire people have been doing their homework for their entire lives. As soon as you get a radio or your parents bring some records into the collection, you start getting a preparation. When Terry Jennings was four he was playing Beethoven four hands with his mother at the piano; when he was twelve he was working on the *Sonatas and Interludes*; when he was thirteen he was sight-reading the B-flat clarinet [part] of the Schoenberg *Suite*, Op. 29, on an E-flat clarinet. He grew up in a situation that automatically prepared him for concerts of modern music. Sure, the average man on the street is not yet prepared to hear a John Cage concert. I've just heard a concert in South Carolina at the American Spoleto Festival where Merce Cunningham danced. I'm accustomed to the New York hard-core avant-garde audience who've heard it all—nothing fazes them—but for South Carolina this was radical!

PD   It's not just in South Carolina. Paul Zukovsky, for whom Cage wrote the *Freeman Etudes*, had a rough ride in Europe because they're really demanding to listen to. So, does the listener have to come to Cage in a Zen state of mind, ready to take whatever comes as a kind of meditation?

LMY   Absolutely. I do think the listener acquainted with Eastern philosophy, who has involved himself in certain Eastern disciplines and practices, can be in a much better state to hear Cage than somebody who hasn't. However, some Eastern practices might prepare you better than others. The master Indian vocalist Pandit Pran Nath likes Cage very much as a person and heard John do his roaring howling piece in Cologne.[9] He's an ascetic with a strict classical Indian training, but he found it quite amusing and didn't understand that this was high Western art! Being steeped in Eastern traditions can help but is not everything. One has to have an awareness of music and philosophy on a universal level to really appreciate what John is doing.

PD   Is he ahead of his time in leading us into a world music?

LMY   I do feel he's been a leader setting an example to those on the cutting edge. It's not every day you get a composer who influences another composer on the level of Stockhausen.[10] When I was in Stockhausen's seminar at Darmstadt, half the time he was talking about Cage. He used to like to give the example of a fish—he was doing his *Klavierstück XI* at that time, with the little groups on the page where you can go from one to another—and would say: "Any *Hausfrau* can do it. You take the fish, you cut it in pieces and you move them around, but it's still fish!" The class loved it, but this was really coming right out of Cage. Not only was he a long way ahead of his time, but he also had something to offer people who were already ahead of their time.

---

9. Pandit Pran Nath (1918–96), celebrated North Indian vocal master who set up the Kirana Center for Indian Classical Music in New York in 1972. His disciples included La Monte Young and Terry Riley.
10. See interview with La Monte Young and Marian Zazeela in William Duckworth, *Talking Music: Conversations with John Cage, Philip Glass, Laurie Anderson, and Five Generations of American Experimental Composers* (New York: Da Capo, 1999), 232–34.

PD   Cowell did this in his *Mosaic Quartet* in the mid-thirties.[11]

LMY   You can see a line of descent going through Ives, Ruggles, Cowell, Cage—an American tradition.

PD   How do you see the four personalities of the New York School?

LMY   Let's think of John as the philosopher, although Christian is somewhat of a philosopher also. Christian is the most radical of that group. I very much like some of his early works with only a few pitches in each piece. Morty and Earle are very different. Morton has a philosophical bent and knows the New York avant-garde painting scene extremely well but lacks the background and erudition Cage has. He and I did an interview together in an anthropological review called *Res*.[12] We talked a lot about our work and Cage's—some of the differences and interrelationships. One thing that differentiates my work from Morton's and John's is that there's a great deal more improvisation. Morton questioned whether this was composition. I said it was and that when you improvise you prepare a repertoire of licks around which you add, change, and make permutations. I have this material in my fingers, and I bring it forth . . .

PD   Which is exactly what Cage's chance operations are designed to prevent!

LMY   That's true. The chance operations try to remove the individual from the performance to bring a kind of objectivity into it so that one will discover totally new situations and sounds never before heard.

PD   Cage even said that art's day was done, but the other three wouldn't agree!

LMY   Certainly not Earle and Morty. What's interesting in contrasting Earle is that he also has a relationship with jazz musicians and grows more out of an improvisational background. I've played some Earle Brown with him conducting, and I felt the musicians were in effect improvising.

PD   In Cage's *Winter Music*, for example, you may have twelve notes and can play seven in one clef and five in the other—do you regard that as improvising?

LMY   I think it depends on the performer's approach—to what degree you predetermine how you're going to realize a particular page. Some people write it out in advance, but when I perform Cage I sometimes put the page there and do what comes to me.

PD   I don't think you're meant to!

---

11. Henry Cowell's *Mosaic String Quartet* (1935) consists of five movements that can be played in any order. The Colorado Quartet's recording on Mode 72/73 (1999) plays the movements in the order I–IV–III–II–IV–I–II–III–V. Cage knew the work: see *Silence: Lectures and Writings* (Middletown, CT: Wesleyan University Press, 1961), 71.

12. Morton Feldman and La Monte Young, "A Conversation on Composition and Improvisation," *Res* 13 (1987): 153.

LMY   That's a good point—I think you may not be!

PD   What else have you played?

LMY   I played in *Imaginary Landscape No. 4* for radios at Berkeley,[13] and I did *Music Walk*.

PD   Is Cage's work of the last twenty years of the same importance?

LMY   I've heard a good number of performances over the years, including *Cartridge Music* and a big piece at the Armory, which he said had been influenced by me in that it went on for a long time and was one big mass of sound. Then I was at the U.S. premiere of the new string quartet commissioned by the Kronos Quartet about a year ago.[14] That was very nice, but I must say that I found his work most revolutionary when I was a youngster in 1959–60 because I had never been exposed to anything like that. Afterward you begin to accept it as part of music, and I felt a responsibility to go on and discover additional parts of the universe. I'm sure that Cage's work is as important as it ever was, but the immediate impact of the philosophy and the music in the first five years was the most important period for me.

PD   That's very understandable. What about Cage as a writer and graphic artist too?

LMY   Some of his graphics are very beautiful, but I think it's as a writer that he achieves one of his highest peaks. He's one of the finest writers today in the English language, and I also feel that what he has to say philosophically about music and about cultural tradition is not only a breath of fresh air but also an inspiration for those of us who are seeking something that goes beyond our ordinary traditional training.

PD   What about the influence of Cage on younger composers?

LMY   I think it's more on the level of something that has already been absorbed into the tradition—third-, fourth-, and fifth-hand. From what I can see now, I don't think Cage is having the direct influence on young composers that he was having when I was breaking into the classical music scene in 1959–60. Everybody was talking Cage at that time. The main figures were.

    [Marian Zazeela entered the discussion briefly][15]

---

13. Ensemble conducted by Dennis Johnson, University of California, Berkeley, December 2, 1959.

14. *Thirty Pieces for String Quartet* (1983), premiered by the Kronos Quartet at Darmstadt in 1984. There is no full score, and the players sit removed from each other.

15. Marian Zazeela, married to La Monte Young, was one of the first contemporary artists to use light as a medium. Her first New York exhibition was in 1960. She has been part of his ensembles since 1962 and created the visual components of their *Dream Houses*. She has taught at the Kirana Center for Indian Music and performed with Pandit Pran Nath.

MZ   It seems to me he's performed a lot, much more than he was then.

LMY But is he influencing compositional style?

MZ   He often presents his work at universities, so I feel sure the musicians and composers are being more broadly influenced. It was more specialized to be influenced by Cage when you were. You had to go all the way to Darmstadt to get enough information.

PD   Is it necessary to have Cage himself at a performance to get the full magic?

LMY It's always preferable to have John there because he has such charisma, such a radiant personality. You have a remarkable understanding of him through the osmosis of being in his presence. Of course, the work has to stand on its own because John will die at some point. It must be able to go on without him, and I think it does. It requires an outstanding performer to bring John's work off. When David Tudor played Cage, you did not need John there to have a successful performance!

PD   Is his enormous international prestige today due to his personality rather than his music?

LMY The fact that John was a success in his own lifetime is definitely related to his personality. When I was very young and innocent I thought that all one had to do was practice and create great music to be a success. It was only over the years that I discovered how wrong I was. You can be the best in the world and die in oblivion if you don't somehow learn how to bring your music before the people. You have to learn promotion and how to meet people who can take your work into the public eye. What John had in addition to extraordinary talent was the ability to bring his music to the concert audience and his writings to the world.

PD   So, paradoxically, there's no composer, it's not art, and yet it's a success?

LMY John is playing both sides at the same time. I'm impressed by his attitude that there's enough art and he wants to take himself out of it, but you can be sure that at the same time he's doing that he's still meeting people and shaking hands and having a glass of whatever at the party in order to make the next connection. I think John has learned extremely well that you cannot live in a vacuum and you cannot be an ascetic. He still answers the telephone and still writes his letters. He's taken himself out of his art but has not taken himself out of the circuitry that makes things happen in the world today.

PD   It's what Marshall McLuhan meant when he said the medium is the message?[16]

---

16. Marshall McLuhan (1911–80), Canadian media analyst whose best-seller *Understanding Media: The Extensions of Man* (London: Sphere Books, 1964) was

LMY In our own lifetime we have seen the world change completely as a result of the electronic networking that encircles the globe. One of the reasons John and I could become so involved in the East is through records, tapes, telephone, radio—the entire media network. Debussy had to wait for the gamelan orchestra to come to Paris. Today all you have to do is walk into the music library or get on a plane and be there in no time at all.

PD Instant availability—one reason why John doesn't like records or completely repeatable pieces.

LMY Yet he still makes records, whether or not he likes them. I want to make it clear that at the same time John takes that standoffish approach in his work and says he's going to let the work exist for itself, take the creator out of it and let something new happen, he didn't go off and live in a cave. He didn't separate himself from the world. I'm sure you had no trouble reaching him: if I call him he'll pick up the telephone. He realizes that for the art to exist and do its job—that is to communicate with people—he must remain actively connected.

PD So communication today is not a matter of writing tunes but involves making all these separate media function?

LMY Absolutely. It's critical. It's what's known as PR. You have to know how to promote your work as a serious part of your life. I have often wished it were not so because I would prefer to spend all my time practicing, composing, and writing. But I have found, even when taking a few years off to study Indian classical music, that the people who thought you were important yesterday forget about you within only a month! People are always looking for something new.

PD Has Cage managed to provide something new, or is he dated?

LMY In one sense it's new—he has devised a formula through which he can always get something new on one level. But now people understand the formula and know what it can produce. Maybe they say, "When I go to a Cage concert nothing happens that is not within my expectations anymore."

PD How can you say that when chance procedures guarantee that you never know what's going to happen next?

LMY I'm not surprised anymore because a great deal still depends on the imagination of those who realize the works. They will not realize

followed by The Medium Is the Massage: An Inventory of Effects, with Quentin Flore (New York: Bantam Books, 1967). See Jonathan Miller, McLuhan (London: Fontana Modern Masters, 1970) and "Obituary. Professor Marshall McLuhan: Stimulating Writer on Modern Communication," The Times, January 2, 1981.

themselves. It's rare now for somebody with extraordinary imagination to perform John's work so that we hear it as a really new experience. The parameters tend to be very much defined—you get jumps, beeps, growls, and squeaks—and I don't feel it's happening on that level anymore. In the beginning nobody had heard anything like it. It was a brand-new introduction to music. Even Tudor and Cage have more or less stretched their imaginations to the horizon. As a result, I don't find anything shocking anymore.

PD   You're saying that the unexpected has lost its power to surprise?

LMY For me. You can still pull the man off the street who will go crazy when he hears Cage for the first time. But I've heard everything.

PD   And his works don't have the capacity to renew themselves in your experience? But if they're going to have an important position they will have to have that power—like Beethoven, Stravinsky, and Schoenberg.

LMY John has preconditioned us to look for a newness these composers did not. They gave us fully notated works where each performance would basically be the same.

PD   But it was pretty shattering when Beethoven's Fifth Symphony was first performed or the *Rite of Spring*! The audience was just as shocked as they were for the premiere of the *Concert for Piano and Orchestra*.

LMY Yes, right. I still find early Cage as beautiful as Beethoven—*The Wonderful Widow of Eighteen Springs*, the *Sonatas and Interludes*, the *String Quartet*. Cage has achieved his historical position in terms of beauty.

PD   These are Cage's masterpieces?

LMY I think people in later generations, after we are dead, will hear the indeterminate works more in the way you and I hear the *Sonatas and Interludes*.

PD   Unless John's work has succeeded in teaching them to use the sounds of the environment so that we don't need music at all?

LMY That could happen too. One often wonders. Do you think John sees his role as a teacher rather than a great artist?

PD   I do see him as a teacher and have related him to the Zen masters when the whole audience is assembled waiting for a pronouncement. They say—absolutely nothing. *4'33"*—the same gesture? Do you see him as a Buddha?

LMY Very much, but I also think John sees himself as an artist who is going to go down in history. No matter how much he has fulfilled the role of an Oriental master, I think he is also very much in the Western tradition of an artist who sees himself making his mark and whose name will be remembered.

Chapter Thirteen

John Rockwell

Interview with Peter Dickinson, New York City, July 2, 1987

Introduction

John Rockwell was born in Washington, D.C., in 1940 and was raised in San Francisco. He graduated from Harvard with a degree in German history and literature and received a PhD in cultural history from the University of California at Berkeley. After working as a classical music and dance critic for the *Oakland Tribune* and the *Los Angeles Times*, he began writing about music of all kinds in increasingly influential capacities at the *New York Times* in 1972. From 1974 to 1980 he was the chief rock music critic and then became the classical music editor. He was director of New York's Lincoln Center Festival during 1994–96 and then rejoined the *New York Times* as Sunday arts editor, later becoming an arts columnist and currently serving as chief dance critic. He is a Chevalier of the French Order of Arts and Letters. His books include *All American Music: Composition in the Late Twentieth Century* (1983) and *Sinatra: An American Classic* (1984); with Thomson he edited *A Virgil Thomson Reader* (1981); and he has written articles on a remarkable range of topics.

Interview

Approved by John Rockwell

PD   Charles Hamm has claimed that Cage has had "a greater impact on world
      music than any other American composer of the twentieth century."[1]

---

1. Hamm, "John Cage," in Stanley Sadie, ed., *The New Grove Dictionary of Music and Musicians* (London: Macmillan, 1980), 3: 597.

Your own approach in *All American Music*[2] is very broad, but would you agree?

JR   Probably, yes. My instinct is to start casting about among nonclassical composers to see if Little Richard could make that claim or Chuck Berry,[3] but I don't think they could because there were so many early rock pioneers, and then the English wave arrived in the sixties. There are those who claim Duke Ellington was America's greatest composer, but I don't think he had a decisive influence. Cage's influence as a symbol of liberation for classical composers, overlapping to some extent into the art-jazz and art-rock scenes as well, has really been enormous. Even if you regard him as a symbol rather than a direct cause of change, as a philosophical stimulus rather than a model to be copied, the influence is huge and I think Hamm's statement could be sustained.

PD   Do you see any connection with Zen in Cage's determination to remove himself from his music since about 1950?

JR   Obviously, it's directly inspired by Zen. Then the question becomes: "Has he been successful?" You could argue that on one level he has— and deleteriously to the effect of his music—and on another level he has failed profoundly, and it is that failure that has guaranteed his influence, which is primarily through his writings and personality rather than his music. There has got to be at some point, before or after his death, a counterreaction to that position which will argue, "Oh no, there are great masterpieces." I think everyone finds the prepared piano pieces very charming—appealing music that, in contrast to his stated aesthetic, reaches out to the listener and compels him. But to the extent that he removed structure, expectation, sonorous appeal, performer choice, let alone composer choice, from his music, it becomes a meditative exercise rather than a shaped piece of music. He would say that is what he's out to do, but in that case you judge him on his ability to stimulate creativity in his listeners. In other words, his pieces pose philosophical invitations to meditation. But presumably the purest follower of Cage would be one who could derive precisely the same satisfaction from listening to silence—the premise behind *4′33″*.

    I myself find most of his later work really boring. To sit through the *Etudes Boreales*, for cello and piano, is really boring.[4] One could develop

---

2. Rockwell, *All American Music: Composition in the Late Twentieth Century* (New York: Alfred A. Knopf, 1983).

3. Little Richard (1932–), blues singer, songwriter, and pianist; Chuck Berry (1926–), rock and roll singer, songwriter, and guitarist.

4. *Etudes Borealis* (1978) is one of several works based on star charts. Cage wrote: "I had become interested in writing difficult music, etudes, because of the world situation which often seems to many of us hopeless. I thought that were a musician to give

a meditative exercise and get into them that way, but one could do the
same for random noise in a room. Even though he talks about removing
all volition—his or the performer's—from his performances, that is not
really what happens. I was on a panel with Morty Feldman and Christian
Wolff where the discussion revolved around these questions. All of them
said there was a lot more compositional choice and performer choice
than the image of Cage as a non-ego would suggest. For me the impact
lies in the written work and the spoken work as transmitted by this
extraordinary charismatic, guru-like, magisterial, puckish personality.
That is why so many composers have cited him as influential. I've read
interviews with composers who cite the experience of reading *Silence* in
the early sixties as amazingly liberating for them, comparable to listening
to early phase pieces of Steve Reich,[5] Terry Riley's *In C,*[6] or *The Rite of
Spring*—seminal. With Cage it's the reading of the essays, and what that
triggered, and the permission it gave these young composers to break
free from whatever training and traditions they'd been struggling with.
PD   Several composers have confirmed this. But why did they need permission when tonal music was still alive and well?[7]
JR   "Permission" may be a charged word, but I'd stick with it—maybe "inspiration" or "psychological kinship" or a sense that someone else had gone
down that path before. Obviously, when you're young, it takes a certain
strength of character to break from the expectations of your training and
of your elders. The world of American composition was so dominated by
the academy at that time that it seemed almost automatic that if you were
going to compose you had not only to teach, go through the process of

---

the example in public of doing the impossible that it would inspire someone who was
struck by that performance to change the world." In Richard Kostelanetz, ed., *John
Cage: Writer. Previously Uncollected Pieces* (New York: Limelight Editions, 1993), 106.

5. Steve Reich (1936–), minimalist composer who first became known for the repetitive tape-loop pieces *It's Gonna Rain* (1955) and *Come Out* (1956) based on spoken
texts. Reich was interested in "a compositional process and a sounding music that are
one and the same thing." He realized that Cage's processes were not reflected in the
audible results. Steve Reich, *Writings about Music* (Halifax: Press of the Nova Scotia
College of Art and Design, 1974), 11.

6. Terry Riley (1935–), minimalist composer whose *In C* (1964) for unspecified
instruments, with parts but no score, over a regular beat, made a strong impact.

7. In the catalog to *Aspects of Conceptualism in American Work*, Avenue B Gallery, New
York, June 1987, curator Leah Durner includes Cage and wrote: "Conceptual works
operate as information systems, approximating mathematics and language through seri-
ality, measuring, numbering, random ordering and games, instructions, and scores. The
viewer of a readymade and the audience for a John Cage composition participate in
completing the work. . . . Although Cage is said to have given us all permission, this per-
missiveness is not that of a father allowing his children to play, but of a fellow playmate."

getting a degree and a job, but you had to submit yourself to this quasi-medieval hierarchical structure that prevails at universities. You move through these various stages and have to conform, outwardly at least, to the wishes of your superiors. By the time you have reached the full status of glory—tenure and a full professorship—it may be too late to assert your own individuality. An alternative would be, if you are in your early twenties and you suddenly read a book which suggests that it's all right to be a composer and not be an academician; to work for a dance company; to present your own programs; and—more to the point—to throw aside orthodoxy. This would apply equally well if, in 1962, you were a student at some midwestern university where an old American symphonist working entirely in the tonal tradition had provided your models and your expectations or if you were a hard-core serialist coming out of Princeton or Columbia. Whatever the orthodoxy, you could feel that there were people who thought as you did. It's like being a provincial and reading about the excitements of being in a bohemian, gay, or hippie community in a big city. That's what I meant by "permission."

PD   Isn't there a similar pattern to Cage's rejections in painting and literature?

JR   Or parallel. It is one of my theories that vanguard art is at its most vital when it appeals across the board to artists outside the immediate discipline of that art. You have exciting painting if the poets and musicians like it too, and you have exciting music if the poets, painters, and dancers like it. Too much American music, especially at the time when Cage was coming into his own, was locked down into a kind of specialist mind-set, which made it impossible for other artists to like it, let alone the layman. Cage represented, by his career as well as his philosophical presuppositions, which obviously applied to many different arts, a real alternative to that.

PD   You could compare Cage's situation with that of Debussy and Satie in Paris around 1900 where they found painters and writers much more congenial than other composers because they had fewer preconceptions.

JR   That is true, as an extension of what I was saying—that art was vital if it appealed to other artists. What you're saying, and I agree, is that experimental art is often misunderstood by the more conservative practitioners within the art and finds a readier audience outside that immediate field. You could use Berlioz as an example of that too, since he had many friends in the artistic community but was misunderstood by the conservatory musicians in Paris.

PD   In the end, doesn't the composer have to come to terms with some aspects of the musical profession as it is? A paying audience has to stomach what Cage does!

JR   That's Cage's genius—he's not a wandering Zen priest, he is a very, very successful careerist. I don't put him down for that; that's the American way. He's played the grants game, the in-residence game, the birthday honorific game, the recordings game—all very brilliantly. Although his impact has certainly been worldwide—if you wish, as a kind of Orientalized second half of the twentieth century extension of the *épater le bourgoisie* experiments of the futurists, the Dadaists, and all of them— he strikes a particularly sympathetic chord with Americans, or a particular kind of American. As Emerson realized, some American artists look to Europe and regard America as a rough and crude place. Fulfillment comes with making American art as good as, and on the model of, European high-art traditions. There is another strain that either picks up on the vernacular tradition or just consists of cranky maverick outsiders who don't particularly go for any established school. Ives has been the obvious prototype of that, but others such as Billings and Heinrich preceded him.[8] Cage speaks to those people, and the success of his speech is attested to by the complete kaleidoscopic diversity of people who have written music supposedly inspired by him. If people talk about followers of Steve Reich, of which John Adams[9] is the most obvious example, their music sounds like Reich, so it seems an obvious emulation. What does Cage's music sound like? Glass[10] is one of those who claims to have been profoundly influenced in the early sixties by reading *Silence*. But there's nothing in Glass's music that sounds like Cage.

PD   Perhaps he gets his regular rhythms from works like the *Three Dances for Two Prepared Pianos?*

JR   That's absolutely true, but what I meant by Cage was the mature work, which fulfills his philosophical precepts. People felt free to "do their own thing," in the argot of the sixties, upon reading *Silence* and other works of Cage—and that could be very different from other disciples and from Cage.

PD   If the prepared piano music is a kind of chinoiserie, then the music after 1951 has got the Oriental thought built into the mechanisms designed to produce a piece of music.

JR   That's true, and you could argue that some of Reich's early music is too obviously indebted to African drumming or to gamelan but that later on he attained a kind of organic quality in his Oriental inspirations too.

PD   So is Cage, with his West Coast background, ahead of his time in anticipating the way a mix of cultures is taking place?

---

8. William Billings (1746–1800), Boston composer and singing teacher who worked as a tanner; Anthony Philip Heinrich (1781–1861), German-Bohemian immigrant known as "the Beethoven of America." Both featured in Michael Broyles, *Mavericks and Other Traditions in American Music* (New Haven: Yale University Press, 2004).
9. John Adams (1947–), currently the most prominent serious American composer.
10. Philip Glass (1937–), the most commercially successful of the early minimalists.

JR   I think that's right. I speak as someone who comes from California and shares an allegiance with that West Coast sensibility. The world is coming together, and Americans looked back to Europe for a long time; to some extent they looked down to Latin America, especially during the twenties and thirties; then they began looking more and more to the West, also known as the East, the Orient. I don't know how pathbreaking it was for Cage to course around the world looking for new ethnic inspirations, but the West Coast is oriented, as Roger Reynolds[11] liked to say, toward the Pacific Rim. There's Lou Harrison, Colin McPhee,[12] Mantle Hood at the UCLA Enthomusicological Institute and Henry Cowell. Cage definitely came out of that syndrome and represents something that is endemic to the West Coast and California. On the other hand, Ives and Ruggles represent a similar kind of New England variant of that cranky sensibility. Moving outside music and away from the Oriental influence, the school of southern writers is also an example of a strong regional sensibility that breaks away from the dominant Northeast—William Faulkner, Truman Capote, Carson McCullers, even Tom Wolfe. I think Cage does represent a vital regional sensibility in America, part of a wider tradition.

PD   At the end of his chapter on Cage in *American Music Since 1910*, Virgil Thomson says: "Cage's aim with music, like Samson's in the pagan temple, has long been clearly destructive."[13] He treats the B Minor Mass as on a par with the noise in the street. Is the medium really the message? Is the mélange what matters rather than highly wrought individual components, as in the past?

JR   A good question. I myself, and most people who were inspired by Cage, don't go as far as he does. You can't very well provide scientific proof of standards. I can't prove to you that *Così* is better than *Phantom of the Opera*, but I believe it to be and I'm not going to be argued out of it by a Zen logical chain! To place the stress of the artistic experience a little bit back in the perceiver's court and to use arguments of that sort to break down ossified traditions, categories, and ways of doing things on the compositional side is only healthy. I think that has been Cage's impact, whether or not that was his intention. I'm not cosmic enough to think that we're all going to be like Stockhausen or Cage, sitting in a circle humming the primordial Om together, and that will be art, culture, and civilization. I don't believe it to be true, but his impact has been beneficial.

---

11. Roger Reynolds (1934–), West Coast composer who published interviews with Cage in 1962 and 1979.
12. Colin McPhee (1901–64), Canadian-born American composer, authority on Balinese music.
13. Thomson, *American Music Since 1910* (London: Weidenfeld and Nicolson, 1971), 81.

PD I said to Cage that it was all very well to make assumptions about discipline in the listener, but these are based on him or somebody very sympathetic, a superior kind of listener.[14] Cage seems to demand an ability the ordinary listener will never possess.[15]

JR Also, Cage's freedom only removes him one step from the decision-making process. Yes, the dice tell him where to place the star maps, but he makes the rules. He picks the star maps, he throws the dice, he decides you do it in a certain way, and he has rather rigid instructions for the performers to be followed in almost dictatorial fashion. Where he loosens things and where he keeps the clamps on are idiosyncratically arrived at. A Cage piece is by no means a free-for-all—just going in there in a higher state of consciousness doing your thing is not a Cage score. It may be a La Monte Young score from the early sixties. Cage has a certain window through which he allows chance to operate, but after that the rules are as tight as Toscanini perceived scores to be.[16]

PD Virgil Thomson was saying John was very rigid.

JR I think that's true, and he's also a little thin-skinned when it comes to criticism. Even that does not invalidate him but makes it even more wonderful that he would perhaps secretly perceive his own weaknesses and then evolve a philosophy designed to overcome them—even if he failed. I think it's interesting that Virgil is now moving to the other position of trying to eradicate the bad taste left by his attack on Cage in *American Music Since 1910*. On the other hand, how much of that change of heart is an intellectual position reconsidered and how much of it is a personal thing where he feels uncomfortable having enmity exist in the world? I think it was a little odd for Virgil to make that attack, to describe Cage as destructive. On the one hand, of course he was—and deliberately so. He is out there with a sledgehammer trying to break down what he perceives to be useless and actively unhelpful conditions in society. On the other hand, I think the position of absolute anarchy as espoused in the writing is not one that's going to hold water.

PD I'd like to come back to Cage requiring a special kind of disciplined listener—how can this happen?

---

14. See interview with Cage, chapter 1, 46.

15. Christian Wolff commented: "You often bring up the question of the 'ordinary concertgoer.' I'm not sure this is a viable category—is there such a creature? Would she, for instance, respond readily to a late Beethoven string quartet or the *Art of Fugue* or Ockeghem—not to mention, say, Schoenberg, Varèse, or Kurtag—any more than to one of John's number pieces? There's quite a lot of fairly specialized music out there, with its small audience, and John, along with a number of other wonderful composers, is part of that." E-mail, September 20, 2005.

16. See Rockwell, "Cage Merely an Inventor? Not a Chance," *New York Times*, August 23, 1992, B21.

JR Cage was speaking of a spiritual revolution in which the entire world, not just a professional cadre of musicians, will rise in consciousness and then create an art that will best respond to its new and higher needs and sensibilities.

PD We won't need separate composers because the composers, performers, and the audience are the same?

JR One comes back to that ancient saw, which Cage quotes, that in Bali we don't need artists because everyone is an artist. Bali, from Colin McPhee onward, became Gaugin's Tahiti for the experimental composers of the mid-twentieth century. In other words, it was the Garden of Eden paradise in which everybody floated together in a state of higher consciousness and everybody made and perceived art.

PD This is the flower power of the sixties. We know it's not going to work. We've admired Beethoven and Stravinsky because they were Beethoven and Stravinsky. Why are we led to agree with John Cage?

JR Who is "we"? Are we quite sure it doesn't work? As an ideal statement of position it never could assert itself, but as a hope for mankind or as a metaphor for possible betterment of social conditions? I agree with you that great individuals working on their own and creating influential and powerful work remains the way that art progresses. That, in my taste, is exactly what Cage has done—against his own philosophy perhaps. His influence is as a powerful personality who produced work—his writings—that had an enormous impact. He was inconsistent.

PD His inconsistency makes him consistent in terms of Zen opposites?

JR Maybe, but Oriental guru-disciple literature from ancient traditions through Gurdjieff[17] is full of deliberately paradoxical statements by the master and outrageous pretenses that aren't really meant to be taken seriously by the true disciples. Maybe Cage is operating on that principle. What I'm saying is that I don't take him really seriously as a composer or as a philosopher. He doesn't stand up with the great religious leaders or philosophical speculators of our time, but he's made his impact as a remarkable influence on other composers.

PD When the Buddhist masters come to address everybody to say something momentous, all the audience is in a state of anticipation, and they say—nothing!

JR That may be Cage; the Buddhist audience may be everybody else. Maybe the Buddhist audience comes away from the masters' nothingness with a higher state of mind, and maybe so have younger composers.

---

17. George Ivanovitch Gurdjieff (1866?–1949), religious philosopher and writer born in Russian Armenia but active in Europe and America, with societies devoted to his work in various parts of the world.

Chapter Fourteen

Pauline Oliveros

Interview with Peter Dickinson, New York City, June 30, 1987

Introduction

Pauline Oliveros was born in 1932 in Houston, Texas, where her mother and grandmother were piano teachers. As a child she preferred noises to concerts but came into her own playing the accordion. She attended the University of Houston and San Francisco State College and was a cofounder with Ramon Sender of Sonics at the Conservatory. Sonics later became the San Francisco Tape Music Center (SFTMC) founded by Ramon Sender and Morton Subotnik. In 1966 she became director of the Mills Tape Music Center when SFTMC moved to Mills College. In the following year she moved to the University of California, San Diego. In 1985, having left the academic world, she became director of the Pauline Oliveros Foundation, which later became the Deep Listening Institute Ltd in 2005. She is now distinguished research professor at the Rensselar Polytechnic Institute, Troy, New York. Initially she investigated tape and electronic music, but in the 1970s, feeling the need for calming activities, she became involved with meditation, ceremony, and ritual using a practice she has developed called "deep listening." In 1989 Cage said: "Through Pauline Oliveros and Deep Listening I finally know what harmony is. . . . It's about the pleasure of making music." Like Cage, she has been concerned to integrate music with the spiritual and social needs of mankind, as John Rockwell recognized: "On some level, music, sound consciousness and religion are all one, and she would seem to be very close to that level."[1]

---

1. Quoted on Oliveros's Web site: www.deeplistening.org

Interview

Approved by Pauline Oliveros

PD When did you first come across Cage?

PO I was aware of John's work by the mid-fifties through the grapevine, so to speak, and through Radio KPFA-FM. I was living in San Francisco at the time—from 1952—and there was a lot of controversy in the Music Department at the University of California at Berkeley, with a polarity between Cage and Schoenberg. In 1960 La Monte Young, a friend of mine who in a seminar at Berkeley, went to Darmstadt. He was very interested at that time in Stockhausen, and when he came back he could only talk about John [*laughs*], and so a lot of Cage's ideas became apparent through La Monte's interest. In 1963 I met David Tudor in San Francisco and within a year we had planned a festival, which I organized at the San Francisco Tape Center where I was. In that festival we performed a number of John's works as well as others by Lucier,[2] Ichiyanagi,[3] and so on. That was an amazing festival because the performers included Terry Riley, Morton Subotnik, Loren Rush, Stewart Dempster, John Chowning, Douglas Leedy,[4] and me—all composers who have continued to be quite visible.

PD Was it particular works that made the impact or his whole ethos?

PO It was the whole thing and the incredible devoted performance of David Tudor. The combination was quite potent. The learning that took place involved care in the preparation of performance materials. David transmitted a wonderful knowledge in his performance practice so everyone could use it in his own way.

PD When did you meet Cage?

PO At that festival, which started out to be performances by David and we called it the Tudor Festival. But we had so many of John's works that we decided we should invite John, who came on his way to Hawaii. That was our first meeting and we did an interview on the radio together, talking about various things including Beethoven! [*laughs*]

PD What about the connection between the work and the personality?

PO I consider the work of Cage to be extremely disciplined in the sense of the sitting practice in Zen. I've come to have a tremendous amount of

---

2. Alvin Lucier (1931–), American composer, primarily of electro-acoustic works.
3. Toshi Ichiyanagi (1933–), Japanese composer and pianist.
4. West Coast composers: Morton Subotnik (1933–), specialist in electronic and multimedia works; Loren Rush (1935–); Stewart Dempster (1936–), trombonist and composer; John Chowning (1934–), computer music pioneer; Douglas Leedy (1938–).

respect for the commitment he's made to that and how he's continued to follow it and let the fruits of it unfold. A practice with this amount of devotion shows in the character of the person. Over the years, having seen John from time to time, I think his work affects him and he affects his work: a reciprocal relationship.

PD How important do you think Zen was in his development after 1951?

PO Extremely important—a path he translated into Western terms. A very valuable translation because tossing coins, consulting the *I Ching*, or using chance operations to arrive at a result, as he does, is a discipline that translates perfectly from the austerity of Zen practice.

PD The Zen connection, which led to him taking himself out of his music, has sometimes created problems with an audience if they don't understand Oriental philosophy. Is this why he encountered opposition from the New York Philharmonic in 1964?[5]

PO There was an element of misunderstanding, a lack of respect, and some emotional immaturity among the players to act in that manner— a lack of integrity for a performer to try to sabotage a person's work because of personal opinion. Ironic in terms of the discipline John has followed. Performers should be devoted to the practice of interpreting a score and not dismissing it because they don't understand it. Part of it is due to the attitude surrounding a professional in New York, which is that such a performer knows it all, can do it all, and if it falls outside what he or she knows it's to be dismissed out of hand. That attitude is destructive. It's promulgated in this country and elsewhere by not educating a performer for change. It's because education is one-sided and not encouraging creative activity.

PD John breaks down the barriers among composer, performer, and audience. Do you think people are ready for that?

PO I absolutely do. My generation of composers has come to terms with a lot of ideas that come from his work. I believe it is seed work, which has opened the field of sound and has made it possible to do many different things, not as imitators but as ways of growth, development, and change.

PD He aims to take himself out of his music, but his personality is pervasive, strong, and consistent. How does this work?

PO This is the apparent irony of Oriental discipline or Zen practice—the realization of oneself by getting oneself out of the way, [*laughs*] which seems to be a paradox but is not. You can't get yourself out of the way unless you realize yourself. I think this is very much what has happened. If you look to the Buddha as a model, he threw over everything

---

5. See interviews with Cage, chapter 1, 44, and Earle Brown, chapter 10, 142.

and went his own way. Then there's an irony there because of the following of the Buddha. [*laughs*] It's paradoxical to follow someone who has thrown over everything to find himself!

PD   "I have nothing to say and I am saying it?"[6]

PO   Right! [*laughs*]

PD   The parallels are extraordinary because when the Zen masters are asked to give a special revelation they say nothing. It's the silent piece?

PO   It's that, but it's also a demonstration of the other side of consciousness and communication. It isn't all verbal. There's the nonverbal side, which can speak even louder than words—many times.

PD   Do you see the illogical contradictions of Zen in John's work too?

PO   I think so.

PD   Have Cage's ideas become dated with the arrival of minimalism? Is he less relevant than in the 1960s?

PO   I think his work will become more and more relevant rather than less and less. Only the surface [*laughs*] has been seen. I don't think that some of the things I've stated in our interview are widely perceived: they require some understanding and practice. I spent twelve years as a practitioner of karate, which is also a form of meditation. It was very austere and strict. I understand the results of that and the levels of change in one's perception.

PD   But how are we going to get professional musicians and concert audiences into this? Isn't he way ahead of his time?

PO   I never relate to that phrase very well—you just are where you are. There are always those who are at a different level of perception and those who are not yet awake in certain respects. I think of it from a different perspective.

PD   It was Varèse who said he wasn't ahead of his time but the public was behind! Do you see Cage's development as consistent, from percussion through prepared piano to chance?

PO   The work is quite consistent, following the path he's chosen. However, the results do produce what appear to be very sharp changes.

PD   In some ways John's adoption of chance can be compared to Schoenberg's use of twelve-tone technique. Do you see 1951 for Cage as a turning point with historical implications?

PO   In another sense there's a similarity because twelve-tone technique can be seen as a discipline as well, which has its own austerity. You could

---

6. Cage, "Lecture on Nothing," in *Silence: Lectures and Writings* (Middletown, CT: Wesleyan University Press, 1961), 109.

make a case for twelve-tone technique and chance operations as being at opposite ends of the spectrum but in a similar vein. The results are very different. One system is open and the other closed.

PD   Charles Hamm has claimed that Cage had "a greater impact on world music than any other American composer of the twentieth century."[7] Is that true?

PO   I think we can say that from this perspective. An overview later on may be tempered by other things. It's tempered by the tools of the time—technology, media exposure, the availability of documentation of world music. This was not available to me as a young person but it is now. John's work, along with [that of] his teacher Henry Cowell and others, forms a collective effort that seems to focus on John, who's managed to present such a powerful image.

PD   Would you feel lost without his example?

PO   I don't know if I'd be lost or not, but I certainly would never discount the influence. It was a very important meeting.

PD   You remember that John said he found the sounds of the environment more useful aesthetically than music. Do you subscribe to that?

PO   It depends on how one would interpret that statement. When you say the sounds of the environment are more useful than music—what is the music we are talking about, and how does it function in our lives? What are the sounds of the environment more useful for? In my own perspective, I would say listening is useful. It's absolutely necessary for one's survival! [*laughs*] Listening critically and crucially can change one's consciousness instantly. That can be very useful! [*laughs*]

---

7. Hamm, "John Cage," in Stanley Sadie, ed., *The New Grove Dictionary of American Music and Musicians* (London: Macmillan, 1980), 3: 597.

Chapter Fifteen

Paul Zukofsky

Interview with Peter Dickinson, New York City, June 30, 1987

Introduction

Paul Zukofsky was born in Brooklyn in 1943 and became a child prodigy as a violinist, studying with Ivan Galamian from age seven. His official Carnegie Hall debut was in 1956, and he took his degrees at the Juilliard School. Since then, as violinist and conductor, he has specialized in twentieth-century works, giving many significant premieres and making first recordings. He has taught at a variety of institutions in the United States and Europe. Since 1975 he has been president of Musical Observations Inc. In 1992 the Museum of Modern Art in New York devoted its Summergarden music series to Cage, and Zukofsky was artistic director. Cage wrote the *Freeman Etudes* for him: his texts on music are available at www.musicalobservations.com.

Interview

Edited by Paul Zukofsky in February 2005

PZ   The first time I met John was when I was in Buffalo as a creative associate, probably in 1965. I certainly knew the name and some of the music well before that, around 1960, when I was sixteen or seventeen.

PD   Do any particular pieces stand out in your mind?

PZ   My primary love of his music came about through *Six Melodies*.[1] In Buffalo I also knew about the theater pieces, as well as the graphic solo

---

1. *Six Melodies* for violin and piano (1950).

violin works, neither of which particularly appealed to me, primarily because my interests are with control. How to control the technical aspects of playing fascinates me. The idea of being allowed to do more or less whatever you wish to do was a type of anarchy I simply could not deal with. Anarchy is not what John had in mind, but he ended up being misinterpreted for many years. He was hoist with his own petard because politically he could not admit that people could not always be allowed to do whatever they wanted to do or that they would not always behave as they should behave toward society.

PD How do you account for his desire for anarchy?

PZ I think that is part of the American character. A British friend of mine once pronounced that we do not have a democracy here but controlled anarchy. This pervades everything we do.

PD I don't see Cage as completely American in that he has taken on something else through his Zen studies and commitment.

PZ To me, the Zen aspect is opposed to the anarchy—it opens the window to freedom through control. I think the forced retreat from the (somewhat) false position in which John found himself (in other words, the conflict between what John thought politically proper as opposed to what he believed musically) began to be resolved through Zen. But I wasn't working with John when this first took place, and I am looking at it from the point of view of an outsider.

One of the most wonderful examples I know of the problem John has dealing with "John" took place in 1978 when the first eight *Freeman Etudes* were finished, and we went to Europe to present them.[2] I've had my problems with the *Etudes*, which is no particular secret. It was in Basle that we got into a squabble. We were walking across the Rhine, not tipsy but somewhat lubricated, and John was bawling me out, saying that he was a revolutionary trying to create change in the world but [that] I simply wanted to do what I wanted to do and to hell with anything else; therefore, there was no conceivable way we could continue to collaborate in the future. I said I was very sorry to hear that, as he had been, and was, an enormous influence. I valued our working relationship and had learned extensively from him, and he had been very important to me musically and personally. But before we never spoke again, would he object if I asked a couple of questions? He said, "No,

---

2. Paul Zukofsky recorded the first eight *Freeman Etudes* in 1981 and issued them on LP in 1983 with his own record label cp2/12. CD release as $CP^2 103$ (1991). The original recording was issued with a discussion between Cage and Zukofsky, reprinted in Richard Kostelanetz, ed., *Writings about John Cage* (Ann Arbor: University of Michigan Press, 1993), 225–28.

of course not." I said, "You remember Mr. Thoreau?[3] He went off by himself to do whatever he wanted to do and didn't want to be bothered with anybody and to hell with anything else?" John agreed. I said, "So why is it that when I behave this way—and nowhere near as extremely—it is a reason for us to never work together again, but with Mr. Thoreau it is something to be admired?" We were smack in the middle of the bridge, and John stopped and looked at me and said: "There's one major difference. Mr. Thoreau isn't alive!" [*laughs*] We've been the best of friends ever since. If we ever run into trouble, one of us says "Mr. Thoreau isn't alive!" and we go on.

PD   With your concern for precise details in performance, it must have been risky when you got together with John to do the *Freeman Etudes*.[4]

PZ   He started out with extremely detailed concerns. You can tell in (for example) the prepared piano scores that anybody who spends that amount of time to generate those pages of detailed information regarding the precise type of screw between which strings and at what distance is a person who cares about detail. His music gradually moved away from that for various reasons, which aren't quite clear to me. Then came the period when the more freedom John appeared to give the performer, the more outrageous the performances became, the more the performances were insulting to the intent of the piece, and the more the freedom was misused and abused. Eventually, it got to a point where he simply walked out and refused to have a piece played.[5]

---

3. See introduction to interview with Jackson Mac Low, chapter 5, 93.

4. Betty Freeman (1921–), influential American patron of the arts who initially befriended and collected abstract expressionists, pop artists, and David Hockney but turned to contemporary music in the 1960s. She supported Harry Partch until his death in 1974 and also supported Cage for many years. She took up photography for her TV documentary on Partch in 1972. There was an exhibition of her photographs at The Royal Festival Hall, London, from April 13 to June 16, 1996. See Max Bygrave, "Betty Freeman: Patron Saint of Modern Music," *Guardian*, March 30, 1996, arts section, 28.

5. Presumably a reference to the orchestral performance of *Cheap Imitation* at The Hague in 1972, which Cage had to cancel. See Cage, *For the Birds: John Cage in Conversation with David Charles* (London: Marion Boyars, 1981), 183–84, n. 1. Cage worked with Zukofsky to produce the violin solo version of *Cheap Imitation* before starting on the *Freeman Etudes*. When Zukofsky gave the European premiere of *Cheap Imitation* at The Queen Elizabeth Hall, London, on June 13, 1978, Max Harrison reported: "The mood is uniquely Cage's, the music conveying an atmosphere of absolute purity and stillness the more affecting for the absence of even the suggestion of an emphatic gesture. Characterized in particular by a cool vibratoless tone, Mr. Zukovsky's performance was a devoted one. It was heard in rapt silence" ("Zukovsky, Queen Elizabeth Hall," *The Times*, June 14, 1978). See Paul Zukofsky, "John Cage's Recent Violin Music," in Peter Gena, Jonathan Brent, and Don Gillespie, eds., *A John Cage Reader: In Celebration of His 70th Birthday* (New York:

I think that progression awoke him to the fact that one cannot believe that every performer is going to be as responsible as one would hope— indeed, the majority of them are not.

PD   Isn't it a spiritual discipline he's asking for, where the performer has to be part composer?

PZ   This is true, but that is not what the majority of performers are bred for. Spiritual discipline is a quality lacking in most performers! Digital dexterity and spiritual/musical discipline are not the same story.

PD   Taking himself out of his music in 1951 seems to have been a kind of crisis.

PZ   For me, the seminal piece of that time is the *Sixteen Dances*.[6] That is when the use of chance, through the use of movements on a chess-board, appeared. At a time of extraordinary musical ferment, taking himself out of his music was one possible solution and perhaps the only one left, as everything else was preempted—by the serialists; by the American school based around Copland, Barber, and Schuman; by the Stravinsky and Bartok imitators, etc. Chance was a way to escape. But despite taking himself out, his pieces still sound like John Cage.

PD   These other composers you've mentioned have a syntax, but Cage doesn't. It's open, empty, like the weather, as he says.[7] Is that what we identify as Cage?

PZ   Being like the weather is a little bit too politicized. It's a statement for the public. You must remember that John makes an enormous number of choices. There's the order in which the events are chosen. There is the question "am I going to allow one of the following number of possi-bilities to occur?" The numbers of those possibilities are predetermined. You may have 10 out of 64 chances of "something" happening; there may be only 2 chances of the some other thing appearing. There are two important points to remember:

C. F. Peters, 1982), 101–6. Cage's *Chorals* (1975) are based on the posthumously published *Douze petites chorals* by Satie; are used as a solo for voice in *Song Books I and II* (1970); and, at the suggestion of Zukofsky, were arranged for solo violin. Cage's nine chorales are Satie's 1, 2, 3, 7, 8, 9, 10, 11, and 12.

6. Zukofsky conducted the *Sixteen Dances* for New Music Concerts, Toronto, and recorded them at Walter Hall, University of Toronto, on January 31, 1982, released on LP cp2/15 in 1984. Now on CD as cp2/112.

7. In the interview with David Sylvester, chapter 16, 193.

1. The *I Ching* does not function under the rules of normal distribution (i.e., the bell-shaped curve). Because of the mutations that are allowed, indeed insisted upon, by the *I Ching* (i.e., when—in the case of coin tosses—both three heads or three tails give rise to alternatives), one can manage to stay in a curiously small world—the *I Ching* is not just a random number generator. Therefore:

2. The distribution of allowed sounds is again not random and not normally distributed and can be quite confined.

For example, when we were doing the violin version of *Cheap Imitation* we used chance to determine most of the bowings in the third movement. We made up rules such as, is this next phrase going to be one bow or completely separate or mixed? I believe we equally distributed that question among all 64 possibilities. Once the decision had been made that the bowing was either to be separate or slurred, there wasn't any further choice. But when you got the result "mixed," where there was a choice about how to split the phrase between separate and slurred bows, then the questions could be manipulated in much greater detail. What was fascinating in the twenty-minute movement was that, with the exception of only about two places, everything worked. I don't think John is as removed from the decision-making process as he would like everybody to believe he is! [laughs] John's genius is in the type of choices made about the distribution of elements.

We had a discussion as to whether the *Freeman Etudes* ought to have been written in proportional notation. I've come to regret that they are—which may be my own narrow-minded viewpoint.

PD   Did you listen to the *Etudes Australes* before starting on the *Freeman Etudes*?[8]

PZ   I saw them, then heard them later.

PD   Do you think they're successful?

PZ   I think they can be, but they're not the most accessible of John's output. They are somewhat too didactic, too much the same over a very, very long period of time.

PD   Were you alarmed by what John might demand technically in the *Freeman Etudes*?

PZ   No, not at first, because it was my idea that we would construct a system that would prevent things from being impossible. It turned out not to be the case!

PD   So the *Freeman Etudes* was a collaborative composition?[9]

---

8. See interview with Cage, chapter 1, 49n72.
9. See also "John Cage and Roger Reynolds: A Conversation," *Musical Quarterly* 65 (October 1979): 591–92.

PZ   We had a great number of discussions regarding what the basic process should be allowed to control and, most important, the order in which it would be allowed to have control. What we succeeded in doing was to invent a system that allowed us to create the most unbelievable combinations, each one of which works individually—without any question. (One project we still have in mind is the creation of a catalog of chords in the *Freeman*, or projected, *Freeman Etudes*, which catalog would be of some pedagogical interest for violinists.) Every single thing works, but they don't work next to each other, as we did not allow enough time. At first we arrived at a massive rumpus, as John had set this up and couldn't, or wouldn't, change it. So I couldn't do what was demanded of me, John wouldn't change it, and I saw no way of getting around that. Merce brought us back together by saying that when he does his chance operations, he sometimes ends up with arms at one end of the hall and feet at the other! Clearly, something has to give. Put in those terms, John understood the problem, but then, in typical fashion, he said, "Go and do whatever you want." At that point I totally balked, as the *Freeman Etudes* were written with the idea of control processes and being able to make, or not make, a performance. If I'm going to be allowed to do whatever I want, then that permission has to be given to everyone else as well. This violates the underlying premise, which was to create a controlled work rather than fall back into the trap of "anything goes" or rely on the good intentions of the potential performer. None of that sat well with me. We ended up at philosophical loggerheads, and we couldn't get out of it. János Négyesy[10] has now gone through the first sixteen *Etudes*—I've not heard them.

PD   You've said that violinists should want to play these Cage works whether they like them or not.[11]

PZ   They should explore them—why they were created and where they lead to from a technical point of view. Contemporary music is not normally so far off the beaten path. One of the most amazing things about working on those pieces was the discovery of things I absolutely never would

---

10. János Négyesy, born in Budapest in 1938, moved to the United States in 1965. He recorded *Freeman Etudes* 1–16 on LP for Lovely Music, VR2051–2 (1985). All 32 *Freeman Etudes* were performed by Irvine Arditti, for whom Cage wrote the last 16 in 1990, at *Anarchic Harmony*, a major Cage Festival in Frankfurt in 1992. Keith Potter was there: "As so often with Cage, the discontinuities of these three-minute *Etudes* rarely focus on anything for long enough to observe a shape. On the other hand, I frequently felt that Cage was gluing sounds together which in the past would have been entirely unrelated." "Rattling Cage's Bars," *Independent*, September 26, 1992.
11. In Gena, Brent, and Gillespie, *A John Cage Reader*, 106.

have conceived of, which appear to be so incredibly violinistic. There were boundaries I could not break through until this came along.

PD Have you had any adverse audience reaction when performing the *Etudes?*

PZ Sure. So what? The worst was in Genoa, where they were making such a racket that I could not hear one note I was playing! Half the audience were screaming and shrieking because they hated the piece and thought I should get the hell off the stage, and the other half were screaming and shrieking because they wanted me left alone to continue what I was doing. I simply stood up there for thirty-odd minutes—I literally couldn't hear myself play—and at the end I got the biggest ovation I've ever had. Everybody stood up to applaud. I was so infuriated that I packed up, walked out of the hall, and wouldn't go back onstage. They told me people just kept clapping for a while. To compound insult on top of injury, they didn't even pay [my] expenses!

Part III

Earlier Interviews

Chapter Sixteen

Cage with David Sylvester and Roger Smalley

BBC Radio 3, London, December 1966

Extracts from an interview recorded at the BBC, London, in December 1966, broadcast in 1967, and printed in the program of John Cage and David Tudor, presented by *Music Now* at The Royal Albert Hall, London, on May 22, 1972.

Reprinted in edited form by permission of Naomi Sylvester and Roger Smalley.

Introduction

The British response to Cage's first visit since 1966, when *Music Now* billed him as "the most influential living composer," cannot have been encouraging. Hugo Cole went to hear Cage and Tudor read and talk at the Institute of Contemporary Arts on May 10, 1972. He reported that Cage emphasized that he used the *I Ching* merely as a utility "to become free of my likes and dislikes," but Cole was perplexed because Cage apparently said he didn't particularly want to compose but people kept asking him for works, adding: "My favorite music is no music at all; I enjoy the sounds round me."[1] Cole interviewed Cage and wrote a sympathetic article as a preview to The Royal Albert Hall concert on May 22.[2] Each half of the concert consisted of a simultaneous performance of a work by Tudor and one by Cage: Tudor's *Rainforest* with Cage's *Mureau*, and Tudor's *Untitled* with Cage's *Mesostics re Merce Cunningham*.

---

1. Hugo Cole, "John Cage," *Guardian*, May 11, 1972.
2. Hugo Cole, "An Easy Composure," *Guardian*, May 22, 1972. Cage also gave an amusing interview to the radio and TV personality Joan Bakewell, "Music and Mushrooms—John Cage Talks about His Recipes to Joan Bakewell," *Listener*, June 15, 1972, 800–802.

Peter Stadlen, the Vienna-born British pianist and critic associated with the Second Viennese School who had given the premiere of Webern's *Piano Variations* in 1937, gained some satisfaction over the poor attendance in the vast Royal Albert Hall in spite of the publicity and added, "What was actually heard, in a darkened hall with two shadowy figures crouching over the usual apparatus, might have been mistaken by the un-Tudored ear (sorry about that) for two low-voiced drunks, making their way home, to the steady accompaniment of high-pitched tinnitus, such as will result from chronically inflamed Eustachian tubes and taking all of an hour over it."[3] The musicologist and editor of *The New Grove Dictionary*, Stanley Sadie, went even further by asking how one could judge something that "conscientiously avoids all points of reference to artistic experience" and "professedly has no standards." Sadie concluded: "The pieces given at the Cage-Tudor concert are not designed as musical experiences which embody planning and organization (built-in or spontaneous), but are actively nihilistic in intention. As far as I was concerned, they were successful: my senses were numbed, my mind left blank."[4] Cage himself was dissatisfied and told Eric Mottram a few days later:

> Even though we desired a situation like the Round House, in which the audience was free to move, we were . . . in the Albert Hall, where the audience was seated. Then, say we accept that fact, we would like to have had at least the loudspeakers around the audience, so that people sitting on one side could later converse with people who had been sitting on the other and discover that they had heard something different. But that too was not possible, simply because of the enormous amount of wiring that would have been necessary and the little amount of time that we had for the setting up of the sound system.

I can confirm that the loud sounds in context were intimidating, and when Eric Mottram asked Cage what he would say if someone said he was panicked he replied: "I too am and I don't know quite why. . . . It is very mysterious to me. But I think that, without meaning to, we touched on something rather urgent. We do not quite know what we are doing."[5] In January 1992, talking to Joan Retallack, Cage used the same words: "I'm in a position when I write music of not knowing what I'm doing. I know how to do that."[6]

---

3. Peter Stadlen (1910–96), "Cage's Music Gets Sparse Audience," *Daily Telegraph*, May 23, 1972.
4. Stanley Sadie, "John Cage, David Tudor," *The Times*, May 23, 1972.
5. Interview with Eric Mottram, "The Pleasures of Chaos," *Spanner 1* (November 1974): 3, private publication.
6. Joan Retallack, ed., *MUSICAGE: Cage Muses on Words Art Music* (Hanover, NH: Wesleyan University Press and University of New England Press, 1996), xli. In 1990

The Participants

David Sylvester (1924–2001) was one of the most influential British art critics concerned with modernism throughout the second half of the twentieth century. His books include *Henry Moore* (1968), *Interviews with Francis Bacon* (1975), *René Magritte* (1992), *Looking at Giacometti* (1994), the five-volume *catalogue raisonné* of Magritte (1992–95), and *About Modern Art* (1996), and he wrote significant essays and reviews. From 1951 he curated major international exhibitions and made films about Matisse and Magritte. He served on the committees of the Arts Council and the Musée d'art moderne, Paris; he was a trustee of the Tate Gallery; and his visiting lectureships included the Slade School and the Royal College of Art. His many honors included the CBE in 1983; he was made an Officier de l'ordre des arts et des lettres; and in 1993 became the first critic to receive a Golden Lion at the Venice Biennale.

Roger Smalley was born near Manchester in 1943. After attending the Royal College of Music in London, he studied composition privately with Alexander Goehr and Stockhausen. With Tim Souster he founded the ensemble Intermodulation, which specialized in improvisation and live electronics and performed widely from 1969 to 1976. He moved to Australia in 1976 and is Professorial Fellow in Music at the University of Western Australia. He has always been active as a pianist, his music has been performed and recorded by leading ensembles, and he has received awards in Australia. The opening page of his setting of Gerard Manley Hopkins's *The Leaden Echo and the Golden Echo* is included in Cage's *Notations* (1969).

Roger Smalley reflected on this interview almost two years later:

> One of the most memorable of my recent experiences was (together with David Sylvester) interviewing John Cage for the BBC in December 1966. We talked for three hours and during that time a picture emerged of the most selfless and humane person I have met to this day. It is paradoxical that this most gentle of men . . . should be the perennial object of the most extraordinarily misinformed attacks. Perhaps it is because Cage presents the unnerving picture of someone with indisputable talent, excellent musical training (study with Schoenberg), the composer of many beautiful and original pieces within a traditional framework, who has consciously and systematically eroded all vestiges of personality and control from his music. Why has he done this considering that he could have done anything?[7]

Cage said the same to Henning Lohner in Berlin about his film: "I don't know what I'm doing. I literally don't know. . . . I don't have any ideas . . . tastes . . . feelings, I'm just doing my work, so to speak, stupidly. And it turns out to be beautiful. It's very hard to explain." "The Making of Cage's *One¹¹*," in David W. Bernstein and Christopher Hatch, eds., *Writings through John Cage's Music, Poetry + Art* (Chicago: University of Chicago Press, 2001), 267.

7. Roger Smalley, "John Cage," *Listener,* September 19, 1968, 377.

Interview

DS   In one of your stories you talk about Schoenberg pointing out the eraser on his pencil and saying, "This end is more important than the other."[8] And you go on to say things that clearly show you are out of sympathy—rather strongly—with that remark. I take it that you might also feel Webern was a composer who used his eraser too much?

JC   He must have.

DS   What's wrong with the eraser?

JC   It means, does it not, that an action has been made that is not an action one wishes to keep, and so it is removed by means of the eraser. Now take the way of painting that we know of from the Far East, where the material upon which one is painting is of such value that one dare not make an action that requires erasure. So the artist prepares himself in advance before he makes a mark. He knows when he is making it that he is going to keep it. The possibility of erasing has nothing to do with that kind of activity.

DS   Right. This is an important moral principle for you, isn't it? In your essay on Jasper Johns you say there are two ways of learning to play chess.[9] One is when you make a mistake to take back the move; the other is, having made a mistake, to accept the consequences.

JC   Right.

DS   And that Johns is an artist . . .

JC   Who accepts the consequences.

DS   This seems to me a marvelous characterization of Johns as an artist, and it's obviously something you feel morally is a very important point in Johns's favor.

JC   Oh yes. Absolutely.

DS   And this presumably is an important principle in your own practice.

JC   It's also an extremely useful principle in all the circumstances of our lives.

DS   The principle of generosity: is that what it is?

JC   Yes, and it leads toward enjoyment, experience, and all those things and away from the things we know about through Freud, which brought about [the] inability eventually to act at all—guilt, shame, conscience.

---

8. Cage, *Silence: Lectures and Writings* (Middletown, CT: Wesleyan University Press, 1961), 270.

9. John Cage, "Jasper Johns: Stories and Ideas," Jewish Museum catalog, 1964, reprinted in *A Year from Monday: New Lectures and Writings* (Middletown, CT: Wesleyan University Press, 1967), 74. "There are various ways to improve one's chess game. One is to take back a move when it becomes clear that it was a bad one. Another is to accept the consequences, devastating as they are. Johns chooses the latter even when the former is offered."

RS It's an act of faith in your material, then?

JC Okay. It's also an act of faith in yourself.

DS There is another point here with regard to the eraser. One of the reasons for the importance of the eraser for Schoenberg and, if you like, Webern was the desire to make the thing concentrated and pithy—obviously, in the case of Webern, to make the utterance as short as possible. Would I be right in saying that your own works have been growing longer? Is this a conscious decision on your part?

JC I think our time sense is changed, or that we have changed it. With all these pieces that I've written in recent years, they can be quite long, hours long. All of them can also be just a few seconds long: did you know that?

DS No.

JC They don't have to be played for any particular length—that is part of the principle of indeterminacy.

RS But would you prefer them to be longer rather than shorter?

JC It doesn't make any difference to me. I wish to be, as it were, useful and practical so that if, say, there was an occasion when one wanted two seconds of music, one could take *Atlas Eclipticalis* and play it for two seconds. It's unlikely because it takes too long to set the thing up. However, you could set up one part of it very easily and quickly and do it for two seconds. Because I conceive that a long work, which has many parts, can be expressed by any one of its parts or any number of its parts for any length of time. When you started this part of the conversation I found that I was thinking about the difference between prose and poetry—Webern particularly suggests poetry, but this activity on my part suggests perhaps a big book that does not need to be read.

DS And also that can bore you for long passages at a time but still leave a mark?

JC Right. And you could read it for any length of time. You could, in other words, have it around, pick it up, put it down, or you could settle down and read it for several hours. And you could, as in the case of *Finnegans Wake*, read it without understanding anything for a long time, and then suddenly you could understand something.

RS But all that you are saying now seems to presuppose that the longer the piece goes on, the more chance you have of getting something out of it.

JC I must confess that I very much enjoy our current ability to listen to things for a long time, and I notice this becoming a general practice in society.

DS Epic films?

JC Epic films and the Warhol films that go on and on or the music of La Monte Young, which goes on for hours and nothing much seems to happen—and large audiences enjoy it.

RS I was going to mention that because it seems that La Monte Young, although his compositions could, like yours, be short or long, would much prefer them to be long. In fact, it's only after the first half hour or so that aural things begin to happen to you. You don't feel your pieces are in the same category?

JC   No. La Monte is focusing one's attention, whereas I'm not focusing it.

RS   You don't make any distinction between a kind or type of musical material or form that might be different if one was to write a piece an hour long or the length of a Wagner opera than it would be if you were going to write a Chopin Prelude.

JC   Well, if you looked over all my work, then I have to say yes, I do make such a distinction, but my recent work has all been such that it has this indeterminate quality with respect to its length. I tend, given the practicality of it in social terms, to make it long. I like, for instance, to start a piece without the audience knowing it has started—that can be done in several ways—and to conclude it without their knowing it has stopped. That appeals to me very much.

DS   At a performance in London of *How to Improve the World*,[10] a lot of people left before the end and there was slow clapping. People were obviously bored and exasperated. They were actually looking at the sheaf of papers in your hand and seeing you get near the end, thinking, "Good, it's near the end." And then, when you got to the end of that sheaf, you rather annoyed them by picking up another lot and starting on that. I think you were probably conscious of what you were doing, but . . . [*Cage laughs*]

JC   That's my wicked laugh, by the way! [*laughter*]

DS   Some people who did find the thing interesting nevertheless said: "Why did it have to go on so long? The point could have been made in ten minutes."

JC   Now, why are people so stingy about their time?

DS   Yes.

JC   Why are they so ungenerous? What in heaven's name is so valuable about thirty minutes? Or forty-five minutes? Or an hour and a half?

DS   I think you want people to give something. Isn't that what it's about?

JC   I assume—and I think by assuming it I invite it—I assume generosity, on my part and theirs.

DS   You quote this saying somewhere: "If something bores you after two minutes, listen for four; if it bores you after four minutes, listen for eight."[11]

JC   Yes, and I consider that generosity can be expressed in at least two ways—that is to say, by giving or by receiving.

---

10. For the contents, see interview with Lederman, chapter 6, 107n17.

11. Cage, *Silence*, 93: "In Zen they say: 'If something is boring after two minutes, try it for four. If still boring, try it for eight, sixteen, thirty-two, and so on.' Eventually one discovers that it's not boring at all but very interesting."

DS   That's at the heart of your whole doctrine, is it not? The idea of the spectator's active participation in the work so that he is not passive but has to supply something—he has to interpret and select?

JC   But active at the point where he has disciplined himself, not at the point where he has not disciplined himself.

DS   But you are asking him to give something?

JC   "Give" in terms of the person who is disciplined to giving.

DS   But the giving of time, you feel, is a part of that which has to be given?

JC   Well, if something that is being given takes time, then its receiving must take an equal time. We don't know, when we get into situations, how much time it's going to take. We ought, through our discipline— that's why I'm harping on it—to be able to endure things for a short time, a long time, or middling times.

RS   This sense of generosity especially applies to your performers, doesn't it? I mean, you were generous enough to give them music in which they could make a variety of actions at any time.

JC   Yes.

RS   So you expect them to be generous enough, I presume, to discipline themselves to decide the best sound they could produce at any particular point. Then produce it as well as they could.

JC   I wouldn't say the best sound. I would say to make certain that what they do is done in the spirit of the piece, which itself is indeterminate and admits of many sounds. You see, I'm averse to all these actions that lead toward placing emphasis on the things that happen in the course of a process. What interests me far more than anything that happens is the fact of how it would be if nothing was happening. Now, I want the things that happen to not erase the spirit that was already there without anything happening. Now, this thing that I mean when I say "not anything happening" is what I call silence; that is to say, a state of affairs free of intention, because we always have sounds. Therefore we don't have any silence available in the world: we're in a world of sounds. We call it silence when we don't feel a direct connection with the intentions that produce the sounds. We say it's quiet when, due to our non-intention, there don't seem to us to be many sounds. When there seem to us to be many, we say it's noisy. But there is no real essential difference between a noisy silence and a quiet silence. The thing that runs through from the quietness to the noise is the state of non-intention, and it is this state that interests me. Therefore I don't go along when you say the making of the best sound, you see.

RS   I mean by that the most appropriate sound.

JC   Well, then I agree, that is to say appropriate in the sense of being appropriate to silence.

DS   You reiterated the importance of the spectators and the listeners being disciplined. What exactly do you mean by that?

JC   Free of intention.

DS   This whole point about duration also relates to your story of when you were taking a class, and you played on the gramophone some Buddhist music that was simply a monotonously repetitive cymbal; and after fifteen minutes a woman cried out that she couldn't stand any more of it, and you stopped the gramophone playing and a man complained that he was just beginning to find the thing interesting.[12] Obviously, you are concerned that if the thing goes on longer one's attention may improve, one's ear would sharpen itself to what was going on.

JC   Exactly, so if one began such a listening period in a state of nondiscipline, one could move into a state of discipline simply by remaining in the room and being subjected to this activity, which eventually one finds interesting.

DS   What you're really saying is that by submitting oneself to listening for a very long time, one does discipline oneself, one does learn attentiveness, one does learn to focus, which is what the whole thing is about?

JC   Exactly.

DS   But there is a totally other way. I mean, it seems to me that Webern's way is by the very pithiness of it, by its extreme concentration, so you know the thing is not going to go on for long. You achieve from the very start an intense effort of concentration. Webern does create that situation, doesn't he?

JC   He did for me. He no longer does. He might for another now still, and he might two hundred years hence have that usefulness for another person. It's just that it doesn't work for me any longer in that way. It just sounds like art, that's all.

DS   In a sense, what you're doing is to revert to an earlier period because Webern in a way belongs to the reaction against the nineteenth century. You're really reverting to the Wagner/Bruckner/Mahler tradition of making a vast structure, creating a whole world surrounding the listener. It's a reversion to a second half of the nineteenth century attitude toward the spectator.

JC   I'm entertained by what you say, but I would hope it was not true. Now, why would I hope it's not true? It's because I connect those works of Mahler, Bruckner, and Wagner and so forth with the industrial business. They're big machines. I'm not making a machine. I'm making

---

12. Cage, *Silence*, 93.

something far more like weather. I'm making a nothingness.[13] It strikes me as being aerial, whereas all those works you just referred to strike me as being heavy, having to be on the earth.

Sometimes people ask me, what is the goal of technology. I say we really need a technology that will be so excellent that when we have it we won't even know it's there. And I see this occurring in all fields now. The proper goal—I don't like the word *goal* but let's use it—the proper goal of each activity is its obviation. Wouldn't this be a lovely goal now, for politics, for economics?

RS   So you advocate a return of the condition of art perhaps as in the Renaissance, when it existed but people weren't so aware of it? They banqueted in halls, they were surrounded by great paintings, and they listened to music. But they talked while the music was going on. Do you see this as a future position of art, perhaps?

JC   I see it as the present one, actually. This experience began for me in Washington when David Tudor and I were performing my *Variations VI*. First, those left who found the whole thing insupportable; then those who were interested stayed and began moving around the room and conversing; and those who were most interested came close to see what we were doing. Shortly, they began talking with us while we were performing, sometimes relevantly and sometimes irrelevantly. Now, in *Variations IV*—the performance in Hollywood about two years ago— some people came up to me while I was performing (it was in an art gallery), and I was unwilling to talk to them because I thought I was performing. When they talked to me I didn't reply, or if I did—to one person who was quite insistent—I simply said, "Don't you see that I'm busy?" Whereas in the case of *Variations VI*, this whole need to be busy had dropped away.[14] The work was being done, which brings us back

---

13. "A Zen master is a man of action—action in the sense of 'metaphysical' activity. He has achieved, through satori, a thorough reorientation of his whole spiritual being, and all that he utters and performs, even lifting a finger, may indicate a full accord with Absolute Nothingness." Lucien Stryk and Takashi Ikemoto, ed., and trans., *Zen: Poems, Prayers, Sermons, Anecdotes, Interviews* (Garden City, NY: Anchor Books, 1965), xxi.

14. Cage, *Variations IV* (1963), from a live performance at the Feigen-Palmer Gallery, Los Angeles. John Cage with David Tudor on Everest Records 3132 (1968). *Variations VI* (1966). See Tim Souster, "John Cage—Tim Souster Discusses his Live-Electronic Variations VI," *Listener,* December 24, 1970, 892–93, where he explains how listeners could participate during the live BBC broadcast. Tim Souster (1943–94) presented a program called "Thirty Years of the Music of John Cage" for the Institute of Contemporary Arts Music Section at the Purcell Room, London, on April 16, 1979, with several British premieres including *Variations VI*. The performers included Gavin Bryars, Cornelius Cardew, John Tilbury, and Souster.

to that Haiku poem, "Taking a nap, I pound the rice." That is to say, by doing nothing, everything gets done.

DS   That is both true and false.

JC   I think we have to say yes to what you just said. Yes, it is true and false, but it's very true.

RS   Do you see music as at all related to ritual, as a ritualistic act?

JC   Well, I imagine now a music in the future that would be quite ritualistic. By means of technology, it would simply be a revelation of sound even where we don't expect that it exists. For instance, in an area with an audience, the arrangement of such things so that this table, for instance, around which we're sitting is made experiential as sound, without striking it. It is, we know, in a state of vibration. It is therefore making a sound, but we don't yet know what that sound is. Now, if we could simply make it audible, I think it would be ritualistic. I had the experience, for instance, of making myself audible not by speaking but simply by being in an anechoic chamber.[15]

DS   A hostile questioner asked, "Why should I sit and listen to unintelligible nonsense?" and you said, "Because it could be important to you." He said, "Why?" and you answered, "Because it's important to you in your life" or something like that, and he protested. Then you went on to say something about—you put it very politely—"If I may say so, our intolerable world." What are the features of our world that you find particularly intolerable, and how can the disciplines of the kind of art you're involved in help us cure them?

JC   In my mind, what you've just said calls up two different directions: my concern toward the irrational, and my belief that it is important to us in our lives, akin to the use of the koan in Zen Buddhism.[16] That is to say, we are so accustomed and so safe in the use of our observation of relationships and our rational faculties, but in Buddhism it was long known that we needed to leap out of that. The discipline by which they made that leap take place was by asking a question that could not be answered rationally. They discovered that when the mind was able to change so that it was able to live not just in the rational world but wholly, in a world including irrationality, then one was, as they said, enlightened. Now, in connection with the thought of Marshall McLuhan, we know that we live in a period of the extension of the

15. Cage mentioned this experience frequently. See Cage, "Lecture," *Die Reihe* 5 (German 1959, English 1961): 115; also *Silence*, 8, 13–14, where he dates it 1951; and interview with Michael Oliver, chapter 18, 204.

16. For a definition of koan, see interview with Schwertsik, chapter 11, 151n13.

mind outside of us, in the sense that the wheel was an extension of the power we have in our legs to move, so electronics has extended our central nervous system not only around the globe but out into space. This then gives us the responsibility to see enlightenment not in terms of individual attainment but in terms of social attainment, so that at that point we must say that the world, as we see it now, is intolerable. Do you follow? So on the individual level, as ever and forever more, it will be possible to see each day as excellent—"Nichi nichi kore ko nichi."[17] But in social terms of the extension of our minds outside of us, which is our present situation, we must see the necessity for the training and discipline of all creation such that life in this intolerable situation will work. Now I needn't, need I, point out intolerable things going on nowadays? They're too evident. We know them without even mentioning them. Our heads are full of them. You must make the world so that those things don't take place—this divisiveness of intention, purpose, and competition in the world between the nations. The wars, the dog-eat-dog, the piggishness, are utterly intolerable. And we must see—I don't know how to say it in Japanese—that it would be, "Each day is a miserable day as long as one person is hungry, one person is unjustifiably killed, and so on." Is that not true?

DS   Very true.

RS   But how does art help?

JC   I may be wrong, but I think art's work is done. I could be right in terms of my own work, with respect to it. I must be wrong certainly with regard to other people's work, with respect to it, but as far as I'm concerned, in the twentieth century art has done a very, very good job. What job? To open people's eyes, to open people's ears. What better thing could have been done? We must turn our attention now I think to other things, and those things are social.

DS   So you must logically give up composing?

JC   No, no, let's not be logical. We're living in this rational-irrational situation. I can perfectly well do something illogical. I can do something unnecessary. I can fulfill invitations. I can invite myself to do something frivolous. I can be grand at one moment and idiotic the next. There's no reason why I shouldn't. I might even from time to time need a little entertainment!

---

17. Japanese quote by Cage in "Composition as Process III: Communication," *Silence*, 41.

Chapter Seventeen

Cage with Frank Kermode

BBC Radio 3, October 1970

Frank Kermode interviewed Cage as part of a series of three programs
called *Is an Elite Necessary?* broadcast on BBC Radio 3 during October 1970.[1]

Introduction

Frank Kermode was born in 1919 and has held professorships in modern
English literature at University College, London, and at Cambridge. He was
Charles Eliot Norton Professor at Harvard in 1977–78. A contributor to many
magazines and journals, Kermode was coeditor of *Encounter* and editor of the
Fontana Masterguides and *Modern Masters* series. His books include *Romantic
Image* (1957); *John Donne* (1957); *Oxford Anthology of English Literature* (1973);
Selected Prose of T. S. Eliot (1975); *An Appetite for Poetry* (1989); *Uses of Error*
(1991); *The Oxford Book of Letters* (1995); his memoirs, *Not Entitled* (1996);
Shakespear's Language (2000); *Pieces of my Mind* (2003); and *The Age of
Shakespeare* (2004). A Fellow of the British Academy and a member of the Arts
Council from 1968 to 1971, Kermode was knighted in 1991. He has approved
the use of this material.

Preface by Frank Kermode (1970)

When we speak of art, we assume that there is a long historical inter-
relation between "high" art and its audience: the audience understands the

---

1. Other interview subjects in these programs were William Burroughs, J. G. Ballard,
Joe Tilson, Joe Boyd, Tony Garnett, Michael Kustow, Richard Wollheim, Julia
Kristeva, David Attenborough, John Calder, Sue Braden, and Michael Astor.

language, or the code, and the artist presumes on this understanding to enlarge the language in the confidence that there exists an audience that will undertake to scan the new thing. This power to scan the new thing is learned, of course, from existing art, so there is a continuity both of the audience and of the forms of art. Occasionally, there are changes more violent than usual, and the thread is broken or seems to be, but in the long run both continuities are reestablished: the languages of art persist, and so does a public.

But many people would now call such views wrong, including some artists. People who think this way may not simply agree that their acceptance of present art depends in some measure on a past of which they may know nothing. They would not even be interested to know that their opinion was first voiced, with a different intonation but very forcibly, more than fifty years ago by the Dadaists. Their program—more than any other—is now being given an extensive trial. The abolition of the past and of the artist, the violation of codes and expectations—these belong now to a new world where there are new media and new interpretations of what goes on in these media. It can be said, though in my opinion falsely, that we've only now distinguished the message and the medium, that there is no longer any point in using the rear-view mirror, and that the important audience now has been trained not on past art but on the violence, discontinuity, and novelty of a modern environment.

Given this state of affairs, changes in the audience must mean changes in their view of the artist, but it's just as important to remember that the artist's view of the artist changes also. We're now quite used to hearing talk of a total discontinuity with the past and about the artist as we've understood him for the past few centuries being on the way out, together with a number of ideas associated with him. For instance, the disappearance of the artist is accompanied by a number of randomizing techniques that do the work thought to be the work of the artist; it becomes more difficult and less desirable to distinguish art objects and sounds from natural ones; products, which might as well be called art, are the work of groups of people, some with and some without special skills; and what they do might be extremely transient. So if the artist is obsolete, form, as achieved by him, is too; and in the final result, art itself is obsolete, since it cannot be distinguished any longer from events or jokes or natural phenomena.

The way I've chosen to approach this complicated subject is to listen first to what John Cage has to say about it. But I should make it clear that he is very much his own man, that his opinions are idiosyncratic, and that you can't really take them as giving the simple gist of the situation I'm talking about. Perhaps the right thing is to treat them as typical of the whole aesthetic we are trying to describe but as representing it quirkily, as having the flavor rather than the substance of that aesthetic.

Interview

FK   Your music is written through various chance procedures rather than with the usual deliberation, and your treatment of sounds has no obvious order or hierarchy. Why does it differ so much from traditional music?

JC   Sounds are not people. They are central to their own experience so that all of nature is a multiplicity of things, each one of which is at the center of the universe. This is an Oriental idea. These centers are then in interpenetration and, hopefully, nonobstruction. That would mean that a sound is a sound rather than that it's the servant of a human being. Therefore each one of us is able to hear a sound freely in his own way. This interests me more than using sounds to express some idea in my head, which itself is not sounds.

FK   This means that whereas a composer of an older kind felt he had to suggest some pattern of relationships between the sounds he used, you no longer feel that to be part of your task. How would you define your task as a composer?

JC   Well, first I would assume that relations exist between sounds as they would exist between people. Those relationships are more complex than any I would be able to prescribe. So by simply dropping that responsibility of making those relationships I don't lose those relationships, I rather keep them in what you might call a natural complexity that can be observed in one way or another. Now, ordinarily one thought that the function of the artist was to express himself, and therefore he had to set up particular relationships. I think this whole question of art is one of changing our minds and that the function of the artist is not self-expression but rather self-alteration. The thing being altered is not his hand or his eyes but his mind.

FK   Do you study these relationships in nature or in the minds of the people perceiving them?

JC   Given a particular situation, one person will observe certain relationships and another others. Now, if we have the view we used to have, that there was only one right way of observing such relationships, then we have a situation that doesn't appeal to me. We have, in other words, one thing that's right and all the rest are wrong. I would like to have a multiplicity of rights! [*laughs*] Then there's a further thing that comes in here—what we might call life instead of art. That is, while we are listening to a piece of music or looking at a painting, inevitably things outside intrude—shadows or lights on a painting, sounds of people coughing or cars in the street coming into a piece of music to which we may be listening. If we see life as opposed to art, then we will find those shadows or ambient sounds interruptions. But if we engage in self-alteration, we will see them not as interruptions but as enrichments. Just the other day I had the experience of listening to a piece of mine on a record—the *String Quartet*[2]—and while I was listening to it I noticed sounds of insects and traffic superimposing themselves on the sounds of the record. I couldn't help at one point wishing I had written some of the sounds [*laughs*] that were actually simply happening!

FK   You don't have to write them; they're all around. Presumably, what you have to do is create a situation in which they're attended to.

JC   True. So I wouldn't say that we are interested in destroying the barrier between art and life or even blurring it. I would say that we are interested in observing that there is no barrier between the two.

FK   Would it be better to abandon the art and life distinction and say that what you're looking for is that people should pay the kind of attention they normally reserve for music to other sounds, which seem to you to be equally interesting?[3]

JC   True. I'm in perfect agreement with that.

FK   You've used various ways of avoiding the imposition of your own ideas of order on what you're doing—dice, the *I Ching*, and now computers?

JC   I used the computerized *I Ching*. Now that I have arthritis it's difficult for me to toss three coins six times and do that tens of thousands of times, which is necessary in the case of an extended work. I have a large stack of computer printouts, which I use for any work I have to do. Then I make a series of questions, which is what computer programming is, and I relate all numbers to the number 64, which is basic to the *I Ching*, and then I'm able to know from a collection of possibilities which one I'm to use.

FK   What would be the difference between your doing this and somebody else doing it? Duchamp once said that his random is not anybody else's—it's all his. Is your random totally impersonal, or is it Cage random?

---

2. It was very unusual for Cage to listen to recordings. The only commercial recording of the *String Quartet* (1950) available at this time was with the New Music String Quartet on Columbia ML-4495, released in 1952. In 1989 he said, "One of the things I dislike very much about recording in opposition to a performance is that a record tends to be always the same whereas a performance has the opposite tendency." Cage, *Harvard Lectures I–VI* (Cambridge: Harvard University Press, 1990), 171–2. In 1971 Cage told me he did not possess a record player. See chapter 1, 28n11.

3. Four years before this interview, in an article in *Encounter*, Kermode approached a definition: "Art is whatever you provide when the place in which you provide it is associated with the idea, and contains people who are prepared to accept this and perhaps other assumptions." "Modernisms," reprinted in Bernard Bergonzi, ed., *Innovations* (London: Macmillan, 1968), 81.

JC   I try to make it impersonal. I would like to separate myself from these events so they can be themselves rather than being me.

FK   You want to get right out of the whole operation, in fact?

JC   I would like to live my life and let my sounds live their lives! [*laughs*]

FK   If other people knew how to do it, they could do it just as well as you!

JC   I should think so.

FK   The way you do it is affected by your own predilections.

JC   I've also had a good deal of experience and I've not tried to keep this a secret. I've generally explained all the various things I've done. I've even been careful to save what seems to me to be my inferior work so that people could, if they wished, do what I do. However, it's unlikely that someone would want to do my impersonal work in the same way I do.

FK   How do you know that some of it is inferior?

JC   I feel that when there are few ideas in a piece rather than many. If there are only a few ideas it's like that business of relationships. It produces a kind of concentration, which is characteristic of human beings. Whereas, if there are many things it produces a kind of chaos, which is characteristic of nature.

FK   That's what you want?

JC   Yes. That's what we live in.

FK   The fact that we live in it may mean we don't want it.

JC   Formerly we didn't want to, but I think we're growing interested in living the very lives we do live rather than some life, say, in heaven! [*laughs*]

FK   You might think that a composer with your views would publish his work anonymously.

JC   Even though I'm opposed to the principle of ownership, nevertheless I copyright everything I do because at the present time it's necessary for me to make a livelihood. It's symptomatic of the present social situation, which extends from conventions of the past and overlaps what I would call this new view that is beginning. Our lives are full of contradiction at the present time. I agree with Marshall McLuhan that through our electric technology we have extended not our legs but rather our central nervous system. And since we know that an individual can change his mind, and since we see that society at present is, so to speak, a mind, then we hope that society can change. Art that changes our minds can give us examples of how the society might change. In music we have the old tonality structures and in society we have a comparable thing— namely, the national structures. And we speak of nations and of politics and of internationalism. Buckminster Fuller, whose views you know I uphold, refuses to use the word "international" and insists upon the words "world man." We need a view of society that is not divided by political entities but that sees the world and the people living in it as a whole.

Chapter Eighteen

Cage with Michael Oliver

BBC Radio 3, Music Weekly, June 29, 1980

Introduction

Michael Oliver (1937–2002) was one of the leading British writers and broadcasters on music. For many years he presented *Music Weekly* for BBC Radio 3 and *Kaleidoscope* for BBC Radio 4. His hundreds of radio programs included biographies of Verdi and Puccini; he was a critic for *The Gramophone* for over thirty years and founding editor of *International Opera Collector*; he contributed to many books on music and published biographies of Igor Stravinsky (1995) and Benjamin Britten (1996). Oliver's interview shows Cage recycling several familiar aspects of his background, but there are some variations.

Interview

By permission of the Michael Oliver Trust

MO Some people say you're a philosopher rather than a composer, since your ideas can be applied to all your different activities.

JC When I was very young I didn't know whether I would be a musician or a painter or a writer. And actually I'm very fortunate because through music, and the fact that not everyone understood my music, it became necessary for me to write. Then in the course of making music, the magnetic tape recording became of such high fidelity that one could make music on tape. Then it became clear that space and time had a certain equivalence, so much of my notation became graphic. That led people interested in the visual arts to invite me to make etchings [*laughs*], so whereas early I made the decision in favor of music, music has been generous and brought me back to all the things that interested me.

MO What caused the decision to choose music?

JC   Before that, I found myself in an architect's studio in Paris.[1] I had heard
      him speaking to a friend and saying, "To be an architect you must devote
      yourself to architecture." The moment I heard him say that, I knew I was
      in the wrong place because at that very time I was working in his studio
      I was interested in music, painting, and poetry. So I told him, "I can't
      work with you any longer because I refuse to dedicate my life to archi-
      tecture." About three years after that, having studied with Adolph
      Weiss,[2] I wanted to study with Schoenberg, and when I went to him and
      asked him to teach me he said, "You probably can't afford my price." I
      said, "Don't mention it because I don't have any money." And he said,
      "Will you devote your life to music?" And I unhesitatingly said, "Yes."
MO   You've said that you don't have a strong harmonic sense.
JC   No, I don't. Harmony, you see, is not itself a sound; it's a connection
      between sounds that doesn't exist in sounds themselves, but the theory
      books all say it does. The pitches of our music aren't related to the
      overtone series. Our fifths aren't perfect. I imagine that our octaves
      even [*laughs*] and our unisons are probably imperfect too. Certainly
      the fifths aren't [perfect], and this was brought about by the desire to
      modulate from one key to another. Harmony is a theory, and what I
      would like is to have sounds be free of that theory. When I didn't yet
      know that I thought I should study harmony, since to be a musician
      you should study harmony, counterpoint, and orchestration—I could
      learn the rules but I had no facility. I had no feeling. And Schoenberg,
      from his point of view, said I wouldn't be able to compose music—this
      was after having taught me for two years—and I said, "Why not?" And
      he said, "Not having a feeling for harmony you'll come to a wall that
      you won't be able to get through." But he was forgetting that I had
      promised him to devote my life to music, and so I said, "Well, then I'll
      simply have to spend my life beating my head against that wall."[3]

---

1. That of Ernö Goldfinger (1902–87), Hungarian-born architect who was based in
Paris from 1923 to 1934, when he moved to London and designed what came to be
regarded as brutalist high-rise buildings. Cage tells this story in "A Composer's
Confession" (1948) in Richard Kostelanetz, ed., *John Cage: Writer. Previously Uncollected
Pieces* (New York: Limelight Editions, 1993), 28; in *Silence: Lectures and Writings*
(Middletown, CT: Wesleyan University Press, 1961), 261; and in *A Year from Monday:
New Lectures and Writings* (Middletown, CT: Wesleyan University Press, 1967), 114.
2. Adolph Weiss (1891–1971), composer and professional bassoonist. He was
Schoenberg's first American pupil in Berlin in 1926 and introduced serial techniques
into the United States. He taught Cage in 1933, and part of his Trio is included in
Cage's *Notations* (New York: Something Else, 1969).
3. Cage, *Silence*, 261; *A Year from Monday*, 114. However, ten years after this interview, when he wrote the Foreword (1990) to Colin C. Sterne, *Arnold Schoenberg, the*

MO You're distinguishing between harmony and simultaneity. One of the things your music is about is being open to several things happening at once.

JC Yes, and particularly to the fact that we don't understand that simultaneity. Harmony is an attempt to understand it and to make it good rather than bad, whereas a true simultaneity is not concerned with things being beautiful or ugly but is rather concerned with an openness to whatever and particularly to freeing [things] from prejudices of the mind.

MO And prejudices about when the music stops?

JC True. I remember, when I first got involved with studying Zen Buddhism, loving those stories that came from a shakuhachi player who was also interested in cooking. The sound of the music continued in the cooking!

MO When I talked about when the music stops, it was Thoreau I was referring to. Listening to the sounds, the music of nature by Walden Pond, he remarked that music is continuous, only listening is intermittent.[4] It's curious that you—the enemy of imposed order—should have studied with that magisterial imposer of order Arnold Schoenberg.

JC I was devoted to Schoenberg, and I still am. Were he alive I would honor him, as I did earlier, and I think if we could converse together now, he would not consider that I'd been unfaithful to his teaching.

MO He did say you weren't a composer.

Composer as Numerologist (Lewiston, NY: Edwin Mellon, 1993), Cage said: "[Numerology] led Schoenberg not only to expression but to harmony. And what is harmony? . . . It is just what happens when you bring sounds together. We discover it also when we have only one sound. There is an inner harmony in each. I myself prefer the many, and I want, above all, anarchy, an absence of law with regard to coexistence of multiplicity. When Schoenberg was alive, we both thought I had no feeling for harmony. Now I know that I do, though it will not be my last word as it was his. My numbers, though not coming from numerology, but from an ancient Eastern source, the *I Ching*, also bring it about." See also James Tenney, "John Cage and the Theory of Harmony" (1983), in Richard Kostelanetz, ed., *Writings about John Cage* (Ann Arbor: University of Michigan Press, 1993), 136–61.

4. Cage quotes this in Richard Kostelanetz, *John Cage (ex)plain(ed)* (New York: Schirmer, 1996), 121. Cage said about Thoreau: "Reading the *Journal*, I had been struck by the twentieth-century way Thoreau listened . . . just as composers using technology nowadays listen. He paid attention to each sound, whether it was 'musical or not,' just as they do; and he explored the neighborhood of Concord just as they explore the possibilities provided by electronics." Cage, Foreword, *M: Writings '67–'72* (Middletown, CT: Wesleyan University Press, 1973).

JC   Yes, but one's notion of what composition is could change. He didn't have such a closed mind, really. That's why I say that if we had the opportunity to converse [*laughs*] I might be able to persuade him that I was faithful to him and [that] my work was, in a sense, composition. I think of myself as a composer, and the reason I think Schoenberg might agree is that when I was studying with him he sent us to the blackboard with a problem in counterpoint, even though the class was a class in harmony. And he said, "When you have a solution turn around and let me see it." When I showed him my solution he said "that's right" and asked for another solution of the same problem. I gave him that and so on until I'd given seven or eight solutions. He then said—I'd always worshipped the man, but now he seemed to ascend in my estimation— "What is the principle underlying all of the solutions?"[5]

    I couldn't answer him then, but in the last five to ten years I've come to think that the principle is the question we ask. It is important not only in music but [also] in the rest of our lives that we ask important questions so that we get good answers! [*laughs*]

MO   But he is owned as teacher and master by those who want to control every single aspect of their compositions, whereas you abandon that.

JC   Not always, but often. I do abandon it even when I write a composition out in every detail, as I am doing now with the *Freeman Etudes* for violin solo. I don't control it, but I make it very precise through the use of chance operations. I think my work shows different instances of how to proceed non-intentionally.

MO   Where did you get the initial idea of proceeding non-intentionally?

JC   I thought myself at a crossroads in the late forties as a result of many things occurring. One was the experience of going into an anechoic chamber at Harvard University. I expected to hear no sound at all because it was a room made as silent as possible. But in that room I heard two sounds, and I was so surprised that I went to the engineer in charge and said, "There's something wrong: there are two sounds in that room." I described them, and he said the high one was my nervous system in operation and the low one was my blood circulating. So I realized that I was making music unintentionally continuously. So I felt myself to be at a crossroads where I could proceed as my body was proceeding, unintentionally, or I could continue intentionally. But since everyone else was doing that, it seemed more reasonable and more useful to society if I took this other direction.

MO   Is that where Thoreau came in?

JC   He came in later. I had read him in school, but my serious contact comes in the late sixties. I like the language of Thoreau very much, in

---

5. Cage, *Silence*, 93.

the same way I like the music of Erik Satie. Debussy was *enrichi* whereas Satie was *depouillé*—the feathers pulled out. If you look at the early writing of Thoreau and then at the later writing you see the adjectives and adverbs disappearing: the language gets simplified.

MO You've said that chance is not a blind oracle but a means of opening oneself to that which one would not have considered.

JC I'm speaking from my experience. No matter how strictly I fulfill the commitment given to me, chance still enters into all the spaces. I think Thoreau was aware of this. He said that besides what we think we're doing in a day, we also have to get the food and prepare a meal. In the doing of those everyday things so many things happen by chance—there are so many things to see, to hear, and so forth—that, as Thoreau says, we don't need any further entertainment than that.

MO So you would say that you are not going out and deliberately subjecting yourself to chance but accepting that chance is an important element?

JC Right. I only use chance operations as a discipline when I'm making something. I don't think of my life as something being made but rather as a series of experiences. But if I'm making a text, a piece of music, or an etching, then I have recourse to chance operations to free the work I'm doing from my memory, my taste, my likes and dislikes. I chose those chance operations and I use them in correspondence to sitting cross-legged and going through special breathing exercises, disciplines one would follow if we were going inward; but as a musician I am necessarily going outward, and so I use this other discipline.

MO You say you free yourself from memory, taste, and so on, but what for? What are you opening yourself up to?

JC The rest of the world, don't you think? I hope so.

MO I agree, but a large number of people do find it difficult to imagine the creative artist abandoning, they would say, his role as a creator.

JC Not abandoning it, simply changing it from the responsibility of making choices to the responsibility of asking questions. I try to ask radical questions—questions that get at the root of things. If I succeed, then the answers—even though they come through chance operations—will be, I believe, revelatory in the sense of revealing to me more of creation than staying with my mind the way it was. Satie said that experience is a form of paralysis because we get absolutely stuck with our ideas.[6] Through chance operations, and faithfulness to them, we can get free of that paralysis.

---

6. Satie said: "When I was young, people used to say to me: 'wait till you're fifty, you'll see.' I am fifty. I haven't seen anything." Nigel Wilkins, trans., *The Writings of Erik Satie*

MO But it does demand from the perceiver an absolute openness and a willingness to go along with this.

JC That demand on the observer or listener is made by anything. Any other art too, don't you think?

MO Not only art. What I think I'm coming 'round to is that if one accepts what you have been doing, then it isn't confined to music or even to the arts but it is a social thing.

JC And becomes useful in everyday life. If you become open to the world outside of your ideas about it—I mean really attentive to the world outside of you, which you can perceive through your eyes and ears primarily—then you become a Thoreau unto yourself. The pavement you're standing on can become fascinating, or the way the light falls on two different Coca-Cola bottles. So we come to a poetic awareness of the uniqueness of each experience, of the necessity to have the experience at the moment it presents itself because it's constantly changing. There's no other time to live than each moment.

MO What sort of effect does this attitude have on your perception of more structured forms of art?

JC Well, I can have difficulty with it. I remember having difficulty particularly with the "Hallelujah Chorus." I felt pushed and I didn't want to be pushed! I prefer a more anarchic situation in which I can move in one direction or another. I had the feeling that if I responded to that music, I'd have to go exactly where it wanted me to go.[7]

MO Most people are afraid of anarchy, aren't they?

JC I think more and more people are going to be less afraid of it and more friendly to their own centers. This will come about through more leisure. I learned recently that the Olivetti company now retires its workers at age forty-five with a pension, and they have trained them while they were employed. Formerly, they trained them only in gardening, but I think they now train them to be artists. Any training in art is at least a partial training in anarchy! [laughs] People learn not to follow the rules from outside but from inside.

MO That in itself is a subversive thought.

(London: Eulenberg, 1980), 84, and—very relevant to Cage—"The exercise of an art requires us to live in a state of complete self-denial," 113. Also Cage, Silence, 118.
7. "I had just heard Messiah with Mrs. Henry Allen Moe, and she said, 'Don't you love the Hallelujah Chorus?' and I said, 'No, I can't stand it.' So she said, 'Don't you like to be moved?' and I said, 'I don't mind being moved, but I don't like to be pushed.'" In Cole Gagne and Tracy Caras, *Soundpieces: Interviews with American Composers* (Metuchen, NJ: Scarecrow, 1982), 79.

JC   I have some others too! [*laughs*] Each one of us must be subversive. All you have to do to realize that is to pick up a daily newspaper.

MO You used to keep a kind of optimist's diary: *How to Improve the World: You Will Only Make Matters Worse.* Do you still keep it?

JC   I have one half finished, but I put it aside a few years ago even though I carry it around with me. I was more or less stupefied by the news each day. But I have very little experience as a pessimist. Once when I was talking to a group at the art school attached to the Museum of Fine Art in Boston, I told the students I was less optimistic than I had been— and they all begged me to continue in my foolish ways! [*laughs*]

Part IV

Extravaganzas

Chapter Nineteen

About Musicircus, Cage with Peter Dickinson

London, May 20, 1972

Cage's *Musicircus* is an event based on the simultaneous presentation of many concerts under the same roof at the same time, exemplifying Cage's utopian ideas about freedom in society. The first performance was November 17, 1967, at the University Stock Pavilion, University of Illinois, Urbana-Champaign,[1] where another Cage spectacular, *HPSCHD*, would premiere at Assembly Hall on May 16, 1969. The second production of *Musicircus* was at Macalester College Fieldhouse, St. Paul, Minnesota, on April 11, 1970. The European premiere, with Cage cited as director, was during the *Journées de musique contemporaine* at the Halles de Baltard, Pavillon 9, Paris, on October 27, 1970.

Cage told Daniel Charles: "In a *Musicircus* you have the right to bring together all kinds of music, which are ordinarily separated. We're no longer worried about what there is to be heard, so to speak. It's no longer a question of aesthetics."[2] In the same series of interviews he commented on the two American productions where "each group really worked in an independent manner. No one worried about his neighbor. The result was amazing. But if you stick to concentrated attention, or if you retain the principle of discourse, musicircuses may not be of any interest at all."[3] Cage regretted that the Paris production had not included film, and he found the

---

1. See Stephen Husarik's description of the occasion in "John Cage and Lejaren Hiller: HPSCHD, 1969," *American Music* 1, no. 2 (Summer 1983): 4–6.
2. Cage, *For the Birds: John Cage in Conversation with Daniel Charles* (London: Marion Boyars, 1981), 52.
3. Ibid., 172.

performing and auditorium spaces so cramped that the audience could barely move.

The British premiere was in The Great Hall, University of Birmingham, on November 24, 1972, followed by a London performance at The Round House on December 17, presented by the Park Lane Group.[4] My students were involved in both occasions, and the director was Jocelyn Powell. I was anxious to know what Cage had in mind for his *Musicircus*, so I met him in London on May 20, 1972, and took notes about his recommendations. These are the points he made:

1. There are serious differences between societies, such as the United States and Germany, so *Musicircus* gets various receptions. The first American performance made the composer Herbert Brün[5] livid, but the audience liked it.

2. In Minneapolis it was good—the organizer was Sue Weil at the Walker Art Center.[6]

3. There should be food and drink, as in a real circus. Ideally, all the senses should be employed.

4. There should be no seats so people can move about.

5. Use the greatest possible variety of participants—church groups, children's choirs, etc.

6. Dancing can be included.

7. There is no score, and therefore no performing fees have to be paid.

8. The piece "should be fun"—people "should get the joyousness of the anarchic spirit."

9. There must be space for the audience.

10. Do not charge admission—in Paris there was a charge, and it became a mob of people who couldn't move.

---

4. The Park Lane Group was founded by John Woolf in 1956 and has had an influential role in the musical life of London ever since by presenting young artists, commissioning new works, and putting on concerts and opera. Earlier that year I had asked Cage if there was any chance he would be present for these performances, but at that time he was in Michigan, with extended periods of touring.

5. Herbert Brün (1918–), German composer who joined the composition faculty at the University of Illinois, working in electronic music and computer composition. There is an extract from his Trio (1966) in Cage's *Notations* (New York: Something Else, 1969). Richard Barnes reported: "Herbert Brün, whose ideas about composition could hardly be farther from Cage's than they are, said: 'With what he does and what he says, either he's a composer or an idiot. And—and—he's a composer.' Pause. 'His great big goofy smile.'" In Richard Kostelanetz, ed., *John Cage* (New York: Praeger, 1970), 53.

6. Suzanne Weil, coordinator of Performing Arts. See "I'm the Happiest Person I Know (S. W.)," in Cage, *Empty Words: Writings '73–'78* (Middletown, CT: Wesleyan University Press, 1979), 122.

11. No fees are to be paid to participants.
12. Use only people who are willing to take part.
13. Don't pay attention to the discrepancy between, say, a clavichord recital and a jazz band! This has happened—at one occasion people went along and put their ears to the clavichord!
14. If there are more performers than platforms, then stagger their share of time.
15. Five hours would be a "reasonable" duration.
16. Limit the time for a rock group because of the din. Amplification is allowed if a group normally uses it.
17. *Musicircus* is a whole evening on its own.

Twenty years later, after a performance in the Braun Music Center at Stanford on January 29, 1992, Cage again referred to the clavichord caught in the melee.[7] This time he said, "It would be good if the *Musicircus* lasted at least three hours," and he arranged to read his text *Muoyce* (*Writing for the Fifth Time through Finnegans Wake*) himself—in a separate room, not mixed up with everything else like his speaking in *Roaratorio*.

The first British performance of *Musicircus* at the University of Birmingham was billed as "an environmental extravaganza." John Falding, covering the occasion for the *Birmingham Post*, got the message: "By moving around, the listeners were able to become the performers, because they could exercise control over the sound they were experiencing. It was occasionally exciting, frequently interesting, and always fun, thereby fulfilling the composer's intentions exactly."[8]

Back in 1972 the London newspapers covered classical music far more generously than they do today—a major concert was liable to have four or five reviews in the weekly papers and two or three in the Sundays. In terms of reception history in one of the world's major musical centers outside the United States, the response to *Musicircus* is worth documentation. London witnessed *Musicircus* after *HPSCHD*,[9] which was the wrong way 'round since

---

7. Charles Junkerman, "'nEw/Forms of Living Together': The Model of the Musicircus," in Marjorie Perloff and Charles Junkerman, eds., *John Cage: Composed in America* (Chicago: University of Chicago Press, 1994), 61–62, n. 8, and 40 for Cage's letter about how to proceed.

8. John Falding, "Music Circus . . . at the Great Hall, Birmingham University," *Birmingham Post,* November 25, 1972.

9. *HPSCHD* was included in *ICES-72 International Carnival of Experimental Sound Based on a Theme of Myth, Magic, Madness and Mysticism,* presented by the editors of *Source-Music of the Avant-Garde*, organized and produced by Harvey Matuso as a BBC Prom concert at The Round House, London, on August 13, 1972. See Adrian Jack, "Cage's Changes," reviewing Nonesuch LP H 71224 containing *HPSCHD*, in *Records and Recording* (August 1972): 22–23. *Musicircus* was included in the BBC's *John Cage*

it actually came later. But that meant there should have been some preparation for this kind of extravaganza.

Dominic Gill realized *Musicircus* was "an 'environmental' piece, more an event than a concert—a music party to relax and meet friends, eat and talk and drink at, and only incidentally, when and as the mood takes you, to listen to. . . . The result is unpredictable, anarchic and (with luck) occasionally fun." He noted the usual features, with "a large cast . . . deployed around the arena, corridors and balcony, on the seats and music platforms. . . . But fun? Socializing apart, this *Musicircus* was a good, clean, unpredictable bore. Them that likes their fun this way might take a tip, and try the practice studios in Marylebone High Street; the sound is the same, but quieter, easier on the ear."[10]

An unsigned review provided more detail:

> It was like a musical replay of the Battle of Trafalgar. In the center of the Round House was Jane Wynn Owen, a tall, blond mezzo-soprano from Birmingham . . . who could only occasionally be heard for, perched on a balcony to her right was a full choir of demure carol singers . . . cheerfully roaring out "Hark the herald angels sing." As they battled it out . . . heavier guns opened from their left, fired by Mandragona, a gutsy rock group from the North. On the other side of the auditorium the Dorian String Quartet . . . were projecting a delicate tracery of musical bullets[11] into no-man's land where the audience milled around eating cakes and ice cream. Honky-tonk, jazz, folk, classical, romantic and contemporary music competed for attention with brass quintets, mandolin players and bongo drummers. . . . Cage, leading figure of the American musical avant-garde, composed it in the hope that his audience would "get the joyousness of the anarchic spirit." Some did, some did not.[12]

The critic for the *Daily Telegraph* was indifferent, regarding *Musicircus* as "a claustrophobic fairground."[13] On the other hand, Hugo Cole was the most favorably disposed of the London critics. He noted that Cage had said, hopefully, "You won't hear a thing: you'll hear everything," then reported that "the evening ended memorably with Cage's settings of E. E. Cummings, the singer moving off into the outer regions during the last unaccompanied

Uncaged weekend at The Barbican, London, January 16–18, 2004. It was not a whole evening. When Stephen Montague, in his program note, said the British premiere of *Musicircus* was at the 1982 Almeida Festival, he may have confused it with *Roaratorio*.

10. Dominic Gill, "Cage's Musicircus," *Financial Times*, December 19, 1972, 3.
11. Cage's *String Quartet* (1950).
12. "Musicircus," untraced London newspaper review.
13. R. M., "Amplifiers v. Players," *Daily Telegraph*, December 19, 1972.

song—simple but effective music theater."[14] He appreciated the extramusical aspects too: "Visually, the effect was enchanting—so many little islands of activity, a tangle of spotlight beams, occasionally catching the bubbles that drifted up from the outer arcade where the Stoned Parrot were involved in a song and dance act. Players came and went, a cellist nested temporarily in an old farm cart, bursts of applause came from here and there as one group or another came to the end of its performance." He thought the audience "seemed to get the idea, and wandered around, neither outraged nor awed, with their cheese rolls," but he still felt that "musically, *Musicircus* would have come off better at The Royal Albert Hall or in the open air—at the Round House too many sounds of different weights were crammed too closely together for comfort; but as a commentary on listening and performing rituals, it made its point wittily and sharply."[15]

Cage realized that prolonged loud sounds would make others inaudible, as his comment to me showed. In 1980, undercutting criticism, he told Frans Benders that he was concerned with "resolving complexity" through the "notion of a musicircus, of many things going on at once. You can have soft things going on at the same time as loud things, and all you have to do to hear the soft things is go closer."[16] He added, "You can get rid of intention by multiplying intention."[17]

At the same time as *Musicircus,* Cage said: "Art instead of being an object made by one person is a process set in motion by a group of people. Art's socialized. It isn't someone saying something, but people doing things, giving everyone (including those involved) the opportunity to have experiences they would not otherwise have had."[18]

James Pritchett has summarized the situation as "a musical anarchy . . . wherein the performers and listeners were no longer told what to do, and Cage retreated to such a distance that his role as organizer and designer, while crucial, was practically invisible. The circus events represented yet another variation on the music-as-process idea, this time turning music into an activity for society at large."[19]

---

14. Presumably the *Five Songs* (1938), followed by the unaccompanied *Experiences No. 2* (1948).

15. Hugo Cole, "Musicircus," *Guardian,* December 19, 1972.

16. In Richard Kostelanetz, ed., *Conversing with Cage* (New York: Limelight Editions, 1988), 226.

17. Ibid., 234.

18. "Diary: How to Improve the World III," in *A Year from Monday: New Lectures and Writings* (Middletown, CT: Wesleyan University Press, 1967), 151.

19. James Pritchett, *The Music of John Cage* (Cambridge: Cambridge University Press, 1993), 158–59.

A decade after that performance, Keith Potter looked back on avant-garde music in London:

Perhaps my fondest memory of the Round House . . . comes from Cage's *Musicircus*. . . . Our improvisation group had retired from the fray after having been banished upstairs where absolutely no one was even aware of our existence. I took my cello and did some doleful solo improvising behind one of the old pillars watched, I eventually became aware, by a man in . . . a dirty raincoat. He came up so close to me that my bow-arm was severely restricted in its motion. And after what must have been several minutes listening to my long-held notes . . . he leaned even further over and said, very quietly but very deliberately: "You're mad, absolutely bloody mad!"[20]

These occasions brought Cage notoriety in Britain, and he became almost exclusively associated with the lunatic fringe of the avant-garde—to the detriment of his earlier music for percussion and prepared piano. Hardly anyone took him seriously. In 1975 he was featured in a cartoon in the satirical magazine *Private Eye*. The sketch shows five bell ringers in a church belfry, bottles on the floor. Two are drinking; the other three are holding ropes. One of the latter group is almost out of sight, clinging on; one is supine on the ground; and the other is on his knees. The belfry door is ajar; a nose and just part of a face show that someone is trying to get in. The caption is: "Piss off will you Vicar—this one's by John Cage!"[21]

I showed this to Cage, but I am not sure he saw the joke.

---

20. Keith Potter, "How Round Was My House," *Classical Music*, May 14, 1983, 8.
21. Cartoon by Colum Wheeler, *Private Eye*, January 10, 1975, 4.

Chapter Twenty

Introducing Roaratorio, Cage, Cunningham, and Peadar Mercier with Peter Dickinson

BBC Radio 3, July 19, 1987

Cage's Irish Circus

Radio feature containing interviews with Peter Dickinson, broadcast before the performance at the BBC Promenade Concert in The Royal Albert Hall, London, with John Cage, Irish folk musicians, and the Merce Cunningham Dance Company.[1] Producer: Anthony Cheevers.

---

1. This performance in London on July 19, 1987, was announced as the first time the Merce Cunningham Dance Company had taken part in *Roaratorio*. However, Cunningham's *Roaratorio* was given at the Festival de Lille, Roubaix, on October 26, 1983; a month later at Frankfurt; and in July 1985 at the Avignon Festival. There were New York performances at the Brooklyn Academy during October 7–12, 1986. See David Vaughan, "Cunningham, Cage and Joyce: 'This Longawaited Messiagh of Roaratorios,'" *Choreography and Dance* 1, no. 4 (1992): 79–89. The first British hearing of *Roaratorio* was at St. James' Church, London N7, on May 28, 1982, during the Almeida Festival, for Cage's seventieth birthday. Cage, narrator and sound production; John David Fullemann, sound production; Irish musicians Joseph Heaney, singer; Peadar and Mel Mercier, percussion; Séamus Ennis, pipes; Paddy Glackin, fiddle; and Séamus Tanzey, flute; assisted by Nicholas Parker and James Fulkerson. The first British performance of *Roaratorio* outside London was at the Huddersfield Contemporary Music Festival on November 22, 1989, with Cage reading, John Fullemann as sound engineer, and Peadar Mercier and colleagues.

Introduction

Roaratorio was commissioned by Klaus Schöning as a radio play for production
at Westdeutscher Rundfunk, Cologne; Suddeutscher Rundfunk, Stuttgart;
and Katholieke Radio Omroep, Hilversum. The first transmission was
on October 22, 1979.
By permission of the BBC, the John Cage Trust, and Mel Mercier.

Peadar Mercier (1914–91)[2] was born in Cork and began to play the
bodhran and bones in the late 1950s. He was invited by the composer Sean
O'Riada to join Ceoltoiri Chualainn, and during 1966–76 he played with
the Chieftains, the most celebrated Irish traditional music group. As the first
professional bodhran and bones player, he performed and recorded with
the group until 1976, and his playing remained influential after that date.
In the 1980s Peadar and his son Mel performed extensively with Cage and
the Merce Cunningham Dance Company, providing bodhran duets for
Roaratorio and *Duets*. Mercier also wrote poetry throughout his adult life.

Interviews

PD   *Finnegans Wake* is a major document in twentieth-century literature, still
perhaps more discussed than widely read. The richness of its linguistic
games with sound as well as sense has provided a constant fascination
for composers. In *Roaratorio*, using a punning title from *Finnegans Wake*,[3]
Cage matches the visionary complexity of James Joyce.[4] The technique

---

2. This is the correct spelling of Peadar Mercier's name. Other sources are wrong.
E-mail from Mel Mercier, March 8, 2005.
3. "the thrummings of a crewth fiddle . . . caressed the ears of the subjects of King
Saint Finnerty the Festive . . . with their priggish mouths all open for the larger
appraisiation of this longawaited Messiagh of roaratorios," *Finnegans Wake*, 41.
4. Music was always important to James Joyce (1882–1941). As a young man he con-
templated a career as a singer, and his high, light Irish tenor was heard in Dublin
concerts. The musical qualities of his first published book, a cycle of poems called
Chamber Music (1907), have attracted many composers ranging from Geoffrey
Molineux Palmer—Joyce's favorite—to Luciano Berio. Joyce's novels are full of references to popular songs, hymns, and opera. His monumental later works, *Ulysses*
(1922) and *Finnegans Wake* (1939), employ a multilingual stream-of-consciousness
continuity often regarded as musical in its construction. In an extraordinary episode,
Joyce interrupted his work on *Finnegans Wake* in 1930 to promote the international
operatic career of the Irish tenor John O'Sullivan. See Arnold Goldman, " 'Send Him
Canorious'—Arnold Goldman Writes about James Joyce's 'Sullivanising.' " *Listener*,
August 3, 1972, 142–44.

of simultaneous independent layers of music is developed from Cage's *Variations* pieces in the 1960s and mixed-media events such as *Musicircus* and *HPSCHD* seen in London during the early 1970s. I asked Cage when he first came across *Finnegans Wake.*

JC   In the 1920s. When we had *transition* magazine I used to read the sections from *Finnegans Wake* that appeared, and I loved them and used to read them to my friends to entertain them.[5] Then in 1939 I remember going to a department store in Seattle and buying the first edition. But then I was already very busy composing, so I didn't think I had time to read the book through. I mostly went on reading the excerpts with which I was familiar. But now and then, when I was asked to write a song, I went through *Finnegans Wake* looking for a text. I wrote *The Wonderful Widow of Eighteen Springs.*[6] That was how it continued until I was writing *Apartment House* and *Renga* for the American Bicentennial. In the midst of that, I was approached by a magazine to write something about *Finnegans Wake.* I wanted to do it, but I was again too busy. So I wrote back and said I didn't have the time, but the editor was very persistent.[7] It was a magazine that was to have an issue called *In the*

---

5. *transition:* the international magazine published by Shakespeare and Co. and launched in Paris in 1927, which was initially edited by Eugene Jolas (1894–1952) and Elliot Paul and ran until 1938. Cage's friend Don Sample introduced him to the journal; and since he first came across the portions of *Finnegans Wake* that were serialized in the magazine, it may be worth indicating the connections between the first versions, which are often shorter and simpler, and the published text. The issue numbers are listed in Appendix I, 233.

6. *The Wonderful Widow of Eighteen Springs* (1942) and *Nowth upon Nacht* (1984) both have texts taken from the same page of *Finnegans Wake*, 556, which appeared in *transition* in November 1929.

7. Elliott Anderson, editor of *TriQuarterly.* See Cage's more detailed account of this approach in *Empty Words: Writings '73–'78* (Middletown, CT: Wesleyan University Press, 1979), 133. For further information see Cage's speech "On Having Received the Carl Sczuka Prize for Roaratorio," given at Donaueschingen, October 20, 1979, and his interview, both included in the CD booklet with John Cage *Roaratorio: Laughtears*—Cage, Schöning, Heaney, Ennis et al., Cage Vol. 6, mode 28–29 (1992). ("laughtears" appears in *Finnegans Wake,* 15.) Cage's speech was also published in Sorel Etrog and John Cage, "Dream Chamber and about Roaratorio," in Robert O'Driscoll, ed., *Joyce and the Dada Circus: A Collage* (Ontario: Black Brick, 1982). After the initial radio broadcasts, *Roaratorio* was produced live at the Festival d'Automne, Beaubourg, Paris, in January 1981. Keith Potter was there and described it as "an hour of sheer delight: a 'circus,' certainly, in that so much is going on that the ear is forced to follow up its own leads from moment to moment . . . a magical mixture of riotous extravagance and calm beauty." "Americans in Paris," *Classical Music,* February 21, 1981, 22. There was also a performance in Toronto by the Celtic Arts of Canada

Wake of the Wake. He wrote saying he would change the deadline if I would write something for him. I said that would still make too much trouble. He continued insisting, and I finally realized that the quickest way to get rid of this interruption was to do what he wanted! [*laughs*]

So I picked up the *Wake* and opened it the way people say they open the Bible, the dictionary, or something. I simply began looking for Joyce's name in terms of mesostics, and I went to the end of that section. I think I wrote twenty-three mesostics and I sent them off. Then, having done that, I became so fascinated that I looked forward to going through the whole *Wake*, particularly because of the end of the *Wake*, which is so beautiful. Well, that's exactly what happened, and I've now made five *Writings through Finnegans Wake.*

PD   In the text you read during the performance of *Roaratorio*, you can see the name of James Joyce picked out in capitals down the middle of the page. How does it all work?[8]

JC   In an acrostic the name goes down the edge, but in a mesostic the name goes down the middle. I looked for the first word on the first page of *Finnegans Wake* that had a J in it but didn't have an A after the J. Then I looked for the next word that had an A but didn't have an M after it. And so on. The first word in *Finnegans Wake* that has a J in it but doesn't have an A after it is "nathanjoe," and I chose to precede it with "wroth with twone nathandjoe." Those words are together and don't break the mesostic rule. The next word that has an A in it but doesn't have an M is the word "A."

---

and New Music Concerts on the centenary of Joyce's birth, February 2, 1982, which was claimed as the complete realization of *Roaratorio* onstage and was a tribute to Marshall McLuhan. However, claims for *Roaratorio* as classic radio include Elissa S. Guralnick, *Sight Unseen: Beckett, Pinter, Stoppard, and Other Contemporary Dramatists on Radio* (Athens: Ohio University Press, 1996), 98. Following discussion of *Roaratorio* she concludes: "Neither stage, nor film, nor television can effectively compete with the radio as a forum for words that make music. It is radio alone that yields appropriate conditions for releasing the music in language: namely a performing space at once empty and dimensionless, from which words can emanate free from any material associations."

8.   "It is a simple measure of Cage's originality that nobody ever made poetry like this before—the method is, like so much of his work, at once sensible and nutty. To my mind, *Writing through Finnegans Wake* is interesting in part because it is so audaciously innovative; it succeeds in part because it recycles James Joyce. Hearing Cage read it aloud, with sensitive precision, was a special pleasure." Richard Kostelanetz, "Empty Words," in *John Cage (ex)plain(ed)* (New York: Schirmer, 1996), 118.

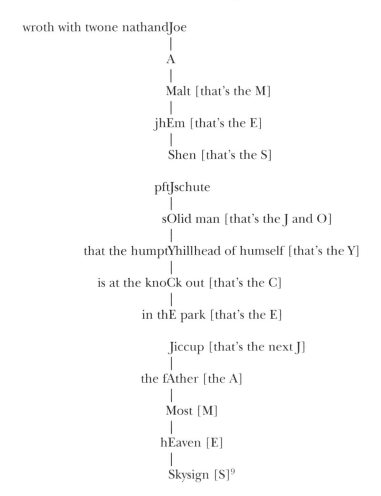

wroth with twone nathandJoe
|
A
|
Malt [that's the M]
|
jhEm [that's the E]
|
Shen [that's the S]

pftJschute
|
sOlid man [that's the J and O]
|
that the humptYhillhead of humself [that's the Y]
|
is at the knoCk out [that's the C]
|
in thE park [that's the E]

Jiccup [that's the next J]
|
the fAther [the A]
|
Most [M]
|
hEaven [E]
|
Skysign [S]⁹

---

9. Joyce's original text for part of this passage on the first page of *Finnegans Wake* is:
. . . wroth with twone nathandjoe. Rot a peck of pa's malt had Jhem or Shen brewed by arclight and rory end to the regginbrow was to be seen ringsome on the aquaface.
. . . The great fall of the offwall entailed at such short notice the pftjschute of Finnegan, erse solid man, that the humptyhillhead of humself prumptly sends an unquiring one well to the west in quest of his tumptytumtoes: and their unturnpikepointandplace is at the knock out in the park where oranges have been laid to rust upon the green since devlinsfirst loved livvy.
Cage's "Writing for the Second Time through Finnegans Wake" is in *Empty Words*, 133–76, with Cage's introduction, and in the CD booklet.

The mesostic, of course, does make the text shorter. *Finnegans Wake* has 626 pages, whereas my *Second Writing* has only 41 pages. I've since made texts that have even less.[10]

PD So you loved the way it turned out even though you didn't know how . . .

JC Yes, and I think Joyce would have been amused!

PD In the performance we're going to see at the Prom and hear over the radio, you speak the mesostics yourself?

JC Right. Otherwise they simply made it possible for me to locate the proper position of all the sounds, which were recorded on tape. Then I was able to identify each line as coming from a particular page in the book. If a dog barked, say, on page 17, line 22, then I would put that in relation to the mesostic where it belonged—between something that preceded it and something that followed it in my poem. Those sounds came from two sources. One, I read through *Finnegans Wake* and listed them as I heard them—dogs barking, roosters crowing, etc. I put those in categories, and I put as many as I could into the tape. When I say "as I could," I'm referring to a deadline of one month at IRCAM;[11] and I worked intensively with John Fullemann, the sound engineer, and we put as many sounds in *Roaratorio* as we could. Half of them came from this listing of dogs, cats, cows, trains and automobiles, and so forth; and the other came from going to places mentioned in Louis Mink's *Finnegans Wake Gazetteer*,[12] which lists all the places in the world that are mentioned in the *Wake*. Nearly half of them are in Ireland, and, of those, half again are in Dublin. So we made a trip, which I actually advise people to imitate.

We went to Dublin, walked to all the places in Dublin [*laughs*] that were mentioned, and this brought about a kind of tourism that was entirely different from the ordinary paths of tourists.

PD Rather like the Bloomsday trip for admirers of *Ulysses*?

JC It was absolutely marvelous. Just as we gave IRCAM a month for the making of tapes, we gave another month for gathering the sounds in Ireland, with a week given to Dublin—maybe a little more. Then we began this fantastic trip all over Ireland, again directed by the book. We had maps that showed the least little roads, almost paths, and we were able to plan each night in a B&B.

---

10. The text of *Finnegans Wake*, Viking Press, starts on page 3, so the count of 626 pages is correct even though the last page is numbered 628. It is less easy to reconcile the page count for Cage's second "Writing through," which runs from pages 137–76 in *Empty Words*; the count of unnumbered pages in the CD booklet is 40.

11. Institute de recherche et coordination acoustique/musique, Paris. Boulez was invited to found a center for research on new music in 1970 and directed it until 1992.

12. Louis O. Mink, *A Finnegans Wake Gazetteer* (Bloomington: University of Indiana Press, 1978).

PD   But you also wrote to some people to get some sounds?

JC   Yes. I wrote to radio stations, universities, and to special organizations interested in sound and sounds of the environment. I was able to collect sounds from all over the world, and people were very cooperative.

PD   So we're building up a picture of this total performance piece. You reading your mesostics, a tape of sounds associated with *Finnegans Wake* and found in the book, but don't you use Irish folk musicians?

JC   Yes. I first found Joe Heaney, who's no longer living, and I met him—strangely enough not in Brooklyn, where he lived at the time, but in England, where he was singing in a pub. I made a trip especially to hear him and to persuade him to sing in *Roaratorio*. I had to explain to each musician that he would be part of a circus—that is to say, that other people would be playing other music possibly at the same time. It's difficult to explain to a soloist that that's the situation they're going to be in—at least I found it difficult. He enjoyed the prospect of it.

PD   Joe Heaney can be heard on the tapes played back during tonight's performance.[13] Later, Cage met other Irish folk musicians. Peadar Mercier with his son Mel has played the drums in all performances of *Roaratorio,* so I asked him how he got involved.

PM   He rang me up to say my name had been given to him by Ciarán MacMathúna, head of the traditional music section here at RTE [Radio Telefís Éireann] in Dublin. He wanted me to come into the studios to play the traditional Irish drum known as the bodhran, which he wanted for some special reason he didn't at that time intimate to me. I said that I had a son called Mel, and often at home we would be playing rhythms and Mel would be extemporizing against the rhythm. Cage said, "That's OK, Mr. Mercier." So that's how I came to meet him. The same day we were there, there was also a marvelous flute player called Matt Malloy, and I understood at the time that we would be playing together. But not so. What John wanted was the sound of a particular instrument to be recorded and to be used in *Roaratorio* but not musicians playing together as such. Subsequently, he went down to Milltown Malbay in County Clare to the Willie Clancy Festival, and there he recorded a great old pipe player named Séamus Ennis—since deceased, Lord rest him. Séamus was the man who did the *I Roved Out* program on BBC radio back in the early fifties. He also recorded a man named Paddy Glackin, a great fiddle player who has presented traditional programs in RTE in Dublin. After Séamus died, his place was taken by another pipe player called Liam O'Flynn. Matt Malloy wasn't available because he'd joined the Chieftains, with whom I played up to that time, and his place had been taken by Séamus Tanzey—quite a character, now domiciled up in Belfast.

---

13. And on the recording.

PD Were the musicians familiar with each other's playing?

PM Well, we knew each other and had regard for each other, but he didn't want a group as such. He wanted the sounds and wanted to present them in their individual attractions without any dependence on anything else. Like all the sounds he has in this marvelous *Roaratorio*, in the sixty minutes it takes for John to decant his beautiful kind of intonation, each musician—Mel and myself as a pair—has twenty minutes only. You are expected to use your discretion in the manner in which you enter and exit. But the normal thing is to try and keep it even, yet not too apparently even. All the other musicians come in at any time playing reels and jigs, which last maybe two or three minutes. They come in and out. Sometimes everybody is playing; sometimes only one.

PD Do the musicians choose the actual pieces?

PM Of course they do, and they change them all the time. Sometimes you can see that there's a little contest going on between the flute and the fiddle where the flute player might start on a jig, making a lovely job of it, and the others are aware of that. Not to be outdone, they'll come in subsequently—not too soon but very clearly—and they'll intrude upon, if you like, the mastery of the flute player. That kind of contention among the musicians is a lovely little byplay that goes on—very enjoyable. None of them would admit it, but I'm well aware that's what they're doing. I think they would, almost unwittingly, be under the influence of the total cacophony and realize the initial sense of discord that comes across. Therefore they would realize it's not their function to be in a kind of affinity with each other. They're there to play the tunes they choose to the best of their ability, with as much melodic excellence as possible, and that's it. But nonetheless, in between there's a bit of one-upmanship going on, which is quite fascinating.

PD There's a fourth layer in *Roaratorio* provided by the Merce Cunningham Dance Company, but the dance was added later.

JC I made it first for the radio at Klaus Schöning's request, but as I made it, and since Merce Cunningham is half Irish, I had in mind that it would be a fulfillment of the work if it included dancing.[14]

PD Will the dance have any connection with what goes on in the other channels of this piece?

---

14. Cage must have been pleased that the name Cunningham, or something close to it, appears several times in *Finnegans Wake*: Lili Coninghams (58), Minxy Cunningham (95), Merkin Cornyngwham (387), Andrew Martin Cunningham (393), and just Conyngham (434). Martin Cunningham appears in "Grace," the story in *Dubliners*, and again in *Ulysses*. Cage must have noticed Xenia (147), would have enjoyed "the science of sonorous silence" (230), and must have found "the Cat and Cage" (563).

JC The connection is taking place at the same time in the same place. It's that kind of connection that exists among all the other parts. My reading, the tapes, and the singing and playing of the Irish musicians are related in the same way.

PD For much of Cage's work with the Merce Cunningham Dance Company, music and movement are completely independent. I asked Merce Cunningham if the Irish folk music had affected his choreography for *Roaratorio*.

MC Not in any strictly material sense, but the dance contains a number of reels and jigs, all made up. I simply took the sense of the rhythm and made them up—they're certainly not authentic. I wouldn't pretend to do that. The *Wake* is so full of references to dancing that I thought it could have that kind of thing. It also has other things in it, but that's where I started. The dance, regardless of the material used, was made totally separate from any strict reference to the sound, and the dancers don't know when the Irish musicians will be playing. So there's no reference but there are certainly coincidences, which happen quite often.

 I decided to think of the company as a sort of family, a large family moving through the space—not in any way trying to do what the *Wake* does. But in the *Wake* there is the sense of this enormous human family continuing and moving around in a kind of spiral fashion. So in my working out of the piece, we start by entering one side of whatever area we're going to perform in, gradually it continues, and then we exit. We leave at the other side as though we are going on someplace else to start all over again [*laughs*] or continue in some other way. That's simply a spatial way for me, and it isn't meant as any kind of strict reference at all. It was like a structure I could use to work on the piece.

PD How did you approach the choreography?

MC I made everything quite separate. As I often do, I would choreograph one of my jigs for the dancers and then put that aside and work on another part, say, that had only three people in it. Then I had this number of elements varying in length, varying in complexity and the number of people involved, and I took all of those things and made a continuity out of it. Sometimes they dance together, sometimes singly, and very often in the pseudo jigs a couple will be dancing but the woman is not doing the same rhythm as the man. There's both opposition and joining. It's to have more than one thing going on rather than two people doing the same thing, although there are couples who do duets.

 From hearing *Roaratorio* and listening to John Cage speak about it, I thought of the dancing as another layer, not supported by other layers or referring to them—just to add more complexity.

PD The actual score of *Roaratorio* doesn't have the name of a book: it's a kind of blueprint for making a whole piece of music out of any book.

JC   Right. What we have now is:
Roaratorio: An Irish Circus on Finnegans Wake
But the score I published is:

_____,   _____   _____ CIRCUS ON _____
(title of composition) (article)   (adjective)   (title of book)

    And I give the directions for translating any book into music or, if you wish, sound.[15]

PD   How should the listener prepare for this?

JC   It would be a good thing to keep the ears open. I think the mind can sometimes get in the way. I don't mean the empty mind but a mind with preconceptions. An empty mind that is nevertheless alert—the kind of mind that would get you across the street safely if you were walking in thick traffic [*laughs*]—I think that kind of attention would be useful! [*laughs*]

PD   You know and I know that our world is concerned with lots of different things happening at once. As you say—it's your word—we've learned to become omni-attentive.

JC   Right.

PD   But not everybody understands: they can accept the fact that in the street we've got masses of things happening at once . . .

JC   And I think people have been, unfortunately, thinking of music and the arts as a kind of escape from that complexity. If it becomes equally complex in the concert hall, then—I don't know, though—I think people are getting more able to listen with pleasure. There are so many kinds of music now, and so much of it is broadcast. Now what happens in the household is extraordinary: it's global. I don't think people have the problems we sometimes think they have.

PD   Finally, I wondered if Peadar Mercier had found the simultaneities of Cage, reflecting those of Joyce, hard to swallow.

PM   Well, I can tell you quite frankly. When I first heard it I really thought it was the weirdest, most astonishing, most unacceptable cacophony I'd ever heard! Now I love every moment of it, and I'm waiting for my pet sounds—there's the blackbird that sings, the waterfall that comes tumbling down at the back of your neck, the Honda revving up on O'Connell Bridge, the seagulls over the tower in Sandymount. It's quite wonderful. There are magic moments when all the cacophony seems to cease and all you hear is John's intonation. Then that precious moment has gone, and down comes the clamor and cacophony again. To say that I love it now is a clear indication of where beauty lies if you look for it.

---

15. Then there are three pages of instructions.

Chapter Twenty One

Europeras *and After, Cage with* Anthony Cheevers

New York City, June 1988

Cage was commissioned by Heinz-Klaus Metzger and Rainer Riehn, the artistic directors of the Frankfurt Opera, to create *Europeras 1 & 2* (1985–87) with the assistance of Andrew Culver.[1] This took Cage's theatrical multimedia involvements—his circus principle—into the opera house itself. At the time of this interview only the first two *Europeras* had been produced, but Cage became so fascinated with the medium that *Europeras 3 & 4* (1990) and *Europera 5* (1991) followed, but these were less elaborate and could be done

---

1. *Europeras 3 & 4* were a Tenth Almeida Festival commission, co-produced by The Almeida; The Hebbel Theatre, Berlin; Musica 90, Strasbourg; and Modus Vivendi, with support from Lufthansa German Airlines, and premiered at The Almeida Theatre, London, on June 17, 1990. The British premiere of *Europera 5* was given by the Cambridge New Music Players, directed by Edward Dudley Hughes, at Blackheath Halls, London, on October 9, 1992. For Cage's notes on *Europeras* see Richard Kostelanetz, ed., *John Cage: Writer. Previously Uncollected Pieces* (New York: Limelight Editions, 1993), 203–4, 206–18, 249, 255; Retallack, *MUSICAGE: Cage Muses on Words Art Music* (Hanover, NH: Wesleyan University Press and University of New England Press, 1996), 220–28, 299–304. See Heinz-Klaus Metzger, "Europe's Opera: Notes on John Cage's *Europeras 1 & 2* (1987)," in Richard Kostelanetz, ed., *Writings about John Cage* (Ann Arbor: University of Michigan Press, 1993), 229–42. From Cage's assistant at the time, Laura Diane Kuhn, "John Cage's *Europeras 1 & 2*: The Musical Means of Revolution" (PhD diss., University of California, Los Angeles, 1992); Herbert Lindenberger, "Regulated Anarchy: The *Europeras* and the Aesthetics of Opera," in Marjorie Perloff and Charles Junkerman, eds., *John Cage: Composed in America* (Chicago: University of Chicago Press, 1994), 144–66; Richard Kostelanetz, "Europera (1987): Before and After," in *John Cage (ex)plain(ed)* (New York: Schirmer, 1996), 133–45.

in concert performance. Cage told Joan Retallack in 1992 that at first the only operas he admired were Mozart's *Don Giovanni* and Debussy's *Pelléas*. Then, through spending time at the Frankfurt Opera, he heard Verdi's *Falstaff*, saw Schoenberg's *Moses and Aron*, described Bizet's *Carmen* as "another nice one," but found Wagner "hopeless" and always disliked vibrato.[2]

Interview

By permission of the John Cage Trust and Anthony Cheevers

AC   What are *Europeras* about?

JC   The opera is an extension to all the elements of theater of the separation that has long existed between dance and music in my work with Merce Cunningham. It's extended to include the lighting, the properties, and costumes. Nothing has anything to do with anything else, following the Oriental belief that everything is related to everything else. All of this was done by chance operations, and I must say I enjoyed the result. When the fire came in November two days before the performance, we lost only about 20 percent of the properties we needed. The Schauspiel, which was not burned, was used a month later. It opened in December and has been going off and on ever since.[3] Now it's coming to Purchase, near White Plains, where there's this Pepsico Summerfare.[4]

AC   Since all the elements are determined by chance operations, does this mean each performance is different?

JC   No. It could in some respects—the way a Beethoven piece is different from one performance to another. You see, when you have things like dance, with the possibility of collision, just to be on the safe side you

---

2. Retallack, *MUSICAGE*, 211–24; Mark Swed, Editor's Introduction to "Synergic Dynamics in John Cage's *Europeras 1 & 2*," *Musical Quarterly* 78, no. 1 (Spring 1994): 127–30; Laura D. Kuhn, "Synergic Dynamics in John Cage's *Europeras 1 & 2*," *Musical Quarterly* 78, no. 1 (Spring 1994): 131–48.

3. The fire at the Frankfurt Opera made it necessary for *Europeras 1 & 2* to be premiered at The Schauspielhaus of The Städtische Bühnen, Frankfurt, December 12, 1987.

4. The American premiere, with the Frankfurt production, at the Performing Arts Festival of the State University of New York. Patrick O'Connor reported ("Back to Collage," *Independent*, July 21, 1988): "The total effect is of a mesmerizing crossword. Without the stage pictures and movement (everything supervised and directed by Cage) [and] the shifting lights, different at each performance, the music alone might be unbearable. . . . Cage says he never goes to the opera, yet *Europeras 1 & 2* presents a sometimes hideously accurate picture."

have to have things more or less fixed. Music is much freer than the other arts because it doesn't bump into itself.

AC So for practical reasons you must have fixed gestures.

JC Right: fixed places and times.

AC Opera is a complex operation, and singers can be resistant to new ideas.

JC Here they had the advantage of being able to choose the arias they would sing. The only thing that was novel to them was what they were doing while they were singing. I think they're all used to being—so to speak—in the limelight, so they don't really mind what else is going on provided they have a chance to do what it is they're doing. [*laughs*] It's marvelous to have the opportunity of hearing five or six of them singing different arias at once.

AC But not in the original context.

JC No, but they're amazingly willing to do anything you ask them to do. I think that's a kind of discipline of the theater. For instance, it came up through chance operations that one of them was to get into a bathtub with water in it and continue singing while she was there. Then she was taken wet, seated on a rug, to make an exit. She didn't object ever! [*laughs*]

AC How did that come about by chance?

JC I used *Webster's Second Unabridged Dictionary,* and I would get a pair of pages through counting the pages of a given letter. I got into the Bs and came to the page that included baptism. That's submersion! [*laughs*]

   I agree with you, though, that opera is very complicated both in terms of the singers and in terms of administration—all of the people who can say "I won't do that" or "I will do it." On top of that the singers, just to make ends meet, are always taking jobs. Unless you have engaged them, you can't dream up a performance any time you wish because the singers may not be available. In fact, coming here to Purchase we have to have substitutes.

AC You'll be directing it here?

JC There isn't any real direction. There's a score and there's the knowledge of the score on the part of a number of people. The person who's been taking charge of getting them to do it is Roberto Goldschlager. I don't have a spirit for telling people to do this and that. I'll talk to them after seeing what they do and tell them what I think. I hear that some, since it's been performed several times, are beginning to foresee the response of the public and so to act in the way the public might want them to act, which is foolish because the masters of comedy never act that way. They always act seriously, and then it's very funny. But if they pretend they think it is funny, then it's silly.

AC It loses spontaneity.

JC Right. In some cases exaggeration can be accepted—the kind of exaggeration one sees in French mime is all right, I think.

AC   You've been invited to give the Charles Eliot Norton Lectures at Harvard. Have you decided what the subject will be?

JC   Yes: it's a long title. I first wrote the text called "Composition in Retrospect" as mesostics in front of the students at Surrey University, England.[5] They're on the subjects that struck me as central to my work. Since that time I've added five more subjects, to make fifteen:

MethodStructureIntentionDisciplineNotationIndeterminacy InterpenetrationImitationDevotionCircumstancesVariableStructure NonunderstandingContingencyInconsistencyPerformance

AC   You're going to talk about each of those subjects?

JC   No. I'm going to continue my work, which is to find a way of writing that comes from ideas but is not about them but produces them. The first example is a book called *Themes and Variations*, then *Mushrooms et Variationes*, then *The First Meeting of the Satie Society*, and more recently *Anarchy* and *Time*, and now there will be these six lectures.[6]

AC   How closely will you be working with the students at Harvard?

JC   I'll be giving six lectures and six seminars. That's all that's planned. In the lectures I'll speak, so to speak, poetry, which doesn't make sense, and in the seminars I'll speak prose the way we're speaking now. [*laughs*] The lectures I will have made before I get there; the seminars will be free.

AC   I imagine it's important for you to be doing this with younger people?

JC   I suppose it's important. It's very funny, though, the relation of age and youth. I find from time to time—for instance, at Wesleyan last February where there was a week of things about my work—that young people know more about it than I do and they have their points of view about it.[7] And sometimes points of view that didn't enter my head. I actually find myself less knowledgeable than they! [*laughs*]

---

5. International Dance Course for Professional Choreographers and Composers, University of Surrey, Guildford, England, August 16–29, 1981. Merce Cunningham, "A Collaborative Process between Music and Dance," in Peter Gena, Jonathan Brent, and Don Gillespie, eds., *A John Cage Reader: In Celebration of His 70th Birthday* (New York: C. F. Peters, 1982), 107–120.

6. Cage, *Themes and Variations* (Barrytown, NY: Station Hill, 1982); *Mushrooms et Variationes* (1983); *The First Meeting of the Satie Society* (1985); *Anarchy* (1988); and *Time* (1988).

7. John Cage at Wesleyan: A Festival-Symposium, February 22–27, 1988. The week covered every aspect of Cage and opened with Electric Phoenix performing his *Hymns and Variations* (1979) and ended with the complete string quartets played by the Arditti Quartet—two British ensembles. Cage gave a major lecture: "Anarchy," in Richard Fleming and William Duckworth, eds., *John Cage at Seventy-Five* (Lewisburg, PA: Bucknell University Press, 1989), also published separately as *Anarchy* (Middletown, CT: Wesleyan University Press, 2001). See R. Wood Massi, "Lectures on Anarchy: John Cage at Wesleyan," *Contact* 33 (Autumn 1988): 27–30.

I hope it'll be fun for both of us. You never can tell. It can be fun for one person, say—somebody we don't know—and miserable for all the others, so there's nothing to worry about. [*laughs*]

AC Minna Lederman said she found it easier to see what you were getting at when she separated your work from classical music—but the system of classical music is all around us.

JC Well, it is and it isn't. Have you heard the statement that there are as many people living at this moment as all added up together from the past? The population curve has gone up so much. When you're referring to classical music, it isn't all of the people.

AC But the trouble is that Eastern culture is almost being destroyed by the prevalence of Western culture.

JC I'm not so sure. I think we're really having an interpenetration of East and West. I think the strength of Russia, apart from its politics, is that it spans from the Orient to the Occident. I find that my work has been used in Russia for at least fifteen years and has encouraged Russian artists to turn in either direction. Before, they wondered which direction to face. Now they know the whole thing belongs together. They really thanked me for that when I was just there. What I'm saying is that we can turn in any direction—we can cite Wittgenstein or Suzuki. There's not so much difference. There's as much pizza in Tokyo as there is in New York! [*laughs*]

People frequently ask me whether my ideas or my music are more important. Those who don't like the music say maybe the ideas. Then if I invited them to lunch, what would they think of the food! [*laughs*] Would they think it was too philosophical? [*laughs*]

AC What comes after the Harvard lectures?

JC I have constant projects—right now it's more writing music after those lectures. I have commissions from the Boston Symphony and the Arditti Quartet. I've just finished a piece for twenty-three strings—seven players in Boston, five players in Germany, two players in Italy, etc.[8] I refused a commission because it involved two trips and it seemed just too much.

AC Are you prepared to write for any combination?

JC Yes: after you've written an opera you'll do anything! [*laughs*] I may be making a second opera for Tokyo, which isn't definite yet.

AC Do you feel you want to give precedence to either your music or writing at the moment?

JC No. Nor my food! [*laughs*]

---

8. *Twenty-three* (1988) for thirteen violins, five violas, five cellos; followed by *101* (1988) for orchestra, where Cage had to explain to Seiji Ozawa that there would be no conductor—referred to in Cage's Harvard lectures, *I–VI* (Cambridge: Harvard University Press, 1990), 181, 352; and *Four* (1989) for string quartet.

Appendix I

Finnegans Wake

Most of James Joyce's *Finnegans Wake* was serialized in the avant-garde literary magazine *transition*. The issue numbers of the periodical are given, with pages, followed by the equivalent passages in the full text of *Finnegans Wake*. This table shows that when Cage was in Paris in 1930 he could have seen all of Part I, all of Part III, and a passage from Part II.

The first installment was headed *Opening Pages of a Work in Progress*, and most of the subsequent ones were called *Continuation of a Work in Progress*. These appearances were a major part of the avant-garde scene for a decade, controversial but strongly supported by most of the *transition* writers. Gertrude Stein appeared regularly in the same period. Richard Budd in his Catalog 87 (September 2005) described *transition* as "the most important of the American expatriate magazines, it lasted longer, published more influential writers, and had a wider readership than any other journal edited abroad by an American," and he offered a complete set for sale at £4,500.

1. April 1927, pp. 9–30 [FW 3–29]
2. May 1927, pp. 94–107 [FW 30–47]
3. June 1927, pp. 32–50 [FW 48–74]
4. July 1927, pp. 46–65 [FW 75–103]
5. August 1927, pp. 15–31 [FW 104–25]
(part reprinted from the *Criterion*)
6. September 1927, pp. 87–106 [FW 126–68]
7. October 1927, pp. 34–56 [FW 169–95]
(appeared in earlier form in *This Quarter*, No. 1)
8. November 1927, pp. 17–35 [FW 196–216]
(concludes Part I)

9. and 10.   Nothing by Joyce who was ill
11.   February 1928, pp. 7–18 [FW 282–304]
(Part III was not ready, so Joyce "consented to detach pages from Part II" for this contribution)

12.   March 1928, pp. 7–27 [FW 403–28]
(this is now Part III)

13.   Summer 1928, pp. 5–32 [FW 429–73]
transition is now described as "An International Quarterly for Creative Experiment"

14.   Nothing by Joyce
15.   February 1929, pp. 197–238 [FW 474–554]
16–17.   June 1929, nothing by Joyce
18.   November 1929, pp. 211–36 [FW 555–90]
19–20.   Nothing by Joyce
21.   Transition 1932. Contains an Homage to James Joyce, pp. 246–82
The magazine is now called *Transition, An International Workshop for Orphic Creation*

22.   February 1933, pp. 50–76 [FW 219–59]
(back to Part II)

23.   July 1935, pp. 110–28 [FW 260–308]
24.   Nothing by Joyce
(now described as *Transition: A Quarterly Review*, with New York office)

25.   Nothing by Joyce
26.   1937, pp. 35–52 [FW 309–331]
(described as "opening pages of part two, section three")

27.   April-May 1938, Tenth Anniversary, pp. 59–78 [FW 338–55]
(described as a "fragment from Work in Progress, Part II, section 3")

Appendix II

John Cage Uncaged

BBC Radio 3, The Barbican, London, January 16–18, 2004

January 16.

Concert 1: Schuman, *New England Triptych*; Cage, *The Seasons*; Cowell, Concerto for Piano and Orchestra; Antheil, *A Jazz Symphony*; Ives, *Central Park in the Dark*; Copland, *El Salón México*; Cage, *4'33"*
BBC Symphony Orchestra/Lawrence Foster, Philip Mead (piano)

Concert 2: Feldman, *Piano*; Wolff, *Bread and Roses*; Schoenberg, Piano Pieces Op. 33a & b; Cage, *Solo for Piano*
Nicholas Hodges (piano)

January 17.
Concert 3: Cage, *String Quartet in Four Parts; Four*
Duke Quartet

Concert 4: Varèse, *Amériques*; Cage, *Aria*; Satie, *Parade*; Ruggles, *Sun-Treader*; Cage, *Atlas Eclipticalis* with *Winter Music* and *Cartridge Music*
BBC Symphony Orchestra/David Porcelijn, Loré Lixenberg (soprano), John Tilbury (piano), Sound Intermedia (sound design)

Concert 5: Cage, *Imaginary Landscape No. 3; Construction in Metal No. 1; Living Room Music; Credo in US; Child of Tree;* Tudor, *Rainforest;* Garland, *The Three Strange Angels*; Cowell, *Ostinato Pianissimo;* Cage, *Construction in Metal No. 3*

January 18.
Concert 6: Cage, *Variations 1 for Stephen Montague*; Choral music by Billings, Virgil Thomson, Hovhaness, Ives, Randall Thompson; Cage: prepared piano works

BBC Symphony Chorus/Stephen Jackson, Rolf Hind (prepared piano), Deborah Miles-Johnson (mezzo-soprano)

Concert 7: Feldman, *Madame Press Died Last Week*; Cage, Concerto for Prepared Piano; Wolff, *Spring* (UK premiere); Brown, *Centering*; Cage, *Apartment House 1776* (UK premiere of original version)
London Sinfonietta/David Porcelijn, Clio Gould (violin), Ralph van Raat (prepared piano)

Concert 8: Cage, *Song Books*, songs and piano pieces; Harrison, Symphony No. 4; Feldman, *Cello and Orchestra*; Cage, *101* (UK premiere)
BBC Symphony Orchestra/Pierre-André Valade, Rolf Hind (piano), Frances M. Lynch, Nicole Tibbels (sopranos), Paul Watkins (cello), Annilese Miskimmon (director)

The three-day festival also included performances of Cage's *Musicircus*, Satie's *Vexations*, and several films and discussions.

Selected Bibliography[1]

Acton, Sir Harold. *Memoirs of an Aesthete.* London: Methuen, 1948.

Anonymous. "Chance and Spec." Review of *An Anthology,* by La Monte Young. *Times Literary Supplement,* August 6, 1964, 688.

———. "Obituary. Marcel Duchamp: True Father of Dadaism Who Was Noted for 'Ready-mades.' " *The Times* (London), October 3, 1968.

———. "Obituary. Professor Marshall McLuhan: Stimulating Writer on Modern Communication." *The Times* (London), January 2, 1981.

———. "Obituary. Dr. R. Buckminster Fuller. Philosopher of a Technological Future." *The Times* (London), July 4, 1983.

———. "Obituary. John Cage." *Daily Telegraph* (London), August 14, 1992.

———. "Obituary. John Cage." *The Times* (London), August 14, 1992.

———. "Obituary. David Tudor." *The Times* (London), September 5, 1996.

———. "Obituary. Norman O. Brown. Wide-ranging Thinker Whose Unorthodox Vision Made Him a Hero of the Sixties Counterculture." *The Times* (London), October 8, 2002.

———. "Obituary. Lou Harrison." *The Times* (London), February 5, 2003.

Bergonzi, Bernard, ed. *Innovations.* London: Macmillan, 1968.

Berkeley, Michael. "The Music of Chance." *Guardian* (London), January 16, 2004, 11.

Bernstein, David W., and Christopher Hatch, eds. *Writings through John Cage's Music, Poetry + Art.* Chicago: University of Chicago Press, 2001.

Boulez, Pierre, Herbert Weinstock, trans. *Notes of an Apprenticeship.* New York: Alfred A. Knopf, 1968.

Brecht, George. *Chance Imagery.* New York: Great Bear Pamphlet, 1966.

Brindle, Reginald Smith. *The New Music.* Oxford: Oxford University Press, 1975.

Brooker, Joseph. *Joyce's Critics: Transitions in Reading and Culture.* Madison: University of Wisconsin Press, 2004.

Brooks, William. "Music and Society." In *The Cambridge Companion to John Cage,* ed. David Nicholls. Cambridge: Cambridge University Press, 2002, 214–26.

Brown, Carolyn. "Carolyn Brown." In *Merce Cunningham: Edited and with Photographs and an Introduction by James Klosty.* New York: Limelight Editions, 1986, 19–32.

---

1. This is not a comprehensive bibliography—theses are not included—but references in the text and in the footnotes are listed along with some further, mostly British, citations that seemed relevant and would otherwise be impossible to trace.

Brown, Kathan. "Towards the End of His Life the Great American Composer John Cage Turned His Hand to Etching—with the *I Ching* as His Guide. Kathan Brown Remembers the Years He Spent in Her Studio. The Uncertainty Principle." *Guardian* (London), August 3, 2002, arts 14.

Brown, Norman O. "John Cage: A Lecture by Norman O. Brown at Wesleyan University, February 22–27, 1988." In *John Cage at Seventy-Five*, ed. Richard Fleming and William Duckworth. Lewisburg, PA: Bucknell University Press, 1989, 97–118.

Broyles, Michael. *Mavericks and Other Traditions in American Music.* New Haven: Yale University Press, 2004.

Bryars, Gavin. "Vexations and Its Performers." *Contact* 26 (Spring 1983): 12–20.

———. "The Music of Chance." *Guardian* (London), January 16, 2004, 10–11.

Bygrave, Max. "Betty Freeman: Patron Saint of Modern Music." *Guardian* (London), March 30, 1996, arts 28.

Cage, John. "To Describe the Process of Composition Used in *Music for Piano 21–52.*" *Die Reihe* 3 "Reports Analyses" (German 1957, English 1959): 41–43.

———. "Lecture." *Die Reihe* 5 "Musical Craftsmanship" (German 1959, English 1961), introduced and trans. Hans G. Helms, 83–120.

———. *Silence: Lectures and Writings.* Middletown, CT: Wesleyan University Press, 1961.

———. *Merce Cunningham & Dance Company.* New York: Foundation for Contemporary Performance Arts, 1963.

———. *A Year from Monday: New Lectures and Writings.* Middletown, CT: Wesleyan University Press, 1967.

———. *Notations.* New York: Something Else, 1969.

———. *To Describe the Process of Composition Used in Not Wanting to Say Anything about Marcel.* Cincinnati, OH: Eye Editions, 1969.

———. *M: Writings '67–'72.* Middletown, CT: Wesleyan University Press, 1973.

———. *Writing through Finnegans Wake.* Tulsa, OK: University of Tulsa Press, 1978.

———. *Empty Words: Writings '73–'78.* Middletown, CT: Wesleyan University Press, 1979.

———. *I–VI.* Cambridge: Harvard University Press, 1990.

———. *For the Birds: John Cage in Conversation with Daniel Charles.* London: Marion Boyars, 1981.

———. *Themes and Variations.* Barrytown, NY: Station Hill, 1982.

———. *X: Writings '79–'82.* Middletown, CT: Wesleyan University Press, 1983.

———. Introduction to Ornella Volta. *Satie Seen through His Letters*, trans. Michael Bullock. London: Marion Boyars, 1989.

———. *I–VI.* Cambridge: Harvard University Press, 1993.

———. Foreword to Colin C. Sterne, *Arnold Schoenberg, the Composer as Numerologist.* Lewiston, NY: Edwin Mellon, 1993.

———. *Anarchy.* Middletown, CT: Wesleyan University Press, 2001.

Cage, John, and Joan Bakewell. "Music and Mushrooms—John Cage Talks about His Recipes to Joan Bakewell." *Listener*, June 15, 1972, 800–802.

Cage, John, and Geoffrey Barnard. *Conversation without Feldman.* Darlinghurst, NSW: Black Ram Books, 1980.

Cage, John, and Alan Gillmor. "Interview with John Cage." *Contact* 14 (Autumn 1976): 18–25.

Cage, John, and Jeff Goldberg. "John Cage Interviewed by Jeff Goldberg." *Transatlantic Review* 55–56 (1976): 103–10.

Cage, John, and Kathleen Hoover. *Virgil Thomson: His Life and Music.* New York: Thomas Yoseloff, 1959.

Cage, John, and Stephen Montague. "Significant Silences of a Musical Anarchist." *Classical Music,* May 22, 1982, 11.

Cage, John, and Roger Reynolds. "Interview with Roger Reynolds." In *John Cage,* ed. Robert Dunn. New York: Henmar, 1962, 45–52.

Cage, John, and Roger Reynolds. "John Cage and Roger Reynolds: A Conversation." *Musical Quarterly* 65 (October 1979): 573–93.

Cage, John, Roger Shattuck, and Alan Gillmor. "Erik Satie: A Conversation." *Contact* 25 (Autumn 1982): 21–26.

Cage, John, and Michael John White. "King of the Avant-garde." *Observer* (London), September 26, 1982, color supplement.

Cage, John, and Robin White. "View: Interview by Robin White." Oakland: Crown Point, 1978.

Canning, Hugh. "Sound Investment in the New." *Sunday Times* (London), September 30, 1990.

Cardew, Cornelius. "Cage and Cunningham." *Musical Times* 105, no. 1479 (September 1964): 659–60.

———. *Stockhausen Serves Imperialism and Other Articles.* London: Latimer New Dimensions, 1974.

Carlson, Michael. "Jackson Mac Low." *Guardian* (London), December 20, 2004.

Chang, Jung, and Jon Halliday. *Mao: The Unknown Story.* London: Cape, 2005.

Chilvers, Ian. *Concise Dictionary of Art and Artists.* Oxford: Oxford University Press, 1996.

Clarkson, Austin. "The Intent of the Musical Moment." In *Writings through John Cage's Music, Poetry + Art,* ed. David Bernstein and Christopher Hatch. Chicago: University of Chicago Press, 2001, 79.

Clements, Andrew. "John Cage." *Financial Times* (London), August 14, 1992.

Cole, Hugo. "John Cage." *Guardian* (London), May 11, 1972.

———. "An Easy Composure." *Guardian* (London), May 22, 1972.

———. "Musicircus." *Guardian* (London), December 19, 1972.

———. "John Cage." *Guardian* (London), June 14, 1978.

———. "Breaking the Sound Barrier." *Guardian* (London), August 14, 1992.

Cook, Nicholas, and Anthony Pople, eds. *The Cambridge History of Twentieth-Century Music.* Cambridge: Cambridge University Press, 2004.

Coomaraswarmy, Ananda K. *On the Traditional in Doctrine of Art.* New Orient Society of America, 1938.

Cope, David. *New Directions in Music.* Dubuque, IA: W. C. Brown, 1976.

Copland, Aaron. "The Music of Chance." In *The New Music 1900–1960.* New York: W. W. Norton, 1968, 176–81.

Cowell, Henry. *The Dancer and the Dance: Conversations with Jacqueline Lesschaeve.* New York: Marion Boyars, 1985.

———. *New Musical Resources,* ed. David Nicholls. Cambridge: Cambridge University Press, 1996.

Cowell, Henry. *Selected Writings on Music 1921–1964*, ed. Dick Higgins, Preface by Kyle Gann. Kingston, NY: McPherson, 2001.

Crawford, Richard. *America's Musical Life*. New York: W. W. Norton, 2001.

Cunningham, Merce. *Changes: Notes on Choreography*, ed. Francis Starr. New York: Something Else, 1968.

———. "A Collaborative Process between Music and Dance." In *A John Cage Reader: In Celebration of His 70th Birthday*, ed. Peter Gena, Jonathan Brent, and Don Gillespie. New York: C. F. Peters, 1982, 107–20.

Cunningham, Merce, and Debra Crane. "Let's Get with the Program." *The Times* (London), September 6, 2002, T2, 14.

Cunningham, Merce, and Alan Franks. "One Step Beyond." *The Times Magazine* (London), October 21, 1995, 45–48.

Cunningham, Merce, and Donald Hutera. "Dancer to the Musics of Time." *The Times* (London), September 30, 1998, 37.

Cunningham, Merce, and Laura Kuhn. "Merce Cunningham in Conversation with Laura Kuhn." In *Art Performs Life: Cunningham/Monk/Jones*. Minneapolis: Walker Art Center, 1998, 22–43.

Cunningham, Merce, and Judith Mackrell. "Me and Mr. Cage." *Guardian* (London), November 24, 1997, 13.

Cunningham, Merce, and John O'Mahony. "Guardian Profile: Merce Cunningham. The Dancing Master." *Guardian* (London), October 7, 2002, Saturday Review, 6–7.

Delio, Thomas. *The Music of Morton Feldman*. New York: Excelsior, 1996.

Dickinson, Peter. "The Avant-garde in New York." *Musical Times* 101, no. 1408 (June 1960): 377–78.

———. "The Living Theater." *Musical Courier* (June 1960): 26.

———. "Way Out with John Cage." *Music and Musicians* (February 1965): 32–34, 54, 56.

———. "London Meets Stockhausen." *Music and Musicians* (February 1966): 24–25.

———. "Erik Satie (1866–1925)." *Music Review* 28, no. 2 (May 1967): 138–46. [Includes score of *Vexations*]

———. "Case of Neglect 3: Cage String Quartet." *Music and Musicians* (January 1972): 28–29. Also in Kostelanetz, *Writings about John Cage*, 77–81.

———. "Stein Satie Cummings Thomson Berners Cage: Towards a Context for the Music of Virgil Thomson." *Musical Quarterly* 72, no. 3 (1986): 394–409.

———. Review of *The Music of Henry Cowell: A Descriptive Catalog*, by William Lichtenwanger. *Music and Letters* 69, no. 2 (April 1988): 292–93.

———. "Virgil Thomson." *Independent* (London), October 2, 1989.

———. Review of *Erik Satie*, by Alan Gillmor; *Satie the Composer*, by Robert Orledge; and *Satie Seen through His Letters*, by Ornella Volta (Foreword by Cage). *Musical Quarterly* 75, no. 3 (1991): 404–9.

Doran, Sean. "The Music of Chance." *Guardian* (London), January 16, 2004, 11.

Dreier, Ruth. "Proms 1987: A Joycean Circus." *Listener*, July 16, 1987, 28–29.

Driver, Paul. "Obituaries: John Cage." *Independent* (London), August 14, 1992.

———. "The Follies of Cage." *Sunday Times* (London), January 25, 2004, culture section, 29–30.

Duberman, Martin. *Black Mountain: An Exploration in Community.* New York: E. P. Dutton, 1972.

Duckworth, William. *Talking Music: Conversations with John Cage, Philip Glass, Laurie Anderson, and Five Generations of American Experimental Composers.* New York: Da Capo, 1995.

Dufallo, Richard. *Trackings: Composers Speak with Richard Dufallo.* New York: Oxford University Press, 1989.

Dunn, Richard, ed. *John Cage.* New York: Henmar, 1962.

Durner, Leah. *Aspects of Conceptualism in American Art Work.* New York: Avenue B Gallery, 1987.

Eimert, Herbert, and Karlheinz Stockhausen, eds. *Die Reihe* 3 "Reports Analyses" (German 1957, English 1959). 5: "Musical Craftsmanship" (German 1959, English 1961). Vienna: Universal Edition.

Ellman, Richard. *James Joyce.* New York: Oxford University Press, 1982.

Falconer-Salkeld, Bridget. *The MacDowell Colony.* Lanham, MD: Scarecrow, 2005.

Feldman, Morton. "Give My Regards to Eighth Street." In *The Music of Morton Feldman,* ed. Thomas Delio. New York: Excelsior, 1996, 199–204.

———. *Morton Feldman Says: Selected Interviews and Lectures 1964–1987,* ed. Chris Villars. London: Hyphen, 2006.

Feldman, Morton, and La Monte Young. "A Conversation on Composition and Improvisation." *Res* 13 (1987): 153.

Fleming, Richard, and William Duckworth, eds. *John Cage at Seventy-Five.* Lewisburg, PA: Bucknell University Press, 1989.

Flynt, Henry. "Cage and Fluxus (1990)." In *Writings about John Cage,* ed. Richard Kostelanetz. Ann Arbor: University of Michigan Press, 1993, 279–82.

Ford, Andrew. *Composer to Composer: Conversations about Contemporary Music.* London: Quartet Books, 1993.

Fox, Margalit. "Jackson Mac Low, 82, Poet and Composer, Dies." *New York Times,* December 10, 2004.

Fuller, Buckminster. *Operating Manual for Spaceship Earth.* New York: Simon and Schuster, 1969.

Fuller, Buckminster, and John Donat. "Our Spaceship, Earth—John Donat Presents the Discourses of Buckminster Fuller." *Listener,* September 26, 1968, 392–96.

Gagne, Cole, and Tracy Caras. *Soundpieces: Interviews with American Composers.* Metuchen, NJ: Scarecrow, 1982.

Gann, Kyle. "La Monte Young: Maximal Spirit." *Voice,* June 9, 1987, 70.

———. *American Music in the Twentieth Century.* New York: Schirmer, 1997.

Gena, Peter, Jonathan Brent, and Don Gillespie. *A John Cage Reader: In Celebration of His 70th Birthday.* New York: C. F. Peters, 1982.

Gill, Dominic. "Cage's Musicircus." *Financial Times* (London), December 19, 1972, 3.

———. "John Cage." *Financial Times* (London), June 14, 1978.

Gillmor, Alan M. *Erik Satie.* London: Macmillan, 1988.

Goldman, Arnold. " 'Send Him Canorious'—Arnold Goldman Writes about James Joyce's 'Sullivanising.' " *Listener,* August 3, 1972, 142–44.

Griffiths, Paul. "Cage: Young Vic." *The Times* (London), July 23, 1974.

———. *Cage.* London: Oxford University Press, 1981.

Griffiths, Paul. *Modern Music and After: Directions Since 1945*. Oxford: Oxford University Press, 1995.

———. *The Substance of Things Heard: Writings about Music*. Rochester: University of Rochester Press, 2005.

Guralnick, Elissa S. *Sight Unseen: Beckett, Pinter, Stoppard, and Other Contemporary Dramatists on Radio*. Athens: Ohio University Press, 1996.

Hamm, Charles. "John Cage." In *The New Grove Dictionary of Music and Musicians*, ed. Stanley Sadie. London: Macmillan, 1980, 3: 597–603.

———. *Music in the New World*. New York: Norton, 1983.

———. "Epilogue: John Cage Revisited." In *Putting Popular Music in Its Place*. Cambridge: Cambridge University Press, 1995, 381–85.

———. Introduction to *John Cage: Music, Philosophy and Intention 1933–1950*, ed. David W. Patterson. New York: Routledge, 2002, 1–13.

Harris, Dale. "Spheres of Influence." *Guardian* (London), June 14, 1976.

Harrison, Max. "Zukofsky, Queen Elizabeth Hall." *The Times* (London), June 14, 1978.

Harvey, Jonathan. "John Cage: Four Envois." *Perspectives of New Music* 31, no. 2 (Summer 1993): 133–34.

Henehan, Donal. "The Random Cage." *New York Times*, August 23, 1981.

Hicks, Michael. "John Cage's Studies with Schoenberg." *American Music* 8, no. 2 (Summer 1990): 125–40.

Hines, Thomas. "Then Not Yet 'Cage': The Los Angeles Years, 1912–1938." In *John Cage: Composed in America*, ed. Marjorie Perloff and Charles Junkerman. Chicago: University of Chicago Press, 1994, 65–99.

Hitchcock, H. Wiley, with Kyle Gann. *Music in the United States: A Historical Introduction*, 4th ed. Upper Saddle River, NJ: Prentice-Hall, 2000.

Holzaepfel, John. "Cage and Tudor." In *Cambridge Companion to John Cage*, ed. David Nicholls. Cambridge: Cambridge University Press, 2002, 169–85.

Hoover, Kathleen, and John Cage. *Virgil Thomson: His Life and Music*. New York: Thomas Yoseloff, 1959.

Humphreys, Christmas. *Zen*. London: Hodder and Stoughton, 1962.

Husarik, Stephen. "John Cage and Lejaren Hiller. HPSCHD, 1969." *American Music* 1, no. 2 (Summer 1983): 4–6.

Ives, Charles. "Postface." In *114 Songs*. Redding, CT: n.p., 1922; New York and Bryn Mawr, PA: AMP/Peer/Presser, 1975.

Jack, Adrian. "Cage's Changes." *Records and Recording* (August 1972): 22–23.

James, William. *A Pluralistic Universe*. Cambridge: Harvard University Press, 1909.

Johns, Jasper, and Emma Brockes. "A Rare Interview with America's Greatest Living Artist." *Guardian* (London), July 26, 2004, G2.

Johns, Jasper, and Richard Cork. "Galleries: The Liberated Millionaire Is Not Flagging." *The Times* (London), November 30, 1990.

Jolas, Eugene, with Elliot Paul, ed. *Transition: An International Quarterly for Creative Experiment*. Paris, 1927–39.

Jolly, James, ed. *Redmuse Classical Catalogue 2005*. London: Gramophone, 2005.

Jordan, Stephanie. "Freedom from the Music: Cunningham, Cage and Collaborations." *Contact* 20 (Autumn 1979): 16–19.

Jordan, Stephanie. "Cage and Cunningham at the Laban Centre." *Dancing Times* (October 1980): 38–39.

Joyce, James. *Finnegans Wake.* New York: Viking, 1939; Compass Books, 1959.

Junkerman, Charles. "nEw/foRms of Living Together: The Model of the Musicircus." In *John Cage: Composed in America,* ed. Marjorie Perloff and Charles Junkerman. Chicago: University of Chicago Press, 1994, 39–64.

Katz, Jonathan D. "John Cage's Queer Silence; or, How to Avoid Making Matters Worse." In *Writings through John Cage's Music, Poetry, + Art,* ed. David W. Bernstein and Christopher Hatch. Chicago: University of Chicago Press, 2001, 41–61.

Keller, Hans. "Caged." *Spectator,* June 24, 1978, 27.

Kermode, Frank. "Modernisms." In *Innovations,* ed. Bernard Bergonzi. London: Macmillan, 1968, 81.

Kirkby, Michael, and Richard Schechner. "An Interview with John Cage." *Tulane Drama Review* 10, no. 2 (1965–66): 49–72.

Klosty, James. *Merce Cunningham: Edited and with Photographs and an Introduction.* New York: Limelight Editions, 1986.

Kostelanetz, Richard. *John Cage.* New York: Praeger, 1970.

———. *Conversing with Cage.* New York: Limelight Editions, 1988. [Index: Larry J. Solomon, http://music.research.home.att.net/CageInde.htm]

———, ed. *Merce Cunningham: Dancing in Space and Time, Essays 1944–92.* Pennington, NJ: A Cappella Books, 1992.

———, ed. *John Cage: Writer. Previously Uncollected Pieces.* New York: Limelight Editions, 1993.

———, ed. *Writings about John Cage.* Ann Arbor: University of Michigan Press, 1993.

———. *John Cage (ex)plain(ed).* New York: Schirmer, 1996.

———. *Thirty Years of Critical Engagements with John Cage.* New York: Archae Editions, 1996.

Kozinn, Alan. "John Cage, 79, a Minimalist Enchanted with Sound, Dies." *New York Times, August 13, 1992.*

———. "John Cage, Universal Avant-Gardist, Dies at 79." *International Herald Tribune,* August 14, 1992.

Kuhn, Laura Diane. "John Cage." In *Dancers on a Plane,* ed. Judy Adam. London: Anthony d'Offay Gallery, 1989, 149–52.

———. "John Cage's Europeras 1 & 2: The Musical Means of Revolution" (PhD diss., University of California, Los Angeles, 1992).

Lang, Paul Henry. "Long-Hair Critic Reviews a Glove-Wearing Pianist." *New York Herald Tribune,* March 29, 1960, 14.

Lederman, Minna. *The Life and Death of a Small Magazine (Modern Music, 1924–46).* ISAM Monographs 18. New York: Institute for Studies in American Music, 1983.

Lohner, Henning. "The Making of Cage's *One[11].*" In *Writings through John Cage's Music, Poetry + Art,* ed. David W. Bernstein and Christopher Hatch. Chicago: University of Chicago Press, 2001, 267.

Luening, Otto. *The Autobiography of Otto Luening.* New York: Scribners, 1980.

Mac Low, Jackson. *Representative Works: 1938–1985.* New York: Roof Books, 1986.

———. "Something about the Writings of John Cage." In *Writings about John Cage,* ed. Richard Kostelanetz. Ann Arbor: University of Michigan Press, 1993, 283–300.

———. "Cage's Writings up to the Late 1980s." In *Writings through John Cage's Music, Poetry + Art,* ed. David W. Bernstein and Christopher Hatch. Chicago: University of Chicago Press, 2001, 210–33.

McLuhan, Marshall. *Understanding Media: The Extensions of Man*. London: Sphere Books, 1964.

McLuhan, Marshall, and Hunter Davies. "The Hunter Davies Interview: Joker or Genius . . . or Both." *Sunday Times* (London), August 13, 1967, 17.

McLuhan, Marshall, and Quentin Fiore. *The Medium Is the Massage: An Inventory of Effects*. New York: Bantam Books, 1967.

Mellers, Wilfrid. "From Noise to Silence: Harry Partch, John Cage and Morton Feldman." In *Music in a New Found Land*. London: Barrie and Rockliff, 1964, 177–88.

———. "John Cage at Seventy." *Times Literary Supplement*, June 11, 1982, 637.

Mellers, Wilfrid. "Odd Men In." *Musical Times* 146, no. 1890 (Spring 2005): 111.

Meyer, Leonard B. *Music, the Arts, and Ideas: Patterns and Predictions in Twentieth-Century Culture*. Chicago: University of Chicago Press, 1967.

Midgette, Anne. "Grete Sultan, 99, a Pianist and Mentor to Cage, Is Dead." *New York Times*, July 3, 2005.

Miller, Jonathan. *McLuhan*. London: Fontana Modern Masters, 1970.

Miller, Leta E. "Cultural Intersections: John Cage in Seattle (1938–40)." In *John Cage: Music, Philosophy and Intention, 1933–50*, ed. David W. Patterson New York: Routledge, 2002, 47–82.

Mink, Louis O. *A Finnegans Wake Gazetteer*. Bloomington: University of Indiana Press, 1978.

Mitchell, Donald. "London Music." *Musical Times* 95, no. 1342 (December 1954): 667.

Mottram, Eric. "The Pleasures of Chaos." *Spanner 1* (November 1974), 3, private publication.

———. "Obituary. John Cage." *Independent* (London), August 14, 1992.

Myers, Rollo. *Erik Satie*. London: Dennis Dobson, 1948.

———. "Notes from Abroad." *Musical Times* 95, no. 1342 (December 1954): 671.

Nattiez, Jean-Jacques, ed., Robert Samuels, trans. *The Boulez-Cage Correspondence*. Cambridge: Cambridge University Press, 1993.

Nicholls, David. *American Experimental Music, 1890–1940*. Cambridge: Cambridge University Press, 1990.

———, ed. *The Cambridge History of American Music*. Cambridge: Cambridge University Press, 1998.

———, ed. *The Cambridge Companion to John Cage*. Cambridge: Cambridge University Press, 2002.

Nyman, Michael. *Experimental Music: Cage and Beyond*. London: Studio Vista, 1974; Cambridge: Cambridge University Press, 1999.

O'Connor, Patrick. "Back to Collage." *Independent* (London), July 21, 1988.

O'Driscoll, Robert, ed. *Joyce and the Dada Circus: A Collage*. Ontario: Black Brick, 1982.

Oliver, Michael, ed. *Settling the Score: A Journey through the Music of the Twentieth Century*. London: Faber and Faber, 1999.

O'Mahony, John. "The Dancing Master." *Guardian, Saturday Review*, October 7, 2000, 6–7.

Orledge, Robert. *Satie the Composer*. Cambridge: Cambridge University Press, 1990.

———. "Understanding Satie's 'Vexations.'" *Music and Letters* 79, no. 3 (August 1998): 386–95.

Page, Tim, and Vanessa Weeks Page, eds. *Selected Letters of Virgil Thomson.* New York: Summit Books, 1988.

Patterson, David W. "Cage and Asia: History and Sources." In *The Cambridge Companion to John Cage,* ed. David Nicholls. Cambridge: Cambridge University Press, 2002, 41–62.

———, ed. *John Cage: Music, Philosophy, and Intention, 1933–1950.* New York: Routledge, 2002.

Perloff, Marjorie, and Charles Junkerman, eds. *John Cage: Composed in America.* Chicago: University of Chicago Press, 1994.

Peyser, Joan. *Boulez: Composer, Conductor, Enigma.* New York: Schirmer, 1976.

Phillips, Tom. "Obituary. John Cage." *Independent* (London), August 14, 1992.

Porter, Andrew. *Musical Events, a Chronicle 1980–83.* London: Grafton Books, 1988.

———. "Chance Master." *Observer* (London), August 18, 1992.

Potter, Keith. "Americans in Paris." *Classical Music,* February 21, 1981, 22.

———. "How Round Was My House." *Classical Music,* May 14, 1983, 8.

———"Rattling Cage's Bars." *Independent* (London), September 26, 1992.

Pritchett, James. *The Music of John Cage.* Cambridge: Cambridge University Press, 1993.

Reich, Steve. *Writings about Music.* Halifax: Press of the Nova Scotia College of Art and Design, 1974.

Retallack, Joan, ed. *MUSICAGE: Cage Muses on Words Art Music.* Hanover, NH: Wesleyan University Press and University of New England Press, 1996.

Revill, David. "Obituaries: John Cage." *Independent* (London), August 14, 1992.

———. *The Roaring Silence—John Cage: A Life.* London: Bloomsbury, 1992.

R. M. "Amplifiers v. Players." *Daily Telegraph* (London), December 19, 1972.

Rockwell, John. "A Conversation with Virgil Thomson." *Poetry in Review* (Spring-Summer 1977): 419. Also in Virgil Thomson and John Rockwell, *A Virgil Thomson Reader.* New York: Houghton Mifflin, 1981, 427–41.

———. "The American Experimental Tradition and Its Godfather." In *All American Music: Composition in the Late Twentieth Century.* New York: Alfred A. Knopf, 1983, 47–59.

———. "Cage Merely an Inventor? Not a Chance." *New York Times,* August 23, 1992, B21.

Rorem, Ned. *Knowing When to Stop: A Memoir.* New York: Simon and Schuster, 1994.

Sadie, Stanley. "John Cage, David Tudor." *The Times* (London), May 23, 1972.

Salzman, Eric. "Recital Is Given by David Tudor." *New York Times,* March 29, 1960.

———. *Twentieth-Century Music: An Introduction.* Englewood Cliffs, NJ: Prentice-Hall, 1967.

Satie, Erik. *The Writings of Erik Satie,* trans. Nigel Wilkins. London: Eulenberg, 1980.

Schädler, Stefan, and Walter Zimmerman, eds. *John Cage: Anarchic Harmony.* Mainz: Schott, 1992.

Schwartz, Elliott, and Barney Childs. *Contemporary Composers on Contemporary Music: Expanded Edition.* New York: Da Capo, 1998.

Schwartz, Elliott, and Daniel Godfrey. *Music Since 1945: Issues, Materials, and Literature.* New York: Schirmer, 1993.

Schwertsik, Kurt. "Serious Mischief." Interview with Fiona Maddocks. *Independent* (London), May 29, 1987.

Shepherd, John, Phil Verden, Graham Vulliamy, and Trevor Wishart. *Whose Music? A Sociology of Musical Languages*. London: Latimer New Dimensions, 1977.

Shultis, Christopher. "Cage in Retrospect: A Review Essay." *Journal of Musicology* 14, no. 3 (Summer 1996): 400–423.

———. *Silencing the Sounded Self: John Cage and the American Experimental Tradition*. Boston: North Eastern University Press, 1998.

———. "Cage and Europe." In *The Cambridge Companion to John Cage*, ed. David Nicholls. Cambridge: Cambridge University Press, 2002, 20–39.

Smalley, Roger. "John Cage." *Listener*, September 19, 1968, 377.

Smith, Geoff, and Nicola Walker Smith. *American Originals: Interviews with 25 Contemporary Composers*. London: Faber and Faber, 1994.

Smith, Graeme. "John Cage's *Roaratorio*: The Uses of Confusion." *Contact* 27 (Autumn 1983): 43–45.

Solomon, Larry J. "The Sounds of Silence: John Cage and *4'33"*. http://solomonsmusic.net/cage.htm (1998–2002).

Souster, Tim. "John Cage—Tim Souster Discusses His Live-Electronic Variations VI." *Listener*, December 24, 1970, 892–93.

Stadlen, Peter. "Cage's Music Gets Sparse Audience." *Daily Telegraph* (London), May 23, 1972.

Stefanou, Danae. "Mapping a Museum without Walls: John Cage and Musicology." *Journal of the Royal Music Association* 128, no. 2 (2003): 319–28.

Stein, Gertrude. "Tender Buttons." In *Writings and Lectures 1911–1945*, ed. Patricia Meyerowitz. London: Peter Owen, 1967, 158–99. Also "Composition as Explanation," 21–30; "What Are Masterpieces and Why Are There So Few of Them," 146–57.

Stockhausen, Karlheinz. *Aus den Sieben Tagen (From the Seven Days)*. Vienna: Universal Edition, 1968.

Stryk, Lucien, and Takahashi Ikemoto, eds. and trans. *Zen: Poems, Prayers, Sermons, Anecdotes, Interviews*. Garden City, NY: Anchor Books, 1965.

Suzuki, Daisetz Teitaro. *An Introduction to Zen Buddhism* (Foreword by Carl G. Jung). London: Rider, 1983.

Swed, Mark. Editor's Introduction to "Synergic Dynamics in John Cage's Europeras 1 & 2." *Musical Quarterly* 78, no. 1 (Spring 1994): 127–30.

Sylvester, David. *Interviews with American Artists*. London: Chatto, 2001.

Taruskin, Richard. *Oxford History of Western Music 5, Late Twentieth Century*. Oxford: Oxford University Press, 2005.

Tawa, Nicholas. *American Composers and Their Public: A Critical Look*. Metuchen, NJ: Scarecrow, 1995.

Taylor, John Russell. "Andy Warhol: The Ultimate Image-Maker." *The Times* (London), September 13, 1989.

Thomson, Virgil. "Minna Lederman." *New York Herald Tribune*, January 12, 1947.

———. *Virgil Thomson*. New York: Alfred A. Knopf, 1966.

———. *American Music Since 1910*. London: Weidenfeld and Nicolson, 1971.

———. *Selected Letters of Virgil Thomson*, ed. Tim Page and Vanessa Weeks Page. New York: Summit Books, 1988.

Thomson, Virgil, and John Rockwell. *A Virgil Thomson Reader*. New York: Houghton Mifflin, 1981.

Thoreau, Henry David. *Walden*. London: J. M. Dent, 1910.

———. *The Journal*, ed. Bradford Torrey and Francis H. Allen. New York: Dover, 1962.

Tindall, William York. *A Reader's Guide to Finnegans Wake*. New York: Farrar, Straus and Giroux, 1969.

Tomkins, Calvin. *The Bride and the Bachelors: The Heretical Courtship in Modern Art*. New York: Viking, 1965.

———. "Duchamp." London: Chatto, 1997.

Vaughan, David. "A Lifetime of Dance." *Filmmaker Interview*, 2000, available at http://www.merce.org

Vaughan, David. "Cunningham, Cage and Joyce: 'This Longawaited Messiagh of Roaratorios.' " *Choreography and Dance* 1, no. 4 (1992): 79–89.

———. "David Tudor: Black Mountain Sounds." *Guardian* (London), August 28, 1996.

Waddington, Conrad Hal, ed. *Biology and the History of the Future: An IUBS/UNESCO Symposium with John Cage, Carl-Goeran Heden, Margaret Mead, John Papaioannou, John Platt, Ruth Sager, and Gunther Stent*. Edinburgh: University of Edinburgh Press, 1972.

Watts, Alan W. *The Way of Zen*. Harmondsworth, Middlesex: Penguin Books, 1962.

Weld, Jacqueline Bograd. *Peggy: The Wayward Guggenheim*. New York: E. P. Dutton, 1986.

White, Michael. "An Artist Who Dared to Be Indifferent." *Independent on Sunday* (London), August 18, 1992.

Whittall, Arnold. *Musical Composition in the Twentieth Century*. Oxford: Oxford University Press, 1999.

Wilhelm, Richard, trans., Cary F. Baynes, ed. (Foreword by Carl G. Jung). *The I Ching or Book of Changes*. Princeton, NJ: Bollingen Edition and Princeton University Press, 1950.

Wolff, Christian. "Cage, John." In *Dictionary of Contemporary Music*, ed. John Vinton. New York: E. P. Dutton, 1971, 115–19.

Wood Massi, R. "Lectures on Anarchy: John Cage at Wesleyan." *Contact* 33 (Autumn 1988): 27–30.

Wörner, Karl H. *Stockhausen: Life and Work*. Introduced, trans. ed. Bill Hopkins. London: Faber and Faber, rev. 1973.

Yates, Peter. *Twentieth Century Music: Its Evolution from the End of the Harmonic Era into the Present Era of Sound*. London: George Allen and Unwin, 1968.

Young, La Monte. "Lecture 1960." *Tulane Drama Review* 10, no. 2 (1965–66): 73–83.

Young, La Monte, and Jackson Mac Low, eds. *An Anthology*. New York: Heiner Friedrich, 1963–70.

General Index

Index of Works by John Cage

Alternative titles are those of Cunningham's dances where these are different.

Eastman Studies in Music

Ralph P. Locke, Senior Editor
Eastman School of Music

ISBN 1–58046–237–5

John Cage was one of America's most renowned composers and one of the most influential thinkers in the field of twentieth-century arts and media from the 1940s until his death in 1992. From a West Coast American background, as a kind of homespun avant-garde pioneer, he gradually achieved international acclaim.

The increasing numbers of performances, recordings, and studies demonstrate beyond question the relevance of Cage's music today. But he was also a much-admired writer and artist, and a uniquely attractive personality able to present his ideas engagingly wherever he went. As an interview subject he was a consummate professional.

CageTalk: Dialogues with and about John Cage is different from some studies in that it emanates from outside the United States. The main source of CageTalk is a panoply of vivid and compulsively readable interviews given to Peter Dickinson in the late 1980s for a BBC Radio 3 documentary about Cage, whom he had first met around 1960 when living in New York City. The original BBC program lasted an hour but the full discussions with Cage and many of the main figures connected with him have remained unpublished until now.

CageTalk also includes earlier BBC interviews with Cage, including ones by authorities such as literary critic Frank Kermode and art critic David Sylvester. And the editor Peter Dickinson contributes little-known source material about Cage's *Musicircus* and *Roaratorio* as well as a substantial introduction exploring the multiple roles that Cage's varied and challenging output played during much of the twentieth century and continues to play in the early twenty-first.

Apart from the long interview with Cage himself, there are discussions with, Bonnie Bird, Earle Brown, Merce Cunningham, Minna Lederman, Otto Luening, Jackson Mac Low, Peadar Mercier, Pauline Oliveros, John Rockwell, Kurt Schwertsik, Karlheinz Stockhausen, Virgil Thomson, David Tudor, La Monte Young, and Paul Zukofsky. Most of the interviews were given to Peter Dickinson but there are others involving Rebecca Boyle, Anthony Cheevers, Michael Oliver, and Roger Smalley.

Peter Dickinson, composer, pianist and writer, has had a long history of dedication to American music. After his first degree at Cambridge, England, where he was Organ Scholar of Queens' College, he went to the Juilliard School, New York, where he studied with Bernard Wagenaar, was a contemporary of Philip Glass and Peter Schickele, and met John Cage. Dickinson spent two further years based in New York and during this period wrote reviews for the *Musical Courier* and represented the *Musical Times*. He worked as an organist and pianist, his music was performed, and he had a spell on the music staff of the New York City Ballet. Finally he spent a year as a lecturer at Fairleigh Dickinson University in New Jersey before returning to London.

When Dickinson started the Music Department at the University of Keele in 1974, he included a Centre for American Music—well before such programs were common in the United States. He took part in a TV documentary for the centenary of Ives and, with his sister, mezzo Meriel Dickinson, gave many recitals of American music in the United Kingdom and Europe, especially around the Bicentennial. They made first recordings of songs by Carter, Cage, and Thomson. Visitors to Keele included prominent figures in American music such as Aaron Copland, Elliott Carter, George Crumb, Steve Reich, and Philip Glass. The two Keele interviews with Copland were published in *Copland Connotations*, edited by Peter Dickinson (Boydell Press, 2002). He has also written *Marigold: The Music of Billy Mayerl* (Oxford University Press, 1999) and *The Music of Lennox Berkeley* (Boydell, 2003).

After Dickinson left Keele in 1984, his commitment to American music continued. He regularly interviewed American composers for the BBC, reviewed publications, and made Radio 3 documentaries including Barber and Cage. From 1997 to 2004, Dickinson was Head of Music at the Institute of United States Studies, University of London. For some time he has visited the United States most years to lecture and hear performances of his own music.

"John Cage had, as he says of himself in this kaleidoscopic volume, 'very little experience as a pessimist.' Here the breeze of his optimism—challenging, questioning, refreshing—can be felt as nowhere else. With contributions also from Merce Cunningham, David Tudor, and other close associates, this is an indispensable portrait of an artist whose spirit continues to fascinate, chide, and tease."

—Paul Griffiths, author of *The Sea on Fire: Jean Barraqué* and
The Substance of Things Heard: Writings about Music

"Succeeds in capturing in written form the essence of Cage's distinctive, inimitable personality and presence that was experienced by anyone who talked with him, but which was rarely captured in print."

—Charles Hamm, Arthur R. Virgin professor of music,
emeritus, Dartmouth College

"The 'Cage and Friends' interviews are outstanding. In particular David Tudor, the performing musician closest to and most crucial for Cage, is exceptionally forthcoming."

—Christian Wolff, composer

Printed and bound by CPI Group (UK) Ltd, Croydon, CR0 4YY

13/04/2025

14656515-0001